Marriage, Love, Caste and Kinship Support

REVISED EDITION

Marriage, Love, Caste and Kinship Support

Lived Experiences of the Urban Poor in India

Shalini Grover

Routledge
Taylor & Francis Group

LONDON AND NEW YORK

First published 2018
by Routledge
4 Park Square, Milton Park, Abingdon, Oxon OX14 4RN
605 Third Avenue, New York, NY 10017

First issued in paperback 2023

Routledge is an imprint of the Taylor & Francis Group, an informa business

Print edition not for sale in South Asia (India, Sri Lanka, Nepal, Bangladesh, Afghanistan, Pakistan or Bhutan)

British Library Cataloguing in Publication Data
A catalogue record for this book is available from the British Library

Library of Congress Cataloging in Publication Data
A catalogue record for this book has been requested

ISBN-13: 978-1-138-01933-1 (hbk)
ISBN-13: 978-1-03-265284-9 (pbk)
ISBN-13: 978-0-203-73282-3 (ebk)

DOI: 10.4324/9780203732823

Typeset in Antiqua 10/12
by Manmohan Kumar, Delhi 110 035

SOCIAL
SCIENCE
PRESS

CONTENTS

LIST OF PHOTOGRAPHS

LIST OF CASE STUDIES AND NAME INDEX

FOREWORD

The sociology of marriage in India is a field that is rather high on theory and relatively low on evidence. There is the grand theory of the so-called 'Alliance Theorists', represented by Louis Dumont, for whom the institution of Hindu marriage is the veritable key to understanding Indian social structure. There is the middle-level 'regional' theory of Indian kinship organization, pioneered by Irawati Karve, which identifies different regional patterns of kinship and marriage aligned with contrasting features of gender relations. There is an Indological approach to marriage which derives conjugal ideals and practices from normative injunctions in the respective scriptural traditions of Hindus, Muslims and others. There are sociological theories of modernization which postulate certain inevitable changes in kinship and marriage practices as traditional societies modernize and the earlier so-called 'familial' ethos is replaced by an 'individualistic' orientation. And there are varieties of feminist theory which highlight the power asymmetries in the conjugal relationship and seek to assess the potential for the 'democratization' of gender relations within essentially patriarchal family structures.

For well over a century now, marital norms and practices have also featured prominently in public discourse in India – as grounds for social reform, as objects of state control and intervention, and as sites for the assertion and contestation of national and community identities. Throughout this period, and still today, the public sphere has witnessed frequent episodes of moral panic and acts of violent retribution occasioned by the infringement of marital rules and sexual codes of conduct. Racist, sexist, and caste-and class-biased stereotypes of the intimate lives of 'others' flourish, while the description and analysis of subcontinental conjugality has itself been skewed in line with the generally nationalist and modernist orientation of professional sociology. Thus the marital practices of the majority rural population, of lower castes and classes, of religious minorities and of tribal peoples are scripted as pre-modern, heterodox, or in need of reform. Conversely, the enlightened urban middle classes present themselves as the harbingers of social change and leaders in global life-style modernity – albeit with a touch of nostalgia for the supposed traditional Indian family system and its core values.

Despite the proliferation of theoretical literature and public discourse on the state of Indian conjugality, it is remarkable how inadequately theory is put to empirical test or the shibboleths of public discourse challenged in the light of facts on the ground. To some extent, the relative dearth of empirical research in this field may be a reflection of the declining importance of studies of kinship and marriage in the Western academy, even in the discipline of social anthropology which has made this field its special concern. But whatever the reason, it remains a fact that in-depth ethnographic studies of changing aspects of Indian marriage across the range of Indian communities are rather few and far between. Of course, a huge amount of macro-data on household, family and marriage has been generated by survey instruments such as the Census of India, the National Sample Survey series, the National Health and Family Welfare studies, media-commissioned sex surveys and the monumental Peoples of India project of the Anthropological Survey of India which identified and described the social organization of no fewer than 4,635 distinct communities (endogamous groups) throughout the subcontinent. But while all this descriptive and statistical information is a good starting point, it provides little sense of the 'lived experience' of the married lives of Indian men and women, young and old, in different stages of the life-cycle and in varied social settings.

After a long hiatus, during which time one had the feeling that nothing much was happening in the field of the sociology of marriage in India, the last few years have seen the publication of a sprinkling of ethnographic monographs and research papers on aspects of love, marriage and intimacy in India and the South Asian diaspora, accompanied by a parallel burgeoning of interest in aspects of sexuality both inside and outside of marriage. Many of these recent writings are the work of scholars influenced by the Indian Women's Movement and academic feminism, including social historians and literary scholars as well as social activists and social workers, who are together pushing the boundaries of the sociology of marriage in new directions, asking new questions, and undertaking new styles of fieldwork (in courts and police stations, for instance). Dr Shalini Grover's nuanced ethnographic account of the marital lives of poor, Scheduled Caste women in slum and resettlement colonies in New Delhi adds substantially to this gradually expanding literature.

Grover has a healthy respect for received theoretical and interpretative frameworks, whether sociological or feminist, but she also displays a healthy skepticism. According to the prevailing stereotype of North Indian kinship, inflected by scriptural authority and upper caste norms, marriage is an irrevocable, life-time union characterized by the one-way passage of the bride, conceived as a 'gift', from her natal to her conjugal home. Except for childbirth and ceremonial occasions, a married woman's right of return to her parental home is seriously constrained, for the dowry that she is given in marriage is viewed as a substitute for continued rights in natal family assets. Combined with the North Indian rule of patri(viri)local residence (residence after marriage with the husband's paternal kin), these features are interpreted by feminist scholars as imposing severe limitations on a wife's 'bargaining' position in her conjugal family, leaving her with few options and minimal support outside the frame of marriage.

The low caste and economically vulnerable urban community that Grover describes clearly belongs to the North Indian kinship type, and her respondents to a large extent also subscribe to these norms. But their actual kinship practices are highly flexible nonetheless. The marital bond is relatively brittle – divorce, separation, remarriage, elopement, short-term liaisons, widow remarriage, and polygamy are common – and married women may spend long periods in their natal homes, whether for refuge from the emotional and material tribulations of the conjugal home or simply to help out in the parental household. The mother-daughter bond is a particular source of strength and comfort in this regard. On first glance, these 'fall-back' options beyond the frame of respectable monogamous marriage and patrilocal residence may appear liberating, at least when compared to the restricted choices available to women of higher socio-economic and ritual status. To some extent perhaps they are. But Grover's nuanced ethnography and, pertinently, the life-cycle perspective that emerges through her close attention to personal narratives, reveal the limitations of this formulaic interpretation. The bottom line is that the situation of an unattached woman in this community, even when she is economically independent, is almost impossible to sustain: she needs the protection of husband, father, brother or adult son for her social viability. Moreover, as Grover's account clearly shows, the fall-back option of return to the natal home works as a double-edged sword, for while it affords support and refuge in the short term, it is typically unsustainable in the longer term once the older generation passes on and brothers assume increasing responsibility for their own conjugal families. In fact, Grover argues, a wife's over-staying in her natal home will ultimately undermine rather than strengthen her 'bargaining' position in her conjugal home.

Significantly, Grover links her discussion of the dynamics of the wife's exploitation of her customary right of return to her natal home with the type of marriage she has contracted – that is, an 'arranged' marriage or a 'love' marriage (the latter understood as a self-arranged union without parental approval which is very often inter-caste, inter-religious or in some sense in breach of customary marriage rules). Now this antithesis of love versus arranged marriage is a prominent feature of the 'modernization' model of family change, where it serves as a measure of the modern individuation of social values. But it is also a feature of public discourse on intimate relations, fully internalized by her low caste informants. The general opinion of her informants, and of several well-known feminist critics as well, is that love marriages are fragile unions for the reason that the couple's families have no investment in the outcome and no responsibility to mediate marital disputes. A woman who chooses to make a love marriage in defiance of parental approval is deemed to have forfeited her right of support and refuge in her natal home. Grover's case studies show that women who have made love marriages are themselves of the view that they cannot claim a right of refuge in the natal home, whether or not they may in fact receive such support. Paradoxically, however, and in contradiction to conventional expectations, love marriages work out to be more 'stable' and enduring than family-arranged marriages for the rather sad reason that the wives have no-one to turn to if things go wrong, and nowhere else to go: they can only stick it out as best they can with the mates they have themselves chosen. Sadly, too, Grover's case studies suggest that so-called 'arranged love marriage' – the innovative solution to the contradiction of individual choice and social expectation whereby parents come round to endorse the young couple's choice of partner – is a 'filmi' solution that works better at the level of the imagination than it does in real life.

As remarked, the 'arranged' versus 'love' marriage dichotomy is firmly established in both the public imagination and social science understanding. Grover has interestingly complicated this discourse by focusing at some length on what are called 'secondary' marriages, that is, the remarriage of a woman following widowhood, divorce, separation or desertion, or her incorporation as a second wife in a polygamous union. On these types of conjugal arrangement there is as yet very little ethnography outside the case-books of professional social workers, and little theorization either. Though occasionally arranged by parents and family, such secondary unions are more typically self-choice, consensual arrangements based on mutual attraction and, like 'love' marriages, are often contracted across caste boundaries. Grover sees them as a 'critical exit option' for women in unsatisfactory arranged marriages. But, as in primary 'love' marriages, a woman in a secondary union has no automatic claim to parental refuge in the event of a breakdown of the new relationship, and no-one to blame but herself if things go wrong a second time around.

Consistent with her emphasis on understanding her subjects' lived experience of married life, Grover presents much of her ethnographic material in the form of personal narratives and case studies. Significantly, she deploys these narratives and case studies not in order to deduce from them the rules of the underlying 'system' of marriage in this poor and low caste urban community, but rather to illustrate the multiplicity of circumstances, options and outcomes even within a relatively homogeneous group. Nowhere is this better illustrated than in the fascinating chapter on the role of Mahila (Women's) Panchayats in the arbitration of marital disputes. In seeking reconciliation of marital and family problems, Grover's informants take recourse to a variety of institutions, among them the formal legal system, traditional male-dominated caste panchayats, and an innovative new system of Mahila Panchayats which are guided by a prominent woman's NGO but managed by the local women themselves. In these case studies of community-based dispute settlement we gain access to a multiplicity of voices – of aggrieved husbands and wives, natal and conjugal families, the women community leaders and social activists, and the ethnographer herself – as intimate lives are dragged into public view, and grounds of conciliation hammered out. For a blue-blooded feminist, these solutions may often appear to be something of a 'cop-out' for, while husbands are castigated by these grass-roots marriage counsellors for failing to provide adequately for their families, the wives are typically censured for wayward conduct and urged to adjust to circumstances in their conjugal homes as their best option.

Reading between the lines of these case studies, personal narratives, interviews and successful and failed arbitration attempts, one can imagine that fieldwork so close to the grain of the lived experience of love, sex, marriage and domestic violence of the urban poor must have been an emotionally draining as well as intellectually challenging experience for the ethnographer herself. Indeed, I know that to be the case. But the outcome has been an unparalleled, empathetic insight into the intimate lives and loves of poor men and women living precariously at the raw edges of the contemporary urban economy.

Patricia Uberoi
New Delhi, August 2010

ACKNOWLEDGEMENTS

I would like to express my gratitude to all the people who stood by me so generously through the long years of writing this book. My thanks first go to Filippo Osella and Geert De Neve at the University of Sussex. I am fortunate to have had such excellent and dedicated doctoral supervisors. It has been a great privilege to have worked with them. They have offered, at all stages of my academic career, great intellectual inspiration, and immense patience and unwavering support. Their insights into the anthropology of marriage, and their call for an exacting ethnography will always stay with me.

I am also grateful to Ann Whitehead, Clare Rogers, Caroline Osella and Katy Gardner, who gave me valuable feedback and guidance during my years as a doctoral student.

It was possible to write this book because I was awarded the Sir Ratan Tata Post-Doctoral Award Fellowship in Sociology at the Institute of Economic Growth (IEG), New Delhi, for 2007–2010. I am indebted to the Sir Ratan Tata Trust for this generous fellowship and to Kanchan Chopra and Bina Agarwal who are the previous and present directors of IEG, respectively. At IEG it has been wonderful and inspiring to have had Amita Baviskar, Sanjay Srivastava and Vikram Dayal as close colleagues. Aradhya Bhardwaj, Arup Mitra, Chakraverti Mahajan, Devender Pratap, Moneer Alam, Sushil Sen and many other colleagues have also been more than helpful.

From Patricia Uberoi I have drawn much inspiration for the study of marriage as a 'critical institution'. I thank her sincerely for her meticulous and close reading of my work and for her valuable and helpful suggestions and comments. Patricia Jeffery has also been a truly generous and amazing mentor throughout.

I would like to thank Esha Béteille and Meenakshi Jauhari Chawla from the Social Science Press for their encouragement, an anonymous referee for suggestions, Malini Sood for her editorial inputs, and Sage (Delhi) for allowing me to reproduce an article from *Contributions to Indian Sociology* (43:1, pp. 1–33, 2009). I am grateful to Ravinder Kaur, Srimati Basu, Srila Roy and Sylvia Vatuk who gave me comments on my chapters.

In Delhi I must acknowledge those who directly shaped my fieldwork. I remain deeply moved by the kindness and warmth of the people of Mohini Nagar who so willingly shared their stories of marriage, love and betrayal. In particular, I would like to acknowledge two wonderful women, Balaji and Lakshmi, for the kindness with which they welcomed me to the neighbourhood. My two field assistants, Kalpeshwari and Radha, shared the trials of fieldwork with me. In Radha I could not have asked for a more courageous, intelligent and sensitive field assistant.

The mahila panchayat team and the Action India NGO also assisted me unfailingly. Gouri Choudhury, who runs Action India, allowed me to carry out research at the mahila panchayat. I thank her for sharing organizational lessons based on the experiences of the women who sought the services of the mahila panchayat. Sonya Sinha offered invaluable information and friendship and readily accepted me into her team. Other members of the mahila panchayat—Arati, Mamta, Uma, Usha, Vimlesh and Shakuntala—were also indispensable to my fieldwork. In addition Khatijha an independent human rights activist based in Delhi must also be applauded for her work on helping estranged couples.

To the many friends whose kind generosity I have relied upon, my heartfelt thanks goes to Ajay Kapur, Amy Khazmin, Anand Prakash, Lyla Mehta, Nitya Rao, Radhika Jha, Ruchi Tripathi, Seema Batra, Shankar Ramaswamy and Susannah Graham.

I thank my families in India and Norway for their boundless love and support. My adoring father-in-law Erling Iversen has patiently followed the writing of this book. To Mum, Dad, Radhika, Gauri, Nani and Ritu Maasi, without whom none of this would ever have been possible: thank you all for standing by me and for giving me direction and courage.

Most of all, I thank my husband, Vegard Iversen for always having faith in me. For the last fifteen years, he has inspired me unfailingly and provided much of the necessary support. Our beloved son Kabir has borne the brunt of my strict work schedule. He has waited patiently for Mummy to come out and play with him after locking herself for endless hours in the 'computer room'.

Finally, this book is dedicated in loving memory of my Nana, my maternal grandfather, for his kindness, love and humility, which in his lifetime he so effortlessly bestowed upon his family. It is, of course, also dedicated to the remarkable women of Mohini Nagar who deserve a life of dignity and respect.

PREFACE TO THE REVISED EDITION

Marriage, Love, Caste and Kinship Support (2011) has been fortunate to have been widely noticed in professional journals and by the non-academic community. This has motivated me to add new perspectives on change and structural continuity and it is indeed an honour to have this book as a revised edition. The anthropology and sociology journals[1] have applauded the complex ethnographic weaving of marriage with caste, poverty, and gender. The chapter on Mahila Panchayat NGOs has received sustained praise for its analysis of atypical court rulings and local strategies that prompt readers, feminists, and civil society to re-think normative notions of gender equality. With the book's illumination of conjugality from manifold angles, journalists and documentary filmmakers have approached me with eclectic queries.

In my opinion the content of media reportage is worth critiquing and questioning in instances where marriage and family are represented superficially. Journalists make virtually no reference to authentic statistics, such as the claims of an escalating pan-Indian formal divorce rate.[2] It is vital for the academic

---

[1] See, Mehrotra, Nilika. 2011. *Indian Anthropologist*. 41 (2): 99–100; Parry, Jonathan. 2013. *Contributions to Indian Sociology*. 47 (1):141–3; Chaudhry, Shruti. 2013. *Sociology*. 47 (1): 204–5; Chakraborty, Kabita. 2013. *Journal of the Royal Anthropological Institute*. 19: 894–4.

[2] Note the hyperbole in these newspaper captions: 'Rising Divorce Rates: India Joins the Western Bandwagon,' *Young Muslim Digest*, April 2011 (Qadir Biju); 'In Tradition-Bound India, Female, Divorced and Happy,' *Worldview*,

community to counter the predominance of exaggerated trends through ethnographic examination. My postdoctoral research therefore was conducted in the new Crime Against Women Cells (CAW cells) and the new Family Courts. I observed the mediation sessions of couples and examined the compilation of divorce statistics, which threw new light on my research. (Grover 2016; Grover Forthcoming).

For this revised edition, I would like to conclude by reinstating my greatest appreciation to friends, colleagues, doctoral supervisors, family, and my publisher. Since 2007, the Institute of Economic Growth (IEG) has lent invaluable support. The current Director, Manoj Panda, IEG's very dependable Sushil Sen, and colleague Arup Mitra deserve mention for their immense generosity. From 2011–13, I have benefitted from a Senior Research Fellowship in Social Anthropology, an award granted by the Indian Council of Social Science Research (ICSSR). From November 2014–15, I was part of the IEG faculty, as Associate Professor. This second edition and other research initiatives would not have originated without the hospitable approach of IEG. The University of Edinburgh has been generous in granting affiliation ('Honorary Fellow') from 2014–16. For this I am grateful to Patricia Jeffery for her steadfast encouragement. The Social Science Press has enthusiastically kept up with feedback of my research. More so, Esha Béteille continues to inspire me with new and interesting ideas.

The first publication of my book was followed by the birth of my second child Kristoffer. I cannot thank enough my children's godmother, whose friendship and blessings have enriched our family in ways that are indescribable. My parents, sisters, maasi, and our fantastic child-minders Sarita Topo, Amit Kumar and Suman Devi have been marvelous in raising our two boys, as they let us pursue dual-income careers. Kabir and Kristoffer are experiencing the joys of joint-family life in Delhi in a household with four generations. For maintaining work-life balance, I give my husband enormous credit especially his single-handed pursuit of taking on prolonged periods of sleepless nights and facing

---

September 2008 (Emily Wax); 'What makes Delhi the Divorce Capital?,' *Times of India,* August 2007 (Pallavi Pasricha).

semi-comatose mornings. While the previous edition was bestowed to my maternal grandfather, this edition is for my grandmother ('badi nani') who was our guiding force and the best friend we ever had. Every word and page is dedicated to her love and energy.

Shalini Grover
New Delhi and University of Edinburgh (School of Social and Political Science)
www.drshalinigrover.com

GLOSSARY

Ashram	Spiritual centre
Bahar wala admi	Literally 'an outsider', 'outside man'; unflattering description of a secondary male partner
Bahu	Daughter-in-law
Basti	Shanty settlement or slum
Basti woman	Woman who lives in a shanty settlement or resettlement colony
Bazaar	Market
Beech wala	Marriage intermediary, match-maker, go-between
Beti	Daughter
Bhangi	Derogatory term for the Balmikis (sweeper caste)
Behen	Sister
Biwi	Wife (*see patni*)
Bihata	Husband from the primary (first) marriage
Bindi	A mark (usually a red dot) placed in the centre of the forehead by married

	Hindu women; now also makeup or jewellery or decoration in imitation of the traditional *bindi* worn as a fashion accessory by even unmarried girls and women
Biradari	Members of one's community or caste
Biradari panchayat	Caste association
Chacha	Father's younger brother
Chachi	Father's younger brother's wife
Chunni	Long scarf for covering head, shoulders, and chest, a part of the *salwar kameez* ensemble *(see duppata)*
Doosra admi	Male partner from a secondary union
Doosri shaadi	Second marriage
Dhoka	Betrayal
Dukh	Sorrow, grief
Duppata	Long scarf for covering head, shoulder, and chest, a part of the *salwar kameez* ensemble *(see chunni)*
Gali	Street, row, by-lane, alley
Garib	Poor
Gauna	Ceremony for the ritual transfer of the bride to her conjugal home upon attaining puberty
Ghar wala	Generic term for husband or male partner
Gotra exogamy	Avoidance of three to four prohibited degrees of kinship in matrimony
Hijra	Eunuch, a member of the 'third sex' in India, considered neither male nor female

Ishq	Romantic love, passion, desire *(see muhabbat, prem)*
Jamadar	Derogatory term for the Balmikis (sweeper caste)
Jat	Caste group/identity (used interchangeably with *biradari*)
Jeeja	Sister's husband
Jeevan sathi	Life partner
Jhuggi	Residence that is a semi-permanent structure in a shanty settlement or slum
Jhuggi-jhonpri colony	Shanty settlement or slum area
Jodi	Marital bond or pair
Kachhi naukri	Non-permanent, temporary job
Kahani	Story, tale, narrative
Karva chauth	A festival during which the wife fasts for the entire day for her husband's happiness, well-being, and long life
Kiraya	To live in rented accommodation, to lease or rent
Kharcha-pani	A husband's monthly salary, a maintenance allowance, or household finances
Mahila panchayat	Women's informal court for dispute settlement and NGO
Majburi	Duress, lack of alternatives or options, vulnerability
Manzil	Floor in a resettlement plot
Mera admi	Literally 'my man', term for a husband or male partner
Muhabbat	Romantic love, passion, desire *(see ishk, prem)*

Nasbandi	Sterilization
Pahli shaadi	Primary (first) marriage performed with full rituals
Pallu	One end of a *sari* used for covering a married woman's head and veiling her face in the presence of senior affines as a show of modesty and respect
Pati	Husband
Patni	Wife (*see biwi*)
Pihar	Natal home, family, kin, unit
Plot	Residential unit that is a permanent and solid structure in a resettlement colony
Prem	Love, passion, desire (*see ishk, muhabbat*)
Pakki naukri	Permanent employment
Purdah	Full or partial veiling
Pyar	Love and different types of emotional attachment
Rokna	Ceremony to mark the 'reservation' of a boy in the context of an arranged match
Sak	Male suspicion of female infidelity
Salwar kameez	Long tunic/shirt and pair of loose trousers/pyjamas worn by Indian women, predominantly in northern India, accompanied by a *duppata* or *chunni*
Sanstha	Organization, association, body
Sari	Long, unstitched garment worn by most Indian women
Sarkari naukri	Government job
Sart	Conditions that must be fulfilled by a spouse as an essential part of conflict

	resolution (see Chapter 5 for mahila panchayat agreements)
Sasural	Husband's affines, affinal home
Sat phere wala/wali	Husband or wife from the primary (first) marriage
Shaadi	Primary (first) marriage
Shaadi wala	Husband from the primary (first) marriage
Sindoor	A red powder placed in the parting of a woman's hair symbolizing her status as a married woman
Sukh	Happiness, joy
Tagra ashik	Passionate lover
Teesri shaadi	Third marriage
Yaar	Lover
Zabardasti	Coercion, force, duress

1

Mapping the Debate on Marriage

From Formal Marriage Rules to Everyday Practices

While marriage is recognized as a crucial and life-changing event for most Indian women, their experiences of conjugal relationships, love, commitment, and intimacy have only recently begun to attract scholarly attention. Previously, anthropological and sociological research in South Asia concentrated almost exclusively on the formal structures of kinship rules and relations,[1] ignoring the fluidity, diversity, and dynamism inherent in everyday practices pertaining to marital relations.[2] Patricia Uberoi, who has been instrumental in voicing the need for a theoretical shift, correctly notes how: 'The sociology of Indian family and kinship has focused more on kinship norms than on pathology, deviance and breakdown. For this reason it has largely failed to inform or to confront the practical challenges of social activism and public policy intervention' (Uberoi 2000: 1). Remarking on another type of lacuna in social activism that does privilege women's experiences, Mary John (2005: 721) observes: 'Entering the domain of marriage,

---

[1] For example, Parry (2001; 2004) has examined the stability of marriage across generations and social classes in Chhattisgarh. Earlier, Parry (1979) had looked at caste and kinship structures in Kangra. While his Kangra informants were deeply preoccupied with the exegesis of norms and structures, his Chhattisgarh informants display a strong interest in local marriage events. Parry's present work (2001; 2004) should be seen as an attempt to foreground lived experiences.

[2] For some earlier exceptions, see Jeffery and Jeffery (1996), Kapur (1970), Raheja and Gold (1994), Trawick (1992), Uberoi (1993; 1996; 1998) and Vatuk (1972).

beyond questions of violence and law, is a journey we have barely begun in the women's movement.' With marriage being critically understudied, preconceived notions, often lacking ethnographic validity, have been allowed to pervade academic writing, social activism, and the popular imagination.

In emphasizing the diversity of marriage forms and relationships in an urban poverty setting, this book presents a close and critical scrutiny into 'arranged marriages', 'love marriages', 'secondary unions', and widow relationships as embodied experience and lived practice.[3] Distinct from earlier anthropological texts that attune us to the life-long arranged marriage ideal, my ethnographic explorations will delineate how these conjugal unions and arrangements of the urban poor are rich, complex, unpredictable, and often transient in nature. During the course of a single day, I could be in conversation with a woman whose marriage is *arranged*, another who chose a *love marriage*, and a third who is in a *secondary union*.[4] I would meet widows and widowers and divorced men and women in search of partners, and witness liaisons between married women and unmarried men. Like in Parry's (2001) Chhattisgarh study, my respondents would juxtapose their 'second' and 'fifth' consensual unions. I felt compelled to disentangle women's subjectivities of these diverse relationships and to draw out contrasts and parallels. What are the experiential intersecting and dividing lines of these relationships?

Women's perceptions and evaluations of their marriages can provide valuable insights into the dynamics of conjugality and show whether and how marital practices are transmuting in a particular stratum of urban India. The alleged prevalence of love marriages in contemporary India tends to be interpreted as a modernity-induced marker and effect of incipient changes in social mores and practices. The popular discourse on marriage in the Indian subcontinent makes a sharp distinction between the English terms 'love marriage' and 'arranged marriage'. Although these terms may

[3] John (2005: 721) argues that there has been little sustained debate in the women's movement on different conjugal forms, although sexual choice, orientation, and rights are now being given considerable attention.

[4] Secondary unions are relationships and remarriages that follow the break-up of the first (primary) marriage. In short, they are often consensual in nature, linked as they are too separation, divorce and elopements.

have specific local connotations, arranged marriages are typically caste-endogamous alliances initiated by parents (Chowdhry 2007; Uberoi 1998), while love marriages are self-chosen unions preceded by premarital relationships based on love, which may or may not contravene caste-endogamy norms. In north India, the arranged marriage prevails as the idealized marital alliance (Chowdhry 2007). This book will attempt to shed new light on which form of marriage serves women's interests best and why. So far there has been little analytical inquiry into the egalitarian potential of alternative conjugal forms, in particular marriages based on romantic and consensual love and on women's 'positioning' within these unions. In addition my study calls for greater recognition of the widespread phenomenon of secondary unions and their frequent compulsions, arrangements, and realities in an urban locale. It examines whether secondary unions and the concomitant freedom to initiate successive relationships is suggestive of greater female autonomy.

Marriage, Love, Caste and Kinship Support: Framing the Debate

The majority of urban residents whose marital experiences I present are specifically of Scheduled Caste background (SC).[5] The lives of these lowest castes, the 'Indian marriage', and hegemonic alliances have been subject to a plethora of stereotypes and uniform conceptions. A common notion is that Scheduled Caste women as a category exercise a comparatively high level of social and economic independence. Scheduled Caste (SC) marriages are thus assumed to be less hierarchical. Furthermore, a persistent perception has been that arranged marriages are robust and long-lasting, while love marriages are fragile and ephemeral. Arranged matches are viewed as lifelong unions that remain intact through continuous nurture from the couple's respective

---

[5] Former 'untouchables' also known as Harijans or Dalits, are officially classified as Scheduled Castes (SCs). To compensate for past discrimination, Scheduled Castes (and Scheduled Tribes [STs]) were granted special status by the Constitution of India. In 1990, following the Mandal Commission's recommendation, reservation benefits were also extended to Other Backward Classes (OBCs).

families. Conversely, love marriages are regarded as an inferior form, associated with familial disruption, elopement followed by court marriage, and the absence of religious rituals and the social recognition they confer. Another supposition that derives from kinship models is that throughout north India there is a notable lack of post-marital contact between married women and their natal families. To address some of these themes, I start by synthesizing anthropological insights into marriage and caste in India. This is followed by a review of the literature on love marriages and the responses they elicit from near kin, caste groups, and other social institutions. Next, I introduce the provocative debate facilitated by Madhu Kishwar (1994) on family-arranged marriages and love marriages in India and the recent argument by Chris Fuller and Haripriya Narasimhan (2008) that also deconstructs the schism between these marital forms. Simultaneously, I appraise theories that attribute women's access to support to particular forms of marriage and residence. Finally, I discuss Sudhir Kakar's (1989) portrayal of intimate relations and sexuality.

Scheduled Caste Lives and Labour Force Participation

Anthropologists have noted that amongst the upper castes, the marital bond is distinctly hierarchical with women accorded a lower status (Busby 2000; Deliège 1997; Dumont 1964; Dube 1996). In upper-caste households, male breadwinners are entitled to sexual and domestic control over their wives. This hierarchy is evidenced in women's deference in everyday speech, conduct, and ritual. Amongst the upper castes, ideals of *pativrata*, a good chaste wife who subordinates her life to her husband's welfare and needs, are widely promulgated. Ethnographies on SC communities offer a more optimistic picture of women's marital position. Low caste norms permit divorce and remarriage (Deliège 1997; Parry 2001), while women, being unbound by upper caste chastity norms, have greater sexual freedom (Uchiyamada 1997). Crucially, there has been considerable emphasis on the earning capabilities of SC women and on how their labour contribution in sectors such as agriculture, brick-making, and sweeping is highly valued (Deliège 1997; Kapadia 1996; Searle-Chatterjee 1981). As Deliège (1997) observes about Paraiyar women in Tamil Nadu:

In other respects women enjoy great freedom. They are economically indispensable since, in many households, it is they who do the brick-making and thus their incomes are not negligible. Their economic situation puts them in touch with everybody. They go to work, meet other men and women, know the region, etc. This situation contrasts with that of high-caste women, who only leave their houses once a fortnight, or even less, when their husbands decide to take them to a film or to some relative's (1997: 232).

The argument about female autonomy is made most forcefully in Mary Searle-Chatterjee's (1981: 98) study of Benares sweepers, in which she demonstrates that the marriages of low caste sweepers are characterized by an egalitarian gender division of labour, and conduct.[6] Benares sweeper women command a strong position in their community as they control household finances, earn higher salaries than their husbands do, and are able to exact considerable support with domestic chores. Searle-Chatterjee underscores this aspect of effective spousal cooperation as a principal feature of the sweeper castes. Following Searle-Chatterjee's work, the orthodoxy and general orientation in the social sciences has been to view spousal relationships amongst sweepers as egalitarian. In an exposition of marital roles in Chapter 2, I put forward a distinctly different conception of the working and conjugal lives of sweepers. I illuminate the prevalence of the male breadwinner ideology in the sweeper community and amongst other castes while arguing that female waged work does not necessarily enhance cooperation and nor does it enable women to gain an effective voice in the conjugal home. Alongside, I illustrate how men and women's participation in

---

[6] For insights into other types of egalitarian marriages, see Cecila Busby's (2000) study of gender relations in a Catholic fishing community in Kerala. In Marianad village, gender relations are based on discourses of equality, interdependence, and complementarity. The equality between spouses is symbolized in the everyday sharing of money, food, substance, and emotion. Busby notes that beyond the imagery of equality, Catholic and Hindu patriarchal discourses assert male authority and hierarchy. This contextualization of contradictory discourses on gender makes for interesting reading.

urban labour markets, their work trajectories, and gender division of labour are neither uniform nor stable.

Factoring in Class, Caste, and the Conjugal Life Cycle

Recent studies have investigated how families, communities, and caste groups have responded to modern courtship and marriage based on love. Prem Chowdhry's long-term research on north India (1998; 2004; 2007) shows that couples in Haryana who violate the norm of caste endogamy, or whose marriages breach customary rules of *got* (clan) and village exogamy, have to contend with extreme violence from not only their families but also from powerful and conservative caste panchayats. The violence is often gendered, fatally targeting daughters in the name of family and community honour. Contemporary rural Haryana and urban areas such as Gurgaon and Rohtak typify the extreme rigidity in the interpretation of marriage rules and alliances in north India (Grover 2007). Correspondingly, in her study of the social acceptability of love marriages in Delhi, Perveez Mody (2002; 2007; 2008) describes how couples in such 'unsanctioned' unions faced violence and excommunication from their families and caste groups. Mody also captures the hostile and obstructive stance of the judicial system encountered by couples who attempt to legalize their unions at Delhi's Tis Hazari courts. These insightful studies, and the social and political debate to which they have contributed, have primarily focused on the violence, family exclusion, inadequacies of the law, and socio-legal adversities that couples in north India face when opting for and forming a union of their choice. A productive way of refining and deepening the debate is by shifting the inquiry to the post-wedding phase of love marriages, which has until now received notably little scholarly attention. Exploring the nuances of the couple's interactions with their parents after marriage and investigating the dynamics of their everyday conjugal lives in the later years allows us to better understand the changing character of relationships between spouses and their kin, as these unfold over time.

In an essay that provoked considerable reaction, Madhu Kishwar (1994) drew attention to the parental role in arranged and love marriages.[7] Kishwar argued that the stereotypical portrayal of a family-arranged marriage as 'backward' and of a love marriage as 'progressive' needed to be revisited. Drawing on the marital trajectories of upper class men and women, she cited several examples of unsuccessful love marriages, pointing out that the emotional attachment between the couple was often ephemeral in these unions. Kishwar delineated the distinct advantages of family-arranged marriages; marital stability is more achievable in arranged matches since, over time, the two families establish strong bonds through regular reciprocal exchanges. Further, in family-arranged marriages, the material and psychological support extended by parents mitigates women's vulnerability in the marital home. A disadvantage of being in a love marriage is that a woman, by rejecting parental choice, may have severed family ties. The respective families of the couple may have no contact and communication with one another, and may therefore be unable to mediate during times of marital distress and conflict. Kishwar's critical assessment of love marriages sparked off fierce rejoinders in *Manushi*.[8] Kishwar made it clear that she was not defending family-arranged marriages as an ideal; however, long years of working with women as an activist had compelled her to challenge the received wisdom on 'progressive' marital practices and question whether self-chosen unions did, in fact, make women stronger, more secure, and more satisfied. While Kishwar's essay was valuable in triggering an important debate amongst feminist

[7] The essay has been reproduced in Kishwar (1999).

[8] The journal was inundated with interesting and critical responses from across the world, some of which I reformulate here for the reader. According to Kalpana Vishwanath (1994: 41), Kishwar had presented stereotypical views of marriage and the nature of men and women. Viswanath argued that Kishwar's analysis was based on an inadequate and biased sample since most of her informants were her friends and acquaintances. Hsio-Yen Shih (1994: 38) wrote that Kishwar's reflections fell into the cultural relativist trap of 'east versus west' and 'modernity versus tradition'. Srimati Basu (1994: 38) noted that women's economic position and legal entitlements had received little attention in Kishwar's analysis. Rasna Warah (1994: 37) criticized Kishwar for perpetuating the widely held belief amongst Indians that love marriages are a recipe for disaster. In a more positive reaction, Dagmar Markova (1994: 41) felt that Kishwar had offered fresh insights into the merits of arranged marriages to western readers.

scholars, it was strikingly judgemental in tone. She laid the blame squarely on women for irresponsibly disregarding parental choice. She did not criticize parents for withdrawing support from their children in love marriages. Besides, Kishwar completely ignored the question of class and caste differences. More recent studies, including my own, show how caste and class factors are salient in shaping the responses of kin and other significant social groups, thereby affecting the outcome of the conjugal union.

Adding a new dimension to the marriage debate, Fuller and Narasimhan (2008: 751) in their study of urban Vattimas contend that 'competent academic discussion of arranged and love marriage recognizes that the dichotomy is fluid or fuzzy'. Many middle class Vattimas in Tamil Nadu are today arranging their own marriages, albeit within their caste. Significantly, for the Vattimas a companionate marriage[9] has become an important criterion in both arranged and love marriages. Fuller and Narasimhan argue that while anthropologists acknowledge this cross-breeding of 'arrangement and love', current scholarship continues to ally love marriages with 'modernity' and arranged marriages with 'tradition'. While in concurrence with Fuller and Narasimhan that the dichotomy between 'modern' and 'traditional' marriages is problematic and untenable, my ethnography (Chapters 2 and 3) substantiates that these evolving marriage ideals amongst the Vattimas are class and context specific. The Vattima middle class evidence of change should not be read as transferable to other Indian cultural settings. Amongst Delhi's urban poor, there are differences in the way women experience their arranged and love marriages. Therefore, rather than coalescing or assuming that the dichotomy between arranged and love marriages 'is fluid or fuzzy', these marriages need to be subjected to independent analytical scrutiny.

[9] The notion of companionate marriage, which evolved in Europe, implied a shift from marriage as an economic arrangement to one in which emotions became the centrepiece of the marital dyad. Marriage came to be seen as a joint venture in which couples considered themselves companions and friends, thereby bridging the segregated worlds of men and women (Giddens 1992; Jamieson 1998; Martin 1995). Companionate marriage stands in opposition to those ideologies that affirm a hierarchical and strict separation of gender and marital roles (see Parry 2001). See also Tyagi and Uberoi (1990) and Uberoi (1993) for greater value being given to the idea of 'conjugal love' in middle class India.

Kinship Paradigms and Geographical Models

How different forms of marital alliance affect women's access to kin-based support, and consequently their ability to negotiate within the affinal unit, is also the subject of an older body of literature. Karve (1993 [1953]) and Dyson and Moore (1983) analyse the kinship systems of north and south India, paying considerable attention to women's post-marital kin contact and support structures.[10] Broadly, they note that the northern region is characterized by patrilineal norms and a marked preference for long-distance marriages. In the south, marriages are entered into with close-kin (cross-cousins) in nearby and familiar locations, rather than with strangers in far-off places. Close-kin marriages enable women to exact better treatment from their affines. Overall, these models indicate that kinship in north India is associated with a negative image of long-distance marriages, alienation from natal kin, and female vulnerability in the domestic realm because of the absence of durable support structures.

Chapter 2 discusses how the above characterization of north Indian patterns of marriage residence does not extend to the poor in urban north India. Dyson and Moore (1983) and Karve (1993) fail to engage with women's real-life experiences of kinship and different marriage forms.[11] In a patri-virilocal milieu, Delhi women marry into neighbourhoods that are within easy reach and short distance

[10] In their model, Dyson and Moore (1983) also assess demographic trends. They evaluate north–south differences in labour force participation rates, educational levels, age at marriage, sex ratios, and forms of female seclusion. They acknowledge that their model does not incorporate class and caste differences adequately. For a recent appraisal of Dyson and Moore's model, see Rahman and Rao (2004).

[11] Amali Philips (2005: 109) and Penny Vera-Sanso (1999: 582) argue that the formal models of north–south kinship systems are at variance with regional and local patterns. Based on her fieldwork in Chennai, Vera-Sanso (1999: 582) demonstrates that close-kin marriages may not produce more durable and supportive ties between natal kin and married daughters. Consequently, from Vera-Sanso's account the argument that women enjoy greater natal-kin support in south India appears to have been overstated in the literature. See also Karin Kapadia (1996), who argues that across the social classes, Tamil Nadu women's experience of marriage and affinity is highly ambivalent. This is signalled through the familiar yet hidden discourse of 'kinship burns' whereby women elucidate their negative experience of marriage.

of their natal homes. This enables them to enjoy considerable flexibility in their movements between their natal and conjugal homes. Such post-marital physical proximity fosters durable bonds of support between mothers and daughters, reinforcing ties that were forged before marriage by mutual dependence driven by economic survival needs. The Delhi ethnography highlights the centrality of the mother–daughter dyad, a relationship that remains neglected in anthropological studies where attention has mainly been focused on mother–son bonds and on male models of Indian kinship.[12]

Crucially, my chapters will also underscore that the type of marriage into which a woman enters affects her access to post-marital support. My data resonates with Kishwar's claim that women in arranged marriages have particularly strong claims on natal support structures. Yet I depart from Kishwar's assessments in two fundamental respects. First, my case studies reveal that in arranged marriages, significant parental involvement can contribute to conjugal instability and disruption in a woman's marital trajectory. In other words, instead of stabilizing the conjugal union, complex and unpredictable dynamics between daughters and natal kin (especially mothers) may lead to marital breakdown. Second, my data refutes Kishwar's assertion and the more widespread pan-Indian assumption that love marriages usually tend to fail. My evidence suggests that divorce and marital break-ups are rarer in love marriages since women are deprived of the option of seeking parental shelter and support.

Delhi Slum Women and Intimate Relations

Psychoanalyst Sudhir Kakar (1989) is one of the first to have written about 'the sexual politics of Indian people' and their 'particular language of emotions'. He examines the interstices between love and sexuality through the life stories of two middle-aged women from the Delhi slums. He argues that sexual intercourse is structured through contractual exchanges, gender relations are pervaded by hostility, and that marriage is about intimate strangeness. Here Kakar is making broad, sweeping generalizations about the

---

[12] For exceptions, see Jeffery et al. (1988).

nature of Indian marriage and sexuality (cf. John 1998).[13] One of Kakar's most quoted findings concerns the way in which women conceptualize the *jodi* (marital bond or pair). According to him, slum women idealize the permanence of the marital bond and 'cling to the indissolubility of the *jodi*' (1989: 84). In many academic works, the salience of the *jodi* is now perennially identified with Indian women, and particularly with Delhi slum women. Yet through a very small sample, Kakar substantiates the concept of the *jodi* by invoking folklore, mythology, and religious scripture.[14] In Chapter 4, I highlight that the desire for the *jodi* is unfounded amongst the Delhi slum women whom I studied.

Globalization, Gender Equality, and Radical Shifts

In documenting contemporary changes in marriage practices, it is of particular value to engage with wider debates and processes beyond South Asia. The influential sociologist, Anthony Giddens (1992; 1999), for example, argues that transformations in the realms of marital, same-sex, and parenting relationships are a global phenomenon. Modern relationships are moving in the direction of the 'pure relationship', which he defines as follows:

> It refers to a situation where a social relation is entered into for its own sake, for what can be derived for each person from a sustained association with another; and which is continued only in so far as it is thought by both parties to deliver enough satisfaction for each individual to stay within it (1992: 58).

[13] See, for example, Raheja and Gold's (1994) account of women's lyrics. Women's songs in Rajasthan and Uttar Pradesh assign a positive value to sexual pleasure that is uncontested by male kin. Raheja and Gold's study offers nuanced representations of Indian women's sexuality.

[14] For further discussion on the *jodi*, see Haider (1998), John (1998), Lynch (1992), and Singh (1992). Haider (1998: 254) has a distinctly different take on Delhi slum women. She highlights how her ethnographic data does not support Kakar's analysis. Kakar makes notable use of mythology and of the Ram–Sita dyad as a way of deconstructing conceptions of the Indian *jodi*. Haider argues that Delhi slum women do not see Sita as their role model.

The pure relationship entails greater expectations of emotional and sexual equality, and is an outcome of 'plastic sexuality' or the fissure between reproduction and sexuality. Women's emancipation is tied with accessible contraception and new reproductive technologies, and as such the meaning of sexuality has undergone significant change. According to Giddens, modern societies are highly reflexive about their emotional lives, and the pure relationship is likely to become the future norm. The pure relationship is an enhancement of ideals of romantic love, whose advent has led to sweeping secular changes, making feelings and emotions the vital ingredient in relationships. Indeed, the wider import of romantic love is that individualized emotions take precedence over all other social and family relationships. In brief, Giddens' overarching claim is that the global trend is towards a new ideological stress on the emotional quality of relationships and a model of marriage that is based increasingly on personal choice and founded on ideals of gender equality and the possibility of divorce.

As Giddens' strong assertions are unsupported by empirical evidence, many scholars have begun to query his arguments. With reference to Britain, Lynn Jamieson (1998: 40) argues that Giddens downplays deep-seated gender and economic inequalities. Addressing Chhattisgarh, Parry (2001) explains that while young people have assimilated modern ideas, marriage ideologies have paradoxically led to a decline in divorce and to a reinforcement of gender inequality as marriage is becoming an expression of class status.[15] This paradoxical shift contradicts Giddens' (1992) core contention that the stress on intimacy is synonymous with a decoupling of the relationship when it is no longer fulfilling for either party (i.e. the pure relationship).[16]

---

[15] Parry (2001) argues that the type of employment in which Chhattisgarh locals are engaged engenders a particular notion of marriage and family life. For those who work in the informal sector, divorce and secondary unions are frequent and are tied with fluidity, consensuality, and institutional arrangements. Yet amongst those in secure employment ('the aristocracy of labour') in the organized sector, such as those working for the Bhilai Steel Plant (BSP), there is a perceptible alteration in values, with marriage becoming more emotionally intense.

[16] See also Kapila's (2004) evaluation of Giddens' hypothesis in relation to the Gaddis of Kangra.

Scrutinizing the validity of Giddens' hypotheses in a modern metropolis will add richness to the ongoing discussion on whether globalization is influencing and reshaping marital norms in non-western contexts. Like Parry, I am interested in querying the claim that modern-day marriages embody democratic ideals and that personal choice in mate selection resonates with this new ideology. It is, however, necessary to clarify why Giddens' arguments should be relevant for a poor urban populace. More specifically, what processes and manifestations of modernity are apparent in my fieldwork site? This is a low-income neighbourhood, located in Delhi where socio-economic conditions that are conducive for the democratization of marriage and relationships as emphasized by Giddens are moderately present. Residents of the locality are assimilated into heterogeneous urban labour markets where interaction across social classes is increasingly common. They are exposed to modern media imagery and to several women's NGOs, who generate information on legal change. While neighbourhood residents belong to the lower strata of society, they experience the margins of modernity, connected as they are to processes of social change and globalization. This 'marginal modernity position' is of notable interest and does, I will suggest, establish a pivotal link to Giddens' work.

Women-led Informal Courts and their Transformatory Potential

Marital practices can neither be isolated from the ideologies and politics of non-governmental organizations (NGOs) nor from those of the state. Accordingly, I will elucidate how a certain segment of the urban women's movement is regulating the realm of marriage and domestic life, and the extent to which it may be modifying marriage norms and practices. Primarily, I will analyse the vibrant praxis of mahila panchayats or women-led informal courts in low-income neighbourhoods of Delhi. Mahila panchayat NGOs emblematize a woman-centred juridical system that provides dispute settlement and marriage counselling services. In these intimate yet very public spaces, marital relations are played out, often with great intensity. Mahila panchayats address women's complaints of marital conflict and breakdown, domestic violence, and familial abuse. In comparison with state institutions and caste associations, which are known for their male-oriented structures, mahila panchayats offer different and personalized services to women. Yet feminist scholarship has so far neglected to foreground the transformatory potential of these female spaces, the extent to which they empower women, and their considerable influence in the lives of married women. In what follows in Chapter 5, I set up the structure of the mahila panchayat as a startling example of a non-legal body and an alternative type of feminism, one that instills confidence in women but without posing a threat to the wider asymmetries of marriage. I show how the ideologies and interventions of the mahila panchayat are at variance with Giddens' vision of the emerging importance given to equality in marriage. It is my hope that the mahila panchayat analysis that engages with very ordinary female activists and clients will open up a fresh debate on the conundrums of marital reconciliation, the politics of informal dispute settlement, and the ideological agendas of activism. The mahila panchayat movement also draws into analytical focus the question of 'progressive' feminist agendas, the feasibility of such agendas in specific urban contexts, and the question of who should be in a position to set these agendas.

Structure of the Book

The socio-economic profile of the Delhi neighbourhood is included in this introduction. In Chapter 2, succinct information is first provided on how the urban poor arrange their marriages and whether matchmaking forms are undergoing extensive modifications. Following this, the chapter describes the distinct marital roles that are accorded to adult men and women and the ideal gender division of labour. This discussion includes women's notions of the exemplary husband and local understandings of a happy marriage. The schism between ideals and reality is exposed through an inquiry into women's perceptions of marital conflict, and I analyse why certain conflicts are highly dominant in arranged marriages. The exposition on the pervasiveness of everyday conflict leads to an examination of kinship and how natal kin address their daughter's marital complaints and difficulties. Through this investigation, a more distinct and wide-ranging picture of marriage emerges. A nuanced analysis of the dynamics between parents and married daughters in a city environment also illuminates how virilocal marriage residence patterns are reconfiguring conjugal relations.

Chapter 3 covers love marriages. It examines young people who eschew parental matchmaking and choose their own partners. It unravels the nature of premarital romance and the factors that enhance courtship practices in Delhi. Additionally, it discusses the reactions of parents and examines whether they are subverting caste endogamy and accepting love marriages. Mapping various combinations of inter-caste and inter-religious unions indicate how individuals from certain communities face difficult impediments in gaining familial acceptance. Various forms of love marriages and their new accretions (e.g. 'arranged love marriage' and 'elopement marriage') are also scrutinized. Notably, this chapter elucidates the post-marital phase of love marriages; conjugal stability in love marriages, married women's shifting ties with their natal families, and self-evaluations of love marriages are all analysed in length.

Chapter 4 deals with secondary unions and explores post-marital consensuality, remarriages and other conjugal arrangements. It probes women's motivations for entering into new relationships and looks at how a cross-section of people across the generations can so easily break their primary marriages to form secondary unions. Attention is drawn to how informal secondary unions are consolidated between partners. The focus is not so much on remarriage rituals or the legal status of secondary unions but on powerful forms of oral commitment and symbolic gestures that cement 'togetherness'. This chapter marks inter-generational changes, with the younger generation defining remarriage and secondary unions in distinct ways from previous generations. Yet across age groups, women's very similar evaluations of their secondary unions reveal the emotional depth, longevity, and quality of these relationships.

Chapter 5 focuses on marital disputes and women's recourse to dispute settlement via mahila panchayats. As I am also keen to compare how other informal institutions settle disputes in Delhi, I present brief data on urban biradari panchayats (caste associations). The crux of this chapter lies, however, in documenting how the mahila panchayat resolves women's disputes in arranged marriages, love marriages, and secondary unions, and the discourses that they articulate in relation to these marriages. I concentrate on what women expect to gain from mediation, while particularizing both successful and unsuccessful cases of arbitration. The mahila panchayat model, its composite services, and its methods of arbitration are also all given extensive coverage.

In Chapter 6, I bring together my analysis on which forms of marriage are more democratic for women. The epilogue outlines change and continuity from 2000–16. It interlaces new reflections in the context of India's celebrated economic growth story.

Representation and Lived Experience: The Journey

I have dealt with the subject of marriage by privileging the 'neighbourhood' (De Neve and Donner 2006; Vatuk 1972). I purposely chose a neighbourhood as I am interested in foregrounding a more extensive understanding of marriage – one that takes into account the wider gender ideologies of a particular area, kinship ties in a city, social relations in urban spaces, and the material context of men and women's working lives. While my study was located in one particular neighbourhood, I was also able to observe spousal and kinship ties in other Delhi neighbourhoods by accompanying women on visits to their natal homes. In addition, a large cross section of the urban poor from other Delhi neighbourhoods figures in my mahila panchayat research as disputes are brought before this public forum from across the city.

For the purposes of fieldwork, I did not face the task of having to acclimatize myself to a new city, as Delhi is home to me. To date I have managed to retain close ties with my respondents as I work in Delhi after having returned from the UK, where I was a student for eight years. For the duration of my fieldwork between November 2000 and April 2002, I lived with my parents in an upper middle class colony, making visits to the field site daily. My husband, who had a job in the UK at this time, came to visit me twice in India. At the start of my fieldwork, I employed a female field assistant, Kalpeshwari, who was in her late thirties. Kalpeshwari belongs to one of the higher SC groups. After six months, I had to replace her as she was finding the demands of the research project too exacting. My new field assistant, Radha, who was in her early forties, thereafter assisted me with great commitment. Radha belongs to the lowest caste (Balmiki), and her experiences and perceptions of low caste consciousness have shaped the contents and arguments of this book to a great extent. It is to her that I dedicate the central story in Chapter 4: 'The Love Stories of Radha and Her Sisters'.

I employed a range of anthropological techniques to capture marital relations. At various stages of writing this book, people have been curious as to how I approached a private and sensitive topic like marriage. At the outset, it needs to be stated that in the low-income neighbourhood I studied, marriage is by no means a private matter. In contrast to middle class colonies where people are hesitant to offer accounts of their private lives, most people in my field site conversed about marriage and love with surprising ease and frankness. I was able to observe spousal relationships and elicit marital stories by meandering through *galis* (lanes) where residents openly volunteered to discuss their lives. They were enthusiastic about the prospect of sharing their life histories with a wider audience. Besides, many marriage stories that circulate in the neighbourhood are 'public' in the sense that they may have developed into full-scale disputes. Given that low-income neighbourhoods are permeated by women's NGOs working on dispute settlement, the language of 'cases', 'grievances', and 'marital breakdown' is a striking feature of everyday urban life. So while there were few barriers in conversing about marriage, it was still a challenging subject to capture analytically. In a setting where people are candid about their relationships, deciphering emotions is still not an easy task. More so, marital events tend to be variable, or, as Katy Gardner observes, 'plots' are usually 'multiple, fluid and endlessly shifting' (2002: 33). Marriage also interlaces disparate features such as love, violence, money, reproduction, sexuality, vulnerability, jealousy, and cooperation. Roaming the interlocking bylanes of the neighbourhood to enter into conversations about these diverse streams was a continuous process. I would introduce myself as a researcher interested in marriage, love, and relationships. This research objective was reinterpreted in the vernacular idiom as *'sukh aur dukh ki kahanian'* (people's journeys or stories through happy, sorrowful, and difficult times). Primarily, I collected my data through participant observation, informal chats, spontaneous exchanges, and semi-structured interviews. While the ethnographic process of data collection in homes and *galis* was gradual and evolving, the research on mahila panchayats was slightly different, as marital disputes were brought forward to a public forum. In both settings, I have nonetheless extensively favoured the use of 'narrative' to interpret the emotional complexity of lived experiences. While having drawn chiefly on women's narratives, I have also, wherever possible, integrated representations of men and the male point of view. In her study on Bengali migrants, Gardner (2002: 2, 30) discusses why the narrative approach is an extremely valuable source for understanding elderly people's subjectivities of aging. Gardner, who uses 'story' and 'narrative' interchangeably, defines them as 'conscious and structured accounts of events across time' that are closely connected to gender, class, and life positioning (2002: 31). I endorse Gardner's invocation on the salience of narrative as this approach can insightfully bring together diverse voices and life-positioning perspectives. Moreover, anthropologists and feminist scholars (Butalia 2000; Jeffery and Jeffery 1996; Narayan 2004) have used life histories and narratives to capture the voices of poor and marginalized women who do not have an official history. According to Chanfrault-Duchet (1991: 77), the life-history approach enables us to collect poor women's words and to reach out to a social group whose discourses are usually muted.

Translation and the Case Study Method

The ethnographic account that features in the forthcoming chapters is an amalgamation of elicited narratives and events that I generically refer to as 'case studies'. In all the case studies, I have anonymized men and women's names. The reader should note that the scheme of events presented in the case studies is not conclusive but perennially developing or unfolding. In this regard, Jeffery and Jeffery (1996), who have made comprehensive use of narratives in their Bijnor study, remark: 'We have tried not to overstructure the longer stories or create the impression that they have reached the final scene. These are the unfinished lives, still unfolding, of women in their middle years. Their futures are not absolutely determined; the plots can take on courses that may astonish us' (1996: 28).

Furthermore, a word about how I have dealt with vernacular narratives and speech. I have translated narratives directly from Hindi into English. I have also translated many English words in this book into their original Hindi usage (e.g. wedding translates into *shaadi*) and common Hindi phrases that people use (e.g. 'no marital problem is ever one-sided' translates into '*tali dono hath se bajti hai*' (literally, it takes two hands to clap).

The Setting

Fieldwork was undertaken in Mohini Nagar,[17] a South Delhi neighbourhood comprising both *bastis* (shanty settlements or slums also known as *jhuggi-jhonpri* colonies) and resettlement colonies. I also conducted extensive fieldwork in Mohini Nagar's largest *basti*, which I call Raju Camp.[18] The *bastis* are squatter settlements that occupy vacant public land. Starting off as makeshift shelters usually protected and patronized by local politicians, over time a *basti* is able to stave off the threat of eviction and achieve a degree of permanence despite its illegal status. *Jhuggis* (homes) in the *basti* are semi-permanent structures made of brick, wood, corrugated iron, and plastic. The size of the *jhuggis* varies according to each family's economic status. Some consist of only a small room shared by four to six family members. *Basti* dwellers receive inadequate basic services such as water and electricity. As their *jhuggis* are illegal, they are always vulnerable to eviction by the municipal authorities. *Bastis* are adjacent to resettlement colonies, where inhabitants legally own *pucca* (permanent) housing. The resettlement colonies are low-income housing estates with small plots allotted to the former residents of inner-city slums who were evicted and resettled on the outskirts of the city in the mid-1970s. Houses in resettlement colonies are narrow concrete structures, with one to four-storey units or 'plots' shared by married sons and their parents. At this juncture, it is useful to provide a brief historical overview of how Delhi's *bastis* and resettlement colonies have emerged.

[17] In relation to the location of the study and fieldwork, I have used pseudonyms. When I refer to other colonies in Delhi, I use their actual names.

[18] *Basti* residents call their shanty settlements 'camps' because they want to ascribe respectability to them.

In her excellent studies of Delhi's resettlement colonies, Emma Tarlo (2000a, 2000b) discusses how colonies that have undergone resettlement are unofficially connected with violence, displacement, and the national emergency of 1975–77. Tarlo describes the chaotic ways in which *basti* dwellers were evicted across Delhi and were made targets of a compulsory sterilization programme (*nasbandi*): 'Basically, in September 1976, production of a sterilization certificate became the new prerequisite for the allocation or regularization of resettlement plots in the area' (2000a: 64).[19] According to official figures, 700,000 people were evicted during the emergency and over 161,000 were sterilized (Tarlo 2000b: 69). Men were made targets of vasectomies, given the cost-effectiveness of these operations (ibid.: 63). In exchange for getting sterilized, people were 'resettled' and given land plots ranging in size from 25 to 80 square yards, and were expected to construct houses on these plots by taking out loans. The government's initiative to develop 46 resettlement colonies in Delhi in an attempt to obliterate the *basti* population has failed to curb the growth of new shanty settlements. Rather, the open spaces within resettlement colonies have encouraged a proliferation of shanty settlements (Ali 1990: 17). In the contemporary landscape of Mohini Nagar, *bastis* such as Raju Camp are in close proximity to the resettlement colonies. Sabar Ali (1990) points out how ties of caste, class, and kinship have proved critical in the emergence of *bastis* within resettlement colonies.

Raju Camp is a congested *basti* comprising approximately 1,500 households. In contrast, resettlement colonies are less congested, being divided into blocks fringed by open spaces, parks, local police stations, and market centres. They also have small offices, women's NGOs, and numerous shops. The main roads of the resettlement colonies link the neighbourhood to the city's wider public transport system and to other parts of Delhi (for example, Batra Hospital, Greater Kailash, Panshcheel Park, Saket, Sangam Vihar.) A mix of extended and nuclear families is visible across Raju Camp and the resettlement colonies. In Raju Camp, married sons often live in the

---

[19] Tarlo (2000a, 2000b) studied the Welcome resettlement colony in east Delhi. She deconstructs the emergency through forgotten files from the slum unit of the Municipal Corporation of Delhi. Her studies illustrate how such marginalized colonies became sites where national events were played out at the local level.

same or neighbouring *galis* as their parents. Resettlement colonies have a higher concentration of families living collaterally, as the housing structure is conducive to this arrangement. Household structures also differ according to the type of marriage that couples have chosen for themselves. Couples in love marriages and secondary unions are less likely to live with extended kin (i.e. husband's agnates). I found that couples in love marriages often rent a house, while in secondary unions women usually leave their conjugal homes to join a secondary partner. Couples in arranged marriages, at least in the early years of marriage, tend to live in joint families. More importantly, the size and composition of households in the area is often in flux, since over the life course women constantly shuttle between their natal and conjugal homes, while marital break-ups are also prevalent (Chapters 2 and 4).

The Mohini Nagar Resettlement Colony
The typical exterior of a three storeyed 'plot' (residential home) in a resettlement colony. The separate floors are for parents and their married sons.

Despite the variation in the physical structure of *bastis* and resettlement colonies, they both possess a similar social ambience. A notable feature of house decorations across Mohini Nagar is the display of kitchen utensils, such as steel bowls and glasses, arranged triangularly on shelves. Many households have television sets, second-hand usually paid through monthly instalments, music systems, and mobile phones, which is now a common gadget. On any given day, auto-rickshaw drivers crowd around the exteriors and entrances of the main junctions, while vendors roam the *galis*. Children can be seen playing marbles and cricket with enthusiasm. Young men run errands for their parents and hang around in groups with their friends. Married women cover their heads with colourful *duppatas* (scarf) or the ends of their saris. The Mohini Nagar neighbourhood has an air of conservatism, implying that women's behaviour is closely monitored.

A Jhuggi
The triangular display of kitchen utensils on the shelves of a *jhuggi*.

Economic disparities are visible across the *bastis* and resettlement colonies. In Raju Camp, a family may refer to a neighbour as 'very poor' (*garib*), thereby emphasizing distinctions in wealth and status. In the resettlement colonies, dilapidated and sparsely furnished houses indicate the poverty of particular households, while other houses have decorative balconies, freshly painted exteriors, and modern household gadgets that exude lower middle class consumption aspirations. The residents of resettlement colonies are generally marginally better off than their *basti* counterparts because they own their permanent housing and land. However, there are discernible overlaps between *bastis* and resettlement colonies that need to be explicated. Despite the marginal variations in wealth, residents share similar caste backgrounds and kinship structures. The majority of inhabitants of the neighbourhood work in the informal sector of the economy, which is characterized by poorly paid and insecure jobs. Many families in Raju Camp have close-kin living in resettlement colonies. I came across families who were shifting from the resettlement colonies to Raju Camp because they were heavily in debt. Thus, there are intersecting links between *bastis* and resettlement colonies, and my ethnography indicates that across these sites marital relations are lived and experienced in similar ways.

Migration, Education, and Employment

Families residing in Mohini Nagar have migration histories dating back to the 1960s and 1970s. Migrants arrived from the states of Bihar, Haryana, Rajasthan, and Punjab, with the majority coming from Uttar Pradesh. Some Raju Camp residents have a different migration history, as they arrived in Delhi in 1982–84[20] from the rural hinterland (*gav*) as far as the interiors of Rae Bareilly in Uttar Pradesh, and from bustling towns such as Aligarh, Ajmer, Ambala, and Dehra Dun. The peripheries of Delhi's borders with Uttar Pradesh and Haryana have also been centres of migration,[21] and

[20] These migrants identify the setting up of Raju Camp with Indira Gandhi's assassination in 1984. To date Raju Camp has not been demolished, and is therefore, an established and stable *basti*. For the purposes of fieldwork, it was essential to avoid *bastis* that were in the process of being uprooted as this would have disrupted the data-collection process. Moreover, an established *basti* guarantees that people's marital trajectories are set against a background of residential longevity.

[21] According to Veronique Dupont (2000: 233), the current decline in

many Raju Camp migrants specify their place of origin as a city near Delhi. Migration to Mohini Nagar has been permanent rather than circular in nature and primarily takes the form of 'family migration'. Women's migration has been mainly in the context of marriage (Chant 1992). The current residents of Mohini Nagar are the urban-born children and grandchildren of the original migrants. New or emerging migration patterns are not discernable amongst the inhabitants, and neither does Mohini Nagar exhibit a 'floating population'.

Levels of literacy in Mohini Nagar are low and uneven. Residents of forty years of age or more are barely literate. In Raju Camp, children are sent to poorly funded government schools, and begin to drop out as early as Class 4 (i.e. at the age of nine). The resettlement colonies exhibit higher levels of literacy, and I came across girls and boys who had completed their tenth class (i.e. at the age of fifteen). Furthermore, young girls in Mohini Nagar avail of courses that are offered by women's NGOs. For example, Action India (Chapter 5) runs courses for adolescent girls on 'health concerns' (raising awareness about contraception, pregnancy, and chronic illnesses) and 'legal awareness' (the appropriate age for marriage and for eligibility to legal rights). Such courses provide alternatives to the formal education system as they are aimed at generating social and legal awareness. The demand for these courses is growing.

Most of Mohini Nagar's male population work as construction workers, daily labourers, mechanics, contractors, bus conductors, auto-rickshaw drivers, and market vendors. They may also have jobs in the private sector as, for instance, couriers and security guards, while positions such as drivers, gardeners, and domestic servants in the upper middle class colonies of Delhi are much sought after. Some men are employed in higher-status and prestigious jobs on the lower rungs of government departments (organized sector), such as airports (Safdarjung Airport), telephone

---

Delhi's migration coincides with a redistribution of the population in favour of growing peripheral towns. Prem Chowdhry (1998: 352) underscores the growing urbanization in the neighbouring state of Haryana. From 1961–81, the number of towns in Haryana increased from 61 to 81. She emphasizes that despite extensive urbanization, the distinction between urban and rural is not watertight. For example, one lakh (100,000) people from rural and semi-urban areas of Haryana commute daily to Delhi for work.

companies (Mahanagar Telephone Nigam Limited or MTNL), hospitals (Ram Manohar Lohia Hospital), and postal services. These men earn between ₹ 5000 and ₹ 8000 per month. The women of the neighbourhood are employed as domestic sweepers and housemaids, and they travel to upper middle class colonies on a daily basis (see Chapter 2 for women's employment trajectories that are tied to the prevailing gender and neighbourhood ideologies). Some women work as activists with NGOs and on large-scale projects, such as credit schemes and those that generate income (e.g. stitching clothes, packing food items, etc.). New sources of employment are beauty parlours, which have emerged in surrounding colonies in considerable numbers. Women's labour is also in demand by export companies. Within the confines of their homes, women also single-handedly run STD booths (telephone services) and small food shops.

Caste, Region, and Religion: Heterogeneity and Differentiation

Mohini Nagar exhibits a high degree of heterogeneity, with SCs, Other Backward Classes (OBCs), regional groups, and religious minorities residing in close proximity to each other. Table 1.1 presents the predominant SCs in Mohini Nagar.

Table 1.1: Local Scheduled Castes

Scheduled Castes and their traditional occupations[22]	Other castes and their traditional occupations
Balmiki (sweeper)	Bania (trader)
Chamar (leather worker)	Gujjar (cow herder)
Dhobi (washerman)	Jat (landowning caste)
Jatav (sub-caste of Chamar/ leather worker)	Kumhar (potter)
Khatik (butcher, meat-cutter)	Rajput
Koli (weaver)	Gehlot Rajput
Teli (oil presser)	Sonar (jeweller/goldsmith)

[22] While many castes have diversified their traditional occupations, they are still ranked in the caste hierarchy according to their traditional vocations.

The SCs do not constitute a homogenous category. Each caste has its own unique historical, political, and social standing. The Balmikis (sweepers) are the predominant social group in Mohini Nagar. Christians, Muslims, and Sikhs are few in number, and are outnumbered by the SCs. Inhabitants are also associated with the region from which they hail. Those from Bihar, Garhwal (Uttaranchal), and Punjab are identified as Bihari, Garhwali, and Punjabi. While discussing caste, the Hindi terms *jat* (caste) and *biradari* (community) are used interchangeably. Yet these terms can connote different and wider groupings (De Haan 1994: 176) that suggest flexibility and yet have separate interpretations. For some regional groups, the term *biradari* identifies people speaking the same language. As the Garhwalis point out: 'All who speak our language, irrespective of caste, and are from the Garhwal region belong to our *biradari*.' For the Balmikis, *biradari* extends beyond region and dialect, but is not inclusive of other castes. For example, a close affinity or brotherhood (*bhai aur biradari*) exists between the Balmikis of Haryana and Uttar Pradesh. *Biradari* is used in the context of religion as well (De Haan 1994: 176), and Muslims talk about different *biradaris* such as Ansari and Nai.

Residential blocks in the resettlement colonies may house Balmiki, Bihari, Garhwali, and Muslim families, and while the development of kinship networks may have facilitated the dominance of clusters of caste groups in certain *galis*, there is no caste-based residential segregation. This aspect of having to live together in urban neighbourhoods draws comments about the insignificance of caste in Delhi. The local consensus is that the caste system cannot survive in urban localities, where resources need to be shared amicably. At the same time, city life accentuates anonymity and equality amongst castes. A glance at everyday life affirms the diminishing importance of caste discrimination and the decline in the significance of conventional rules concerning the pollution considered to result from bodily conditions such as menstruation, death, and childbirth. Commensality is no longer confined to an individual's caste group. Residents mix during social activities and occasions, and food is exchanged during neighbourly encounters and visits. On the other hand, most castes try to avoid commensal relations with Balmikis, and by shifting our attention to the Balmikis, a different picture of caste relations emerges, which is at odds with the liberal views currently being articulated on caste.

The Balmikis, Caste Evaluations, and Homogeneity in the Cultural Practices of Mohini Nagar Residents

The Balmikis are identified as a sweeper community whose members clean streets, latrines, drains, and sewers. In Delhi they formally introduce themselves as Balmiki, Harijan, or SC. Their other term of reference is 'Bhangi', a word derived from *bhang* or hemp, and thus indicating addiction (Singh 1999: 235). As Shyamlal observes:

> A caste of the removers of night soil and the cleaners of latrines belongs to a well defined group in the Indian social order. All such workers in India are today included under the general nomenclature 'The Bhangi'. For this occupational group, there are various names and titles in use in different parts of the country, but the better known term is 'The Bhangi' (1992: 11).

Today, the sweeper castes who had previously aligned themselves with different religions have united under one community, calling themselves Balmiki or Valmiki (Sharma 1995; Shyamlal 1992; Singh 1999), and the term 'Bhangi' is now considered derogatory. Through legend, the Balmikis claim common descent from Saint Balmiki, who was once a huntsman (Valmiki), and who went on to author the epic Ramayana (Sharma 1995).[23] Unlike other castes, Balmikis

[23] 'Untouchables' identify with many faiths—Christian, Hindu, Muslim, and Sikh. Searle-Chatterjee (1994: 161) draws a distinction between 'untouchable' and religious identity, arguing that the former can be of more significance to the lower castes. For this reason, many 'untouchables' have not ascribed to the Hindu label, thus maintaining their rejection of the caste system. Parry (2001: 795; 1999: 136) points out that the Satnami caste, descendants of the Chamar in Chhattisgarh, are followers of Saint Ghasi Das, who rejected the worship of Hindu deities. Today, people regard the Satnami as Hindu by religion, but not by caste. Similarly, Searle-Chatterjee (1994: 160), points out that Benares sweepers do not identify themselves as Hindu, since Hindus are perceived as people of higher status and power and are associated with the Brahmanical

celebrate Balmiki Jayanthi on the full moon day in the Hindu month of Asvin (September-October). This is their main festival and form of worship. A Balmiki temple stands in the centre of Raju Camp as an important emblem of their identity.[24]

Balmiki Temple in Raju Camp
The inside of the Saint Balmiki Temple in Raju Camp. The temple is particularly vibrant during the festivities of Balmiki Jayanthi.

framework. The Balmiki of Delhi are ambiguous about their Hindu status, their major identification being with Saint Balmiki.

[24] The Arya Samaj reform movement in 1923 sought to bring the SCs back into the Hindu fold as mass conversions to other religions had not changed their low socio-economic status. Rama Sharma (1995: 137) marks out the identity shift from 'Bhangi' to Balmiki: 'The purification movement amongst the 'Bhangis' took the form of Hinduization through the Balmiki cult.' However, the worship of Saint Balmiki has led to separatism from, rather than integration with, the rest of society. The lack of integration with the larger society is not caused by those who attend Balmiki temples, but by those who are generally associated with those temples, that is, the 'Bhangis' (ibid. : 143).

While many castes have diversified their jobs and relinquished their traditional occupations, Balmikis have retained sweeping as their prime occupation. A large proportion of them work as salaried employees for the Municipal Corporation of Delhi (MCD), in secure government jobs (*sarkari naukri*). According to unofficial figures, 7 lakh (700,000) people work for the MCD, out of which 2 lakh (200,000) are sweepers with 25 per cent of them being women. A non-permanent job (*kachchi naukri*) fetches ₹ 2500 per month, and becomes permanent after fifteen years of employment. A permanent employee (*pakki naukri*) is paid ₹ 5000–6000 per month, depending on the year he or she joined.25 The MCD jobs offer benefits such as sick leave, maternity leave, holidays, pensions, and bonuses. Searle-Chatterjee (1981: 78) observes that the sweepers are committed to their secure occupation and feel it unnecessary to struggle through long years of schooling. This explains their low levels of social mobility and literacy, with only the ambitious amongst them pursuing education past the basic level (ibid.). There is an incentive for them to retain sweeping as their main occupation as it is relatively well paid (ibid.).

In Delhi, the Balmikis are ranked the lowest (*sabse chhoti jat*) in the caste hierarchy and are assigned a separate and inferior status amongst the SCs. Their profession, which brings them into close contact with dirt, filth, and excreta, is regarded as the most polluting, and other castes continually construct Balmikis as impure and inferior. The Chamar and the Dhobi are also ranked low in the caste hierarchy, but their fewer numbers mean that they are subjected to less opprobrium. Balmikis frequently contest their status as the lowest caste, contending that they are higher than Dhobis. Regional and religious identities also feature in caste evaluations, with Muslims (*Momdums*) being placed just a notch above the Balmikis, and with the Garhwalis being perceived as a 'good caste'. Given these visible hierarchies amongst the SCs, the uniformity of residents' economic condition acts as a leveller against social differentiation, producing a shared working-class identity. Furthermore, while caste and regional groups have their own particular characteristics, identities, rituals, food preferences, traditions and customs they have in many

---

25 MCD pay scales have been revised, with salaries having gone up marginally.

respects also all assimilated similar cultural patterns. For example, there is virtually little difference between caste groups in the ways in which parental support is offered (or denied) to daughters, the nature of marital breakdown and conflict, practices of courtship and the unfolding of love marriages, and the endorsement of the male bread winner ideology. Notwithstanding the multiplicity of social groups in Mohini Nagar, there is a visible homogeneity in the realm of marital, gendered, and kinship practices. Having made this point, the intra-caste group dynamics and social relations of the Balmikis are slightly different from those of other castes, as we shall see in Chapters 3 and 4.

2

Revisiting Arranged Marriages
Marital Roles, Conflict, and Kinship Support

Anthropological studies identify arranged marriage as the most common form of marriage in India. Arranged marriage as an institution connotes parental involvement in the choice of a spouse and is constructed as a union between two families. In south Asian anthropology, arranged marriage has been analysed primarily through the lens of the criteria employed in matchmaking, prestations, marital strategies, and social mobility. What happens to the couple after they marry and settle down has been of less consequence to the anthropologist. So while arranged marriage has received more academic scrutiny than other marital forms, there have been few attempts to problematize this alliance from different angles. Moreover, it is often assumed that matches arranged by parents and other relatives are by far the most stable, harmonious, and workable of all alliances. This chapter attempts to significantly broaden the understanding of arranged marriage and to revisit predominant perceptions that continue to be allied with this hegemonic institution. By 'looking inside marriages', and by examining their ideals and actual practices, my data will present a very different understanding about the nature of arranged marriage.

The first section briefly outlines marital arrangements in Mohini Nagar. The second section examines how marital roles are conceptualized in arranged marriages. The third section highlights marital conflict and women's perceptions of conflict, including the perceptions of men and their families on the same subject. The fourth section highlights the role of the emotional, material, and practical support provided by primary natal kin to their married daughters in shaping women's relationships with their husbands and affines. This final part makes a case for a deeper and more nuanced understanding of contemporary natal-kin support structures, mother–daughter bonds, and spousal intimacy in urban north India.

Marital Arrangements in Mohini Nagar

Anthropologists have queried the sheer resilience of the arranged marriage system that allows elders to be prime decision makers in choosing prospective mates. Uberoi (1998) notes that with the modernization of Indian society, it was presumed that arranged marriages would be undermined both by encouraging an individualistic ethos and by subverting the rules of endogamy. In a globalized era of open markets, increased consumption, and Hindi cinema's ongoing projection of romantic love, how or through what is the constancy of parental matchmaking manifested? Primarily, caste-endogamous arranged marriages continue to ensure a family's prestige and status and to preserve the normative kinship order.[1] So in Mohini Nagar a Dhobi bride should marry a Dhobi groom, and this type of endogamy is applicable across castes.

The present-day Hindu marriage consists of an engagement ceremony and the main wedding (*shaadi*),[2] after which the bride

---

[1] For another perspective on the perseverance of caste-endogamy see 'Caste Walls Divide Modern India', *Hindustan Times*, 31 December 2006. In a survey conducted in the metros of India, 57 per cent declared that neither they nor their children would marry into castes considered lower than their own. Only 28 per cent believed that it was acceptable for their children to wed outside one's caste. Shiv Visvanathan, a social anthropologist, was quoted as saying that economic liberalization had, in fact, reinforced caste: 'Caste is now a local membership in a globalised society. In a world that is opening up so much, and to so many uncertainties, it helps to have roots and networks that anchor one's identity. Thus, endogamy is still the ideal.'

[2] The *shaadi* is a public and formal wedding reception in which the couple goes around the sacred fire seven times (*sat phere*), a customary ritual of a Hindu wedding. The *shaadi* is a highly prestigious event, marked by receptions for a number of guests and a display of dowry and affinal gift exchanges. The *shaadi* is also symbolic of a marriage arranged by parents and performed with full ritual. It is referred to as the primary marriage in the anthropological literature (Dumont 1964).

immediately joins her conjugal family. The *gauna* ceremony, practiced in north India to mark the ritual transfer of the bride to her conjugal home upon attaining puberty, is in decline in Delhi as the age of marriage for girls has inched upwards to post-puberty (cf. Parry 2001: 795). The legal age for marriage in India is 18 years for girls and 21 for boys. In actuality, girls are married between the ages of 15 and 18,[3] and boys, between 20 and 25. Marriages are often arranged through a *beech wala* (intermediary), who tend to be fictive kin, acquaintances, neighbours, and close or distant relatives. They are not confined to women, as in Ursula Sharma's (1986: 165) study of urban Shimla. In Delhi, a number of male intermediaries are involved in matchmaking. A young woman stated how the intermediary for her marriage was a man who came once a week to sell food provisions in Raju Camp. Intermediaries operate on the principle of goodwill; when word spreads that a family is seeking an alliance, intermediaries volunteer to arrange a match using knowledge of their local networks. The role of the intermediary is to provide trustworthy information about families and to take responsibility if the couple faces marital discord. The reputations of intermediaries are nonetheless often discussed negatively. There are numerous instances where they do not disclose accurate information and cannot be traced after having negotiated a match. Though deception by intermediaries is widespread, and is a common factor leading to marital breakdown, their initiatives continue to be relied upon.[4]

Conversations with young people suggest that marriage preferences remain the prerogative of parents, who may or may not consult their children in this matter.[5] While young people prefer

[3] Some parents 'reserve' a boy, an event known as *rokna*, when the girl is about fifteen years old. In a *rokna* ceremony, the families exchange sweets and a token sum of money. Families that initiate a *rokna* specify that it is a way of monitoring the groom's behaviour before marriage. If the groom stops earning or develops bad habits such as alcoholism or gambling, the impending marriage can be cancelled.

[4] In contrast, the educated Indian middle classes have an array of choices in seeking mates through matrimonial columns, marriage bureaus, and internet sites. The proliferation of these resources reduces their complete reliance on informal networks and intermediaries.

[5] Many young people attempt to resist parental pressure (see Ahearn 2001 for interesting insights into this topic), although the dominant perception is

to be consulted, they also endorse the critical benefits of parental alliances.[6] It appears that boys have more leeway in the choice of a spouse. Reflecting on changes in matchmaking practices, a young man noted that in recent years there has been an overt shift: 'Previously, we were not allowed to view a bride. If a photograph was shown to us, we were considered lucky. Now, before arranging a match, the bride and the groom are allowed to see each other, just once.' His statement indicates that the process of marital negotiations continues to be strict.[7] Natal families exhibit immense anxiety about finding grooms when their daughters turn fifteen. Investing in a child's full education does not seem to be a priority. Mothers make up excuses about how their daughters failed in school; early arranged marriage therefore constitutes the norm, even though it contravenes the law. The institution of arranged marriage has not undergone fundamental modifications in age at marriage or matchmaking traditions as the latter remains primarily a parental responsibility.

For all social groups, marriage is modelled on north-Indian patrilineal norms. Dowry in the form of cash and household items is widespread, and even the very poorest try to muster respectable dowries. Some women gave the example of a widow in Raju Camp who married off her daughter before I began my fieldwork. As she was very poor, her neighbours and those in surrounding *galis* pooled their resources to contribute to her daughter's dowry. Even the local leader of Raju Camp made a substantial donation. Veronica Magar (2000: 110) observes that the giving of dowry is a cultural

---

that protest against parental unions is lacking in India. I encountered girls and boys using the term *zabardasti* to indicate that their marriages were forced upon them. In this chapter, I do not cover this subject. Chapter 3 describes how young people are subverting arranged marriages in preference for love marriages.

[6] As argued by Sudhir Kakar: 'Perhaps the greatest attraction of an arranged marriage is that it takes away the young person's anxiety around finding a mate. Whether you are plain or good-looking, fat or thin, you can be reasonably sure that a suitable mate will be found for you.' See 'Arranged Marriage: Matchmaking', *India Today*, 5 November 2007.

[7] Chowdhry (2007: 4) notes that most marriages in north India are arranged by senior males and females. During the brokering of marriages, the girl and the boy may be allowed to glance at each other or to see a photograph. In other cases, a formal meeting between the prospective bride and groom may not be permitted at all.

practice that is well entrenched in resettlement colonies. I gathered that some of the following items are presented as part of a standard dowry: television set, stereo music system, refrigerator, motor scooter, bicycle, steel kitchen utensils, *saris*, wristwatch, jewellery, furniture (including beds), and cash. While these standard dowries seem lavish for low-income families, Magar (2000: 63) discusses how in resettlement colonies, natal kin spend between ₹ 45,000 and ₹ 100,000 on dowry.

Jhuggi Dwellers' Possessions

Many *jhuggi* dwellers have television sets, video cassette recorders, and a range of steel utensils. Other *jhuggi* owners may have none of these consumer items.

The SCs follow the rule of *gotra* exogamy whereby three to four prohibited degrees of kinship should be avoided, or where it is not possible to trace descent through previous generations. While caste-endogamous matches are the norm, natal families also state their preference for an alliance of 'equal economic standing'. Yet they point out that bride takers will always be superior in status to bride givers. They are referring here to the custom of dowry that signifies status distinctions between bride givers and takers. Further, whilst they profess economic parity, I noticed how many upwardly mobile natal families would boast about how they had married their daughter to a *'notewallah'* (a wealthy groom), elaborating on the lavish wedding expenditure they had incurred. Thus, in actuality, some natal families do seek marriage alliances with families that are relatively better off. Overall, the type of marriage alliance that families seek reflects their long-term aspirations and current resources. Filippo Osella and Caroline Osella (2000: 81a) make the important point that the goal of those with the least wealth and prestige is simply to get their children married: 'the marriage itself being an end rather than a means to further benefits.'

The Male Breadwinner Ideology

In arranged marriages, the notion of the 'providing husband' is accorded great importance. After marriage, a clear gender division of labour is meant to mark the marital roles of men and women. While the role of women is to stay at home and carry out domestic chores, men are expected to provide for their families. Despite low standards of living in *bastis*, this is the idealized division of responsibility between couples. So amongst the urban poor, we observe a distinctly powerful ideology of the male breadwinner. Adolescent girls who have financially aided their natal families by working in beauty parlours, export companies, cinema halls, and as domestic workers are supposed to relinquish their jobs once they marry. Hitherto, the view that has dominated the social sciences is that the male breadwinner construct, or the 'housewife ethic' (Osella and Osella 2000a) is an ideology that pertains to the upper castes. More so, the usual interpretation is that semi-secluded women hail from aspiring, upwardly mobile families and prosperous households. Where poor low caste women are concerned, the predominant perception is that they display autonomy in their working lives and are free to take up waged work without the consent of their husbands. Searle-Chatterjee's (1981) exemplary ethnography is widely cited by scholars to illustrate that poor sweeper women are autonomous wage earners. Searle-Chatterjee unearths unique and positive aspects of the sweepers' conjugal lives that correspond with feminist constructions of egalitarian marriages. In Benares, women from the sweeper caste have the freedom to work; even the wives of prosperous sweepers work. Through jobs in the municipality and domestic sweeping work, sweeper women often earn higher salaries than their husbands do. They also enjoy considerable freedom of movement and play a role in controlling household finances. Notably, conjugality is not based on segregated gender roles: 'In general there is a very joint type of labour between men and women' (1981: 98). Searle-Chatterjee concludes that Benares sweeper women hold a strong position in their community and attributes such egalitarian conjugal patterns to equal labour market opportunities and to the close-knit nature of the sweeper community.

This narrative of female autonomy and equality in marriage by Searle-Chatterjee is not the case amongst Delhi Balmiki sweepers, and nor does it pertain to the other SCs. In Mohini Nagar, marriage is not seen as an enterprise that allows for the mutuality of gender roles. Interestingly, Balmiki women have parallel labour market opportunities with those of their men folk. Like their Benares counterparts, they, too, have easy access to domestic sweeping work, a profession with which their caste is identified, and one which is largely feminized in Delhi. They can also apply for MCD sweeping jobs. Given these congruent economic opportunities available to the Balmikis, they do not in any measure exhibit egalitarian conjugal patterns. In Mohini Nagar, all social groups have assimilated similar cultural patterns and gendered codes of behaviour. Hence, across castes the prevailing social norms suggest that providing for a family is an overriding male responsibility. This is analogous to Vera-Sanso's (1995: 157) portrayal of male breadwinner ideologies that are deeply ingrained amongst the most Backward Castes (a term classified by the Tamil Nadu state government) who reside in low-income Chennai settlements. In Chennai, there is a cogent ideology of *maanam*, a family's honour and reputation that has female chastity at its core. *Maanam* is not only a household concern. Wider kin and local community members mediate as to whether women should work outside the house. As Vera-Sanso argues, women in Chennai are not driven to seek employment despite the poverty levels they face as *maanam* remains more influential than the need for increased female and household income. Correspondingly, in Delhi, male breadwinner ideologies underpin notions of respectability, family reputation, and female modesty, which counter the essentialized view that SC women are exempt from upper caste notions of patriarchal honour.8 In addition, the Osellas (2006) underscore how across classes in India, the male breadwinner ideal is often tied into normative gendering. On this point, readers need to appreciate why even the poorest may want to cling to the male breadwinner-housewife model. It is not simply because of class aspiration. As I will show, in Mohini Nagar, gender identities are deeply rooted in family service roles and adult status (Jackson 2001; Osella and Osella 2006). Therefore, in instances where husbands earn stable incomes, they seek to restrain wives from taking up paid work. Some husbands nonetheless contend that they are less resistant to the idea of a working wife if she can find a respectable job (e.g. a government job or school-based work).

Conjugal Contracts: Two Prominent Arrangements

Two domestic arrangements in the neighbourhood spell out distinct roles for men and women. The first arrangement, which is a customary norm, is one in which an employed husband is required to hand over his entire monthly salary to his wife, who is meant to judiciously budget for household finances. In the second arrangement, which I observed in Mohini Nagar, husbands cover household expenditures themselves but without handing over their earnings to wives, while wives manage domestic chores. Both these practices of household budgeting are visible in nuclear and joint families, although for the latter other set-ups may be in place as women are residing with their affinal kin. These domestic arrangements are employed specifically in cases where

---

[8] When I visited another resettlement colony, located a considerable distance away from Mohini Nagar, that was inhabited by the Gujarati community, I found a completely different set of practices governing women's working lives. Gujarati women independently traverse the colonies of Delhi, exchanging pots and pans for old clothes, a traditional bartering system. They told me that they never have to struggle with their husbands for permission to work and that their husbands rarely object. The case of Gujarati women is closer to the predominant image of poor women displaying autonomy in their working lives.

the husband is the breadwinner and, as I shall go on to indicate, they are overturned when the husband is unable to provide. To facilitate a comparative perspective, these forms of organizing the household economy are found elsewhere, and are analysed in some depth by Ann Whitehead (1981) in a discussion of inequality in marriage. In Whitehead's seminal study of the diverse economies of industrial Britain and rural Ghana, she conceptualizes institutional arrangements within marriage as a 'conjugal contract' wherein 'husbands and wives exchange goods, incomes, and services including labour, within the household' (1981: 88). As argued by Whitehead, marriage and the household as a collectivity are founded on the necessary existence of such conjugal contracts. Whitehead's elucidation of conjugal contracts illustrates how domestic budgeting arrangements are often asymmetrical: 'These institutional arrangements are one important battleground in the establishment of male domination in the sphere of marital and family relations' (1981: 89). One of Whitehead's principal contributions to the field of gender studies has been to show how practices around money and resources retain gender markers, which are, in turn, expressions of gender power. She underscores the point that gender ideologies govern the distribution and allocation of intra-household resources.

Whitehead discusses a prominent type of budgeting arrangement amongst the British working class that she calls a 'whole wage system', where within a household there is a single male breadwinner. In this form of resource allocation, the wife receives the husband's entire wages. This system has been associated with poverty in particular geographical areas of Britain. As these families have scarce resources, the wife must manage expenses as efficiently as possible. From the wages handed over to the wife, a certain amount of money is returned to the husband for his personal needs. The wife's personal savings lie in putting together what she can once household expenditures have been met. The same principle (i.e. the first arrangement) applies to households in Mohini Nagar where husbands earn a stable income to support their families. In this agreement, whatever the husband earns, he is supposed to hand it over to his wife, such provisioning being equivalent to a maintenance allowance that is called *kharcha-pani* in Hindi. *Kharcha* means 'to spend' or 'to receive money to spend', while *pani*, water, alludes to necessity and provisioning. The conjoined household formulation, *kharcha-pani,* connotes the husband's pivotal role of providing for his family through a monthly allowance.

In contrast to the first domestic arrangement, a second one also exists whereby husbands cover monthly expenditures without handing over their entire earnings. This second arrangement is justified by husbands on the grounds that they are more competent ('*limit mein kharch*') at managing funds than their wives. In line with this discourse, wives are belittled for their shortcomings in money matters. In this second arrangement, wives are recipients of sporadic and nominal earnings, and have very little control over household budgeting. Their husbands do the necessary shopping and payment of monthly bills. Women prefer receiving regular lump sums or their husbands' full earnings, even though, as Whitehead (1981) has argued, being in control of earnings does not mean that resources are shared and distributed equally between spouses. Whitehead (1981) has shown how the control of commonly held financial funds allied with folk ideologies of equal sharing is a fallacy, as inequalities persist in wholly different gendered divisions of labour and economic contexts. This view is supported by Henreitta Moore (1992), who notes that earlier conceptions of household relations were framed around a benevolent male breadwinner, while notions of altruism and cooperation characterized family relations (Becker 1991). Moore states: 'One result of this rapprochement between feminist theorizing and mainstream anthropology/economics has been the emergence of a view of the household which sees it as a locus of competing interests, rights, obligations and resources, which often involve household members in bargaining, negotiation and possibly even conflict' (1992: 132).[9]

What do husbands in Mohini Nagar expect from their wives? If a wife is the recipient of regular *kharcha-pani,* she should perform household chores competently. If a husband is a successful provider, a wife should reciprocate by respecting his authority. There is a discernable notion of adherence to male authority. A wife should respect her husband through idioms signifying his superiority (e.g. not calling him directly by his first name). She should adhere to the customs of her affinal home (e.g. covering her head in the presence of senior affines). Married women must obey the neighbourhood

[9] See also Agarwal (1994) and Kabeer (1994).

codes of propriety, which are marked by gender hierarchies and spatial constraints. A wife's conduct is unreasonable if she nags her husband after he returns from work, as earning for a family is associated with extreme hardship. Husbands constantly comment that 'no conflict or marital problem is ever one-sided' (*'tali dono hath se bajti hai'*). Here they are insinuating that their wives have a duty to conform to their marital roles, whilst during a conflict both spouses (not only the husband) are likely to be at fault. As such, there are plenty of appraisals of a married woman's behaviour, verbal conduct, and actions.

Love, Affection, and the Exemplary Husband

By and large, women associate a good marriage with economic protection; the material context gives significant contours to their emotions. They consider themselves fortunate if their husbands hand them regular *kharcha-pani*; the neighbourhood's first domestic arrangement is highly coveted by women. Husbands who dispense *kharcha-pani* also equate spousal happiness with adequate provisioning, using the phrase 'we are lacking in nothing' (*'koi kami nahi hai'*) to exemplify economic stability.[10] The consistent dispensation of *kharcha-pani* has vital material and symbolic connotations for married women. It gives them self-respect and strengthens their role in domestic budgeting. Women are able to save money for their personal use, even though in practice men are watchful and ultimately in control of earnings (Whitehead 1981). What is more, *kharcha-pani* symbolically reinforces a strong sense of spousal fidelity. The possession of earnings, as women mention, is tantamount to fidelity, as otherwise the money would be spent on another woman (*'pyar karta hai'*). Accordingly, regular *kharcha-pani* enhances trust in marriage. Under harsh poverty conditions, economic fulfilment is thus synonymous with expressions of love, happiness, and contentment (*'pyar aur khushi'*).

Women who are denied a basic maintenance allowance (the second arrangement) assert that they are unhappy and dissatisfied.

[10] Beyond India, this is strikingly similar to the findings of Sylvia Chant's (2001: 207) study of Costa Rican men of low-income communities who measure their worth by keeping their family together; continuous earnings are required to secure women's affections and respect.

They indicate how they struggle to run their households and keep the children well fed and clothed. They equate the second arrangement with ill-treatment, thereby seeking intervention from natal kin and mahila panchayats. I observed how the denial of a maintenance allowance provokes great angst amongst women. Female neighbours will mobilize support not when a woman in their *gali* is encountering domestic violence, but when she is in a distressed state because her husband is refusing to hand over *kharcha-pani*. Showing me her bruises, Somvati describes how she was hit the night before with a pressure cooker and thrown against the wall of her *jhuggi*. When I describe Somvati's painful ordeal to Usha, it elicits a flat reaction: 'She must have done something wrong to be beaten. It is never only a man's fault. No marital problem is one-sided.' When I mention that Somvati's husband has withdrawn *kharcha-pani*, Usha becomes agitated: 'As neighbours we will confront him. What does he mean by not giving her *kharcha-pani*?'

Family Devotion as Durable Love

In the context of western Turkey, Kimberly Hart (2007: 350) has critiqued the arranged marriage literature for its narrow depiction of spousal ties. She contends that researchers have neglected to show how couples are agents of their own intimate and emotional lives: 'They see marriage as a practical financial bond between households and lineages' (2007: 350). Hart is arguing here for an analytical shift from the economics of relationships to the emotional texture of a couple's conjugal life. While Hart presents nuanced data on Turkish marital practices, she gives us little sense of the power dynamics within marriage and of the working of dominant gender ideologies. A good marriage in Mohini Nagar rests upon an ideology of economic dependence and a clear gender division of labour. Yet I have attempted to present a multidimensional picture of spousal ties by describing the enormous connectivity between money, trust, equanimity, and affection. The ethnographic evidence substantiates the fact that women tend to evaluate their husbands and their married lives against the backdrop of spousal expectations. The augmentation of married love *(pyar)* is contingent on the fulfilment of expectations. Time and again, ideals are powerfully deployed as a benchmark for appraising marital happiness and sorrow, success and failure. As it follows, in line with what it means to be an adult, there is an enormous focus on the performance of marital and familial duties (cf. Jackson 2001; Osella and Osella 2000b). More so, the ideal husband (*'achcha admi'*) is one who cares about the long-term welfare of his family: 'We are happy when our husbands look after the interests of the family, come home on time, and avoid drinking with other men.' These qualities—where the stress is on family devotion, practical support, and care—attract considerable praise and are the closest that one gets to a local definition of marital love. This paradigm of 'family devotion', as I am told, establishes a durable foundation for marriage and needs to be distinguished from fleeting sexual attraction. This local understanding of family devotion resonates with Daniel Miller's (1998) valuable concept of love relating to a different field of inquiry, i.e. supermarket shopping in north London. In Miller's view, shopping not only reflects love 'but is a major form in which love is manifested and reproduced' (1998: 18). Specifically his interpretation of love has more to do with obligations, cares, concerns, and routine devotion: 'Love as a practice is quite compatible with feelings of obligation and responsibility' (1998: 20). Miller distinguishes love from a romantic ideal or an idealized moment of courtship by equating it with 'a much wider field to that of which life is seen as properly devoted' (1998: 20). It is precisely this conception of devotion and love with which Delhi women identify. Additionally, wives confer their appreciation on husbands if the latter are able to protect the former against the wrath of affines.[11] Thus, a loving husband is a desired part of conjugality. Raheja and Gold's (1994) deconstruction of Rajasthani songs stresses the importance of an intimate conjugality as separate from the extended family. Susan Wadley (1994) also discusses how women's songs in Karimpur counter discourses of male hegemony that mute the love between husbands and wives. Mohini Nagar women, therefore, express love for their husbands in multifarious ways. While emotional compatibility is

---

[11] There are several examples in the kinship literature on the strained mother-in-law and daughter-in-law relationship, the repetition of which is unnecessary here. As women and men are placed differently in the patrilocal family, age and gender being defining features, this aspect tends to foster conflicts between young women and affines in particular.

less talked about in the open, on closer examination it does prove to be significant for couples (see Chapter 4).

Subaltern Working Lives: Ideals versus Experiences

Amongst the urban poor an undercurrent of tension between ideals and local experiences is apparent in daily life. Let us consider the possible shifts in marital roles and alternative scenarios of domestic arrangements, as when husbands are unable to live up to the ideals of male providing. In reality, men's working lives and job opportunities are severely constrained by high unemployment, economic instability, and low incomes. Men are not always able to sustain their families, as they are employed in the informal sector, which offers no guarantee of secure employment. In situations of male unemployment, and when husbands fail to fulfil their provider role because of personal shortcomings (such as excessive drinking) or a crisis (such as the loss of a job), all common occurrences in poor households, wives are expected to search for work as the male provider ideal is overturned. Rita's husband's factory has shut down. This is the first time in her married life that she has taken up employment: 'My children are alone the whole day. What can I do? My *pihar* (natal kin) and *sasural* (affinal kin) are not there to help me.' Women are also confronted with provider responsibilities when their husbands develop serious health problems. As hard manual work, inadequate nutrition, and excessive drinking adversely affect men's working lives, many husbands fall ill while also dying young. Monu, a vegetable vendor, has a chronically ill husband. She tells me that although he does not financially contribute to the household, he is still a caring spouse. From Monu's description, I note how marriage ideals and expectations can be radically transformed. The reconceptualizations of ideals are linked with unexpected life events.

On the whole, a woman's entry into waged work signifies a dramatic shortfall in family income. The necessity of working (*majburi*) can sometimes occur several years into a marriage. In times of financial hardship, Balmiki women have a marked advantage over other SC women as they can find work promptly. For a start, they can approach the MCD for sweeping jobs. Balmiki widows, for example, have financial security. As per the municipality rules, they are entitled to the deceased husband's jobs and pensions. Other

SC women who do not want to be identified with sweeping will pursue other employment avenues; sweeping for them is a means of last resort, an act of absolute desperation. A woman of the Pan Chaurasaya caste said that her family was in dire need of money. Though sweeping brings in a better income, she had hired an ice-cream van that will enable her to earn petty cash. She revealed that if she were to sweep or clean someone's house (*'kothi saf karna'*), her *biradari* (whose traditional occupation is making and selling *pan*, a stimulant and breath-freshener made from betel leaves, areca nuts, and other ingredients) would object: 'My eldest daughter will then find it hard to marry.'

It must be clarified that even in those marriages where men claim to be breadwinners, many women are found to be contributing to the family's income from within their homes. Women run telephone booths, do tailoring work, and sell products from their houses. A distinction needs to be carefully drawn between waged work that entails employment outside the neighbourhood and work within the boundaries of the home and neighbourhood. The former signifies a drastic decrease in household income, for which women must travel outside Mohini Nagar to find better-paid employment. The terms 'male provider' or 'male providing' that men routinely use can, therefore, be wholly inaccurate, as many Mohini Nagar women are working from their homes or within the neighbourhood to accumulate personal savings. The money they generate is never really valued nor is their labour considered work by husbands. In this regard, it is common for women to repudiate the validity and ideological basis of the male breadwinner–housewife model. Many women are also critical of being denied the right to work and have no qualms in describing how they are 'locked up at home'. Women are particularly disdainful of husbands who will not dispense *kharcha-pani* and nor will they permit them to work.

I have indicated that in actuality many Mohini Nagar women support their entire families. A fairly high proportion of these women are employed as domestic sweepers and workers, travelling daily from Mohini Nagar to middle and upper class colonies in Delhi. Informal sector conditions are not conducive to sustaining the deeply embedded male breadwinner ideologies. Hence, in reality, the designated marital roles in arranged marriages do undergo transformation. To add to this, while household chores and childcare are formally part of women's domain, I found that many men spend time with their children and assist with the housework, although not in the same egalitarian manner as described by Searle-Chatterjee (1981). Interestingly, a recurring discourse amongst spouses is the underlying continuity between ideals and experiences. For instance, while women often end up as family providers in compliance with social norms, they may stop working once their husbands or grown sons can provide again (cf. Vero-Sanso 1995). The active discourse on what is expected from an adult can resurface, or go back and forth, even when the marital roles have undergone fundamental transformations. As such, it is vital to underscore that poor women's work trajectories are never linear; they remain fragmented and changeable over their life cycle. For this reason, SC women have a weak economic status as they, too, depend on low-status jobs and, more significantly, they need to conform to the social norms that govern their lives. It must be reiterated that, by and large, Balmiki women only start working when faced with economic instability, as male breadwinner ideologies also constrain their choices. Yet those women who find municipal employment do not relinquish their jobs once their husbands regain employment. Their husbands grow to value the benefits of a municipality job that offers secure employment. In this regard, compared to other SCs, Balmiki women who are municipal employees have a more consistent work trajectory.

Problematizing Marital Relationships

The previous section has shown that there is variation aplenty between marriage norms and experiences. Consequently, many scenarios unfold between couples when the marital roles ascribed to them undergo transformation. This section analyses frequent causes of marital conflict found in arranged marriages when normative expectations of provider roles fail to materialize. It also looks into other forms of interpersonal differences and stresses that can stem from a variety of causes that are unrelated to the expectation of male as provider.

A discussion of the respective perspectives of Ramesh and Shantha regarding their marriage introduces serious conflicts in arranged marriages.

Ramesh and Shantha: Alcoholism and Provider Responsibilities

Ramesh and Shantha, a Balmiki couple, have been married for twenty years. Ramesh tells me that he is emotionally distressed. He has been sacked by MCD because of an incident in which he bailed a friend, who later absconded, out of a Delhi jail. He is attempting to reinstate himself in the municipality by acquiring a certificate of mental illness from an asylum in Agra, which would clear him of misconduct. In addition, Ramesh is in turmoil because of his wife. An outpouring of complaints follows: 'She does not talk to me as a wife should. She is sharp-tongued. She does not listen to me at all . . . she keeps answering me back with abuse. The fighting is non-stop between us. No marital problem is ever one-sided (*tali dono hath se bajti hai*). I tell her not to keep visiting her *pihar* but she does not listen . . . I am given no respect by her family. She does not even let me joke [sexual joking] or come near her [sexual contact]. In this world, it is so important to be loved (*pyar*). What else is there to live for?'

Shantha, a frail woman has just returned to the resettlement colonies from the upper middle class colony of Greater Kailash, where she now holds a sweeping job. Her relatives have dropped in to see her. Shantha recalls that Ramesh looked after her well in their early years of marriage. Now she has given up on him. A year ago, he lost his MCD job (she expresses anguish at this). She blames his loss of employment on drinking and on 'another woman', because of whom he stopped attending work. He can find work now, but instead he drinks away the whole day. He has sold her jewellery to buy alcohol. She is single-handedly keeping their seven children alive, while he is not even bothered about the family's welfare. She also complains that he has no shame: 'He wants to have sexual intercourse all the time. But now our children have grown up. We all sleep in the same room. There is no privacy with grown children. This is also why we have so many fights. When our children were young, it would happen two or three times at night. He would not leave me alone.' Here her relatives are in agreement; major tensions are escalated when husbands need to be sexually restrained. Shantha adds: 'Now when I restrain him, he beats me badly as he thinks I am having an affair with someone from work. He alleges that I go to work to have sex with other men (*randibazi*).

When suspicion (*sak*) starts to grow, it destroys a marriage. There are no cures for male suspicion.'
Shantha and Ramesh's relationship is deeply affected by a breakdown in communication. Ramesh complains that his wife does not treat him respectfully, is quarrelsome, will not cooperate with him, and is denying him sexual intimacy. Shantha evaluates their marital crisis along different lines. Her main cause of anguish is Ramesh's irresponsible behaviour, especially his wasteful expenditure on alcohol. When the marital roles undergo a fundamental reversal (i.e. when the woman becomes the provider), the wife loses respect for the husband, as seen in the way Shantha speaks about Ramesh. Geert De Neve (2004) shows how Tamil wives and mothers readily criticize and ridicule men who fail to live up to the provider ideal. Delhi women ridicule men by hurling insults such as 'I am the man in this house' or 'he is not a real husband'. While the usual assumption is that marital discord manifests itself in the early years of marriage (i.e. the more critical and sensitive phase when couples attempt to establish compatibility), serious and intense conflicts are equally conspicuous among couples with a longer marital history.

Women like Shantha emphasize men's frequent neglect of their responsibility as providers. They describe how their husbands, elderly fathers-in-law, and even fathers drink regularly and how at any given opportunity they plunge their families into debt (cf. Magar 2000). The women point out that when they enter waged work as a response to male unemployment, they often end up providing for their families for several years while their husbands neglect the search for work. This has led to the widespread perception that men are unreliable. Consequently, there is an outpouring of anger against men (*admi log*).[12] Wider norms and expectations of marriage entail compliant male behaviour. Excessive drinking means that money cannot be judiciously saved, as it impinges on

[12] Jeffery and Jeffery (1996: 134) neatly capture critical interpretations of women's married life in rural Bijnor. Female narratives reveal how 'marriage was no great thing' and that 'marriage was a calamity'. Women in Delhi whose husbands are chronic drinkers express similar views about marriage. These women add that they have stopped celebrating the *Karva Chauth* festival (keeping a day-long fast for the husband's happiness, well-being, and long life) as their husbands are 'drinking away' their lives.

family finances. Cecile Jackson (2001: 1) informs us of how the successful achievement of adult manliness is associated with good money management. The Osellas' (2000: 129) Kerala ethnography on money and masculinity shows that being in possession of resources is not enough; accumulating, consuming, and managing these resources wisely over the life course is the crucial task. While some men in Mohini Nagar have government jobs, signifying social status, they, too, are expected to manage their finances prudently. With further reference to drinking, women and higher Scheduled Castes point towards male MCD employees, who they identify as a group drinking throughout the day whilst abstaining from work. I was told that, in effect, MCD employees pay a sum of money, usually ₹ 1000 a month, to another lay person who covers for them and sweeps their designated area. As MCD employees send out others to work in this way, they are viewed as a pampered and privileged lot, earning high salaries and enjoying job security without actually working themselves. As per my observation, MCD employees, many of whom do pay off others, are not the only ones who drink during the day. Men from all professions and castes gather to drink regularly. Moreover, Ramesh's example of being fired from the municipality suggests that in exceptional cases, whether on account of misconduct, abstention from work, or for other reasons, it is quite possible to lose permanent employment.

While there is much fury over how men squander household finances on alcohol, Jackson (2001; 1999) offers a probing, complex, and subtle analysis of the problem of drinking. She argues that habits like drinking need to be juxtaposed against male subjectivities and the working lives of men. This subject needs further academic attention as the considerable importance accorded to the male as provider suggests that men, too, experience vulnerabilities. Chant (2001) describes how Costa Rican men are confronted with personal crises, low-self esteem, and vulnerability when out of work. They no longer feel needed, valued, or appreciated. In the study by Jasinski et al. (1997: 828), ethnic groups facing poverty, unemployment, and economic instability use alcohol to relieve stress. Moreover, as Jackson (2001: 15) and the Osellas' (2000) discuss, successful provider roles are beset with contradictory expectations, in the face of which men have to maintain a precarious balance. According to Jackson (2001), women simultaneously approve and disapprove of certain male habits, which leaves men 'navigating a path which demonstrates adequate provisioning without becoming "overpowered" by a wife, and socializing with men, but not to excess such that adequacy as a provider is questioned, must require careful management' (2001: 15). Here Jackson is illuminating the overlapping boundaries between work and leisure and the ways in which men are expected to carefully organize their time while also socializing with others. In line with Jackson's observations, male socializing in Mohini Nagar permits entry into valuable networks for arranging marriages, borrowing money, etc., for which women show appreciation. However, excess time and money spent on socializing and drinking leads to conflict and to a reappraisal of men's character. Given that men are expected to maintain these delicate balances and that they use alcohol as an escape from grinding poverty, we must not detract from the salient point made by Mohini Nagar women in relation to drinking. They argue that when in distress, they seldom consume large quantities of alcohol. I have met widows who associate their married years solely with a trajectory of alcohol-induced domestic violence and conflict. They unanimously say that they never received any respect or love from their husbands.

Work, Suspicion, and Violence: Real and Imagined Intimacies

From women's accounts it appears that marital relationships acquire a different dynamic when the wives start working outside the house. Ramesh alleges that Shantha has affairs when she goes to work. When Shantha returns home, she is met with paranoid queries about her whereabouts and actions. Likewise, Usha recounts that her husband knew the exact details of her travel route and the lengthy traffic jam in which she had been held up. He had followed her closely. Ever since she had begun working, her loyalties towards him were under intense scrutiny. Many husbands are unabashed about admitting how they surreptitiously follow their working wives around bus stops and street corners to 'test' their loyalties. This form of male suspicion, labelled 'sak', manifests itself as women's waged work is primarily linked to the threat of extra-marital affairs and to the subversion of male authority. Parry (2001: 807) shows how female employment is associated with sexual freedom. For Chhattisgarh women, contractual work holds the promise of romantic and sexual adventure. Many illicit affairs flourish in mixed gangs of contract workers where sexual joking is legitimized by a system of fictive kinship, facilitating more permanent liaisons. In Delhi, husbands are unsettled by working wives for they recognize that they may interact with male colleagues. For example, men and women employed as sweepers, drivers, and domestic workers in middle and upper class homes in south Delhi are often allotted residential domestic quarters that facilitate intimate interaction. Travel on buses to and from work and the city's public spaces also offer ample opportunities for amorous meetings. Additionally, the work environment of MCD allows for frequent socializing between Balmiki sweepers. While the Balmikis are a tightly knit community, their isolation from others is intensified further through their interactions with and under the aegis of MCD. My Balmiki field assistant, Radha, revealed that MCD employees find lovers fairly easily. She portrayed an MCD job as a *khuli naukri,* i.e. a liberal environment in which it is possible to have consensual affairs (cf. Parry 2001; 1999). From the perspective of husbands, *sak* is, then, partly real and relates to the fear of marital break-up (cf. Chant 2001). Yet *sak* can be equally imaginative. Women like Shantha clarify that instances of male *sak* are often baseless and a mode of exercising male control. Moreover, not all women have affairs in the workplace; rather they venture out of the house to work so that they can feed their families.

Women who do not leave the neighbourhood for work are also not exempt from taunts and charges of suspicion. The congenial sexual joking in the vicinity also provokes male jealousy, although this is fuelled more when women start working. During leisure hours, women and men flirt publicly, using phrases such as 'I wish to marry you', 'Let us run away together', and 'Let us make love to each other'. Women also joke about sex, husbands, and infidelity (cf. De Neve 2005). Sexual banter (*mazak*) is especially popular amongst fictive kin (cf. Parry 2001), many of whom are distant neighbours. Overall, women describe having to face male suspicion as a tiresome ordeal (cf. Geetha 1998). Incessant queries about why they are loitering in *galis*, wearing make-up on certain days, or taking extra time in the toilet lead to heated arguments (ibid.). Fights over suspicion can last as long as one or two years. I witnessed how suspicion destroys the fabric of marriage, as women are embroiled in rebutting hurtful accusations and dealing with violent conflict.

Seema despairs how for years she battled her husband's *sak*, his imaginings of her supposed infidelity. If she happened to be sitting in front of her *jhuggi*, her husband would thrash her and demand: 'Which *yaar* [lover] are you waiting for?' Seema endured *sak* for many years, until a palmist warned her husband that 'excessive suspicion' would wreck his life. Following the palmist's prophecy, the expressions of *sak* and accusations ceased in her marriage.

Suspicion is, then, a striking feature of marriage. *Sak* is equated with an incurable disease ('*sak ki bimari*'), for which there are no doctors, remedies, or medicines. Residents comment that 'this disease is very rampant in the area.' Notably, women specify that while men also conduct affairs in the workplace and the neighbourhood, suspicion is chiefly a male preoccupation. This is a significant point. For while infidelity prevails amongst both men and women, the harbouring and voicing of incessant, unrelenting suspicion is a male feature.[13] Cultural conceptions about the sexual nature of men and women have been addressed in many south Asian ethnographies (Bennett 1983; Östör et al. 1982; Tapper 1979).[14] There is a widely held belief that female sexuality is dangerous, threatening, and uncontrollable, and thus in need of regulation. Traditionally, women's bodily functions such as menstruation are seen as ritually polluting and linked with female desire (Östör et al. 1982). In certain cultural settings, control over female sexuality is relaxed once women reach menopause. In Bruce Tapper's Andhra Pradesh study (1979: 6) of the cultural ideas of femininity and ritual symbolism, discourses link women with excessive passion, lust, and emotion. The concept of *asa*, or women having an abundance of passion, rationalizes male authority and dominance: 'The supposed sexual impetuousness of women is a manifestation of *asa*, which is perceived as a potential threat to society' (1979: 30). These broad cultural conceptions of sexuality provide a valuable framework for comprehending why expressions of male suspicion are more pronounced and more frequent.

---

[13] A handful of husbands whom I met insisted that suspicion is also a female characteristic. I did not find this male point of view to be plausible. I only came across one instance where a woman was routinely suspecting her husband of having an affair with their neighbour. Her outbursts and allegations were creating strife amongst her neighbours.

[14] Vishwanath (1997), an activist-scholar, provides a useful overview of these cultural conceptions and describes how the disciplines of social anthropology and women's studies have displayed divergent concerns over female sexuality.

A regular attribute of male suspicion is that it results in frequent wife beating. Most allegations of *sak* are accompanied by bouts of physical violence and verbal abuse. A disturbing aspect of life in shanty settlements is the high levels of domestic violence attributable to suspicion and to accusations of disobeying a husband's authority. In a study that privileges the voices of working-class Dalit women in Chennai, Geetha (1998) interprets the violent nature of suspicion: 'Battering is symptomatic of the sexuality of everyday life' (1998: 304).[15] While linking male violence to sexual control, she argues that chronic suspicion may develop out of a feeling of deprivation. Equally, Henrietta Moore (1994) insightfully relates male violence to the thwarting of, or inability to conform to, gendered positions where certain expectations and rewards fail to be realized, thus generating a crisis of self-representation or social evaluation. Moore perceives violence as the struggle for the maintenance of certain fantasies of identity and power, which make the marital relationship highly volatile: 'Once again, violence is the consequence of a crisis in representation, both individual and social. The inability to maintain the fantasy of power triggers a crisis in the fantasy of identity, and violence is a means of resolving the crisis because it acts to reconfirm the nature of masculinity otherwise denied' (1994: 154). We have seen that in Delhi, suspicion is exacerbated when men's fantasies of power in general, and their failure to provide in particular, are challenged, prompting heightened insecurity and an extra eagerness to scrutinize women's movements.

Husbands find other excuses to justify wife beating, such as the claim that wives nag them, that they never have food ready on time, and that they spend endless time in the natal unit. Children in Mohini Nagar see their mothers being beaten regularly. Domestic violence is a normal part of their growing years. Many children internalize patriarchal notions of violence, espousing the view that their mothers 'deserve a beating'. Violence is, therefore, highly

---

[15] Geetha (1998), in an essay appropriately titled 'On Bodily Love and Hurt', delineates the violent nature of marriage among low caste men and women in Chennai, Tamil Nadu. Through an examination of her work at a feminist marriage counselling centre, she reveals how women complain of chronic suspicion accompanied by overt violence. She maintains that suspicion in a marriage is part fantasy and part incitement, often fuelled by a vision of the erotic. She argues that men equate suspicion with sexual love, while masculine desire takes the form of bodily possession.

normalized and is tied to the construction of masculine identity (cf. Moore 1994). In a climate of normalized violence, neighbours are usually reluctant to chastise a violent husband for fear of being labelled 'interfering'. Violence and rows are deemed a private family matter. As I have stated, amongst neighbours, the sympathy factor is stronger when women are denied *kharcha-pani*; hunger and disregard for children evoke greater public concern. In finding ways to cope with battering, women are nonetheless able to draw some comfort from their female neighbours who may also be enduring violence. Women meet in all-women groups consisting of neighbours, friends (*sahelis*), and fictive kin. In these informal cosmoses, they confide in each other and compare 'notes'. Consequently, while there is lack of solidarity when it comes to condemning wife beating publicly, women can, and often do, easily converse about the hurtful subject of violence, which happens to be neither taboo nor shameful.[16] This ability to talk candidly strengthens their resolve to cope with or contest the violence they are experiencing. Women's ability to cope with violence is never seamless. Many will accommodate violence as a normal part of their married lives: 'My husband beats me, but he also takes care of me.' Alternatively, others will not tolerate violence. They will fearlessly contact mahila panchayats for redress, and some of them may even terminate their marriages.

Sexual Intimacy and Togetherness

The sexual dynamics of a long-term marriage surfaced in Ramesh and Shantha's case study. Shantha confirms that their existing marital tensions have intensified because she is sexually restraining Ramesh. Currently it is unfeasible for them to have regular sex.[17] Their seven children sleep in the same room as

[16] In contexts of domestic violence, friends (*sahelis*) are more proactive in helping each other. With neighbours, there is more at stake because residents of a *gali* share common resources. Thus, a very different level of politics and dynamics governs the relationship between neighbours.

[17] There is no specific Hindi term for sex or sexual intercourse (cf. Kakar 1989). A range of terms locally connote sex. These include *bhog* (where sex is equated with food), *kam* (where sex is equated with work or wifely duty), injection (used mainly in the context of sexual joking), and *sharirik sambandh* (bodily or physical relations).

them. Even so, Ramesh 'wants to have sex all the time'. Shantha says that in situations where husbands are being denied sex, they start imagining that their wives do not love them anymore or that they are having sex with other men. Women verify how much sexual energy and prowess their husbands have, and their local discourses are congruent with cultural notions of how female sexuality is broadly perceived (i.e. women have excess passion). Women stress that it is their men folk who are lustful, persistent, and exacting. They confide that in their married lives sex occurs at least once a day, and may also happen if husbands are at home in the afternoons. In the early years of marriage, the level of sexual frequency is anywhere between three and five times a day. Remarks such as 'I am relieved my husband comes home tired' reflect men's sexually voracious behaviour and the frequent sexual intercourse to which women must submit (cf. Geetha 1998). A young woman disclosed to me how she abhors sex. The minute her husband returns from work, he demands sex, even when the children are around him. In the domain of sexual behaviour, men clearly do not take responsibility for preventing childbirth. No wonder then that women produce anywhere from three to six children. As the majority of men are unwilling to use contraception, the burden of controlling fertility rests principally upon women. Hence, women normally undergo sterilization (an operation) to prevent childbirth, especially after having sons.

Though women complain that men are sexually demanding, many also speak candidly of the pleasures of sex while believing that regular sex fortifies the marital bond, allowing for 'the hearts to merge'. The close contact and togetherness that are augmented through sexual intimacy is important to them. Women claim that their marriages are in crisis when sex has been effaced. Although they may have other stresses in their marriages, inadequate sex is cited as a major cause of conjugal conflict. Even so, I was told that it is not always possible to sustain regular sexual relations. With cramped living conditions and several children sleeping alongside their parents, an inevitable part of daily life in shanty settlements, sexual contact is restricted. This is in contrast to what women say about the early years of marriage, when sexual contact was intense and easy to accommodate since the children were young then.

With growing children and limited or no privacy, women mention how they 'assist' their husbands hurriedly and furtively, often by performing oral sex, while children are sent out on errands. In her sensitive analysis of dowry murders, Veena Talwar Oldenburg (2002) describes how marital conflict is often tied to lack of sexual intimacy. Oldenburg's research on dowry murders in Delhi led her to examine the problems confronting contemporary arranged marriages. She identifies lack of access to sex in marriage, sexual incompatibility, and infidelity as powerful sources of marital violence and strained relations. The 'troubled area of sexuality' is often overshadowed by the focus on dowry-related violence, as the latter remains an easier explanation for conflict and for obtaining legal redress.[18] Oldenburg argues for the urgent need to counter the silenced and difficult domain of sexuality in marriage. Comparably, I have illustrated how poor women are aware that conjugal conflict spirals out of control when regular sexual relations cease. The absence of sexual intimacy disrupts notions of conjugal togetherness, love, and fidelity.

To summarize, this section has described how strands of conflict develop, overlap, and converge in contexts of male behaviour and responsibility, men and women's working lives, the social ambience of the neighbourhood, and sex within marriage. The ethnography presents a graphic picture of gender conflict, sexual antagonism, and stressful relations in arranged marriages. Parental

---

[18] Oldenburg is one of the few academics to have critically investigated arranged marriages and the interpersonal relations of spouses through her work on dowry violence. Whilst trying to make sense of the escalating number of dowry deaths in the 1970s and 1980s, she discusses how arranged marriages during this period were beset with conflict unrelated to dowry demands. She outlines the many problematic features of arranged marriages, such as instances of mismatched alliances, where either the girl or the boy was not satisfied with the physical attributes of the partner, which led to temperamental incompatibility. There were also cases where fraudulent claims were made by the husband's family when arranging matches, for example, the claims that sons owned flourishing enterprises and possessed exceptionally good educational qualifications. When brides later discovered this fraud, it led to scenes of violence. Other relevant themes that Oldenburg discusses in relation to current arranged marriages include the increased age at marriage and women's greater independence on entering marriage. These factors present new challenges to the institution of arranged marriage.

matches amongst low-income couples are conspicuously marked by an overlapping of ineffective providing, alcohol-related abuse, suspicion, and violence, all of which reveal the inequality of marital relations and the discrepancies between ideals and practices. I now describe the support structures available to women facing marital distress and conflict in arranged marriages.

Kinship Support: The Role of Parental Refuge

Certain local beliefs about the role and significance of parental matches give family-arranged marriages enormous credibility. In evaluating the merits of arranged unions, men and women stress that parental support is a highly valued attribute of the arranged marriage system, especially when it enables a period of refuge or prolonged shelter and stay in the natal home during times of marital difficulties.[19] An examination of the practice of refuge allows me to investigate women's rights as well as their access to, and use of, the support of natal kin.

In the event of a marital crisis, women maintain that they can simply go at any time to their natal homes. Their natal homes are located in the vicinity of Mohini Nagar or in other parts of Delhi, 40 to 60 minutes away by public transport. Long-distance alliances are not seen as desirable by local residents, and, for the most part, daughters and sons born and raised in Delhi are married off locally within the city.[20] Daughters born and raised in Delhi are not married into villages, the explanation being that they are likely to experience village life as alien, and, on the whole, such a marriage

[19] There is no specific Hindi term for the married daughter's right to shelter in the parental home. The phrase 'to sit in the *pihar* (natal home)' comes closest to signifying the practice of absenting oneself from the conjugal home when confronted with marital difficulties.

[20] Other north Indian urban ethnographies pertaining to the SCs suggest that women who have grown up in cities are married locally. Lynch (1969:179) points out that Jatav families in Agra showed a clear preference for marrying daughters within the city. Out of a total of 120 marriages on which he gathered information, 71 marriages were arranged within Agra city. Searle-Chatterjee (1981:55) observes that Benares sweepers prefer to marry daughters outside their neighbourhood and into new families in the city. Yet she notes that marriages have occurred within the neighbourhood and are not considered to be irregular.

is regarded as unkind and unjust. Marriages are not arranged between girls and boys who have grown up in the same *basti*, as they are seen to share a sister–brother relationship. Alliances are sought with families who reside in adjacent *bastis* and resettlement colonies. In resettlement colonies too, natal families arrange their daughters' marriages with families who reside in blocks close by. Whether in *bastis* or the resettlement colonies, many natal families reside within walking distance of their married daughters' conjugal homes. In response to the question of why marriages are arranged with families who live so close by, natal kin specify that as their *biradari* members reside in close proximity, it is easier to search for suitable alliances from within that pool. Maintaining checks over daughters in relation to marital problems, or offering them support and shelter in times of marital distress, is equally cited as a motive for seeking marriage alliances close by. Marriage residence patterns are virilocal or patri-virilocal, the wife staying with the husband or his agnatic family, but within easy reach of the natal kin. I shall now address the subject of parental refuge by focusing on the marital problems of Lata, Rajbir and Rani.

Rajbir, Lata, and Rani: Refuge as a Moral Entitlement

Rajbir, a Balmiki, who lives in Raju Camp, tells me that his wife, Lata, is sitting in her *pihar*. They have been married for sixteen years. Rajbir is currently unemployed, so his wife has taken up a sweeping job. He says: 'Look, I tell you frankly that I drink. Which man does not drink these days? At least I care for my children. They all attend school.' According to Rajbir, the problem lies not with Lata but with her *pihar*: 'She has gone to stay with her parents because I have no work . . . she stays with them whenever we have problems. But they never bring her back or try to explain things to me nicely. Do you know that Lata's sister, Rani, has stayed with her parents for most of her married life? Since we got married, Lata has been shuttling back and forth between her parents and me. I am fed up with this.'

I meet Lata in a colony, situated 25 minutes away from Mohini Nagar, where she is staying with her natal family in a two-storey house. She is angry: 'Rajbir drinks heavily with other men. Look at the other husbands who make their wives happy by handing over their monthly salaries. My mother has given me her job because

Rajbir is unemployed. My parents have given me shelter and are taking out loans to support us.' She adds: 'He suspects me all the time of having affairs when I am at work, which leads to fights. In the early years of marriage, I never left the house because of his suspicions. I would be taunted and beaten if I did.' She shows me marks where she has been previously hit. Lata's parents join us: 'That Rajbir is terrible, and so is Rani's husband. Why does Lata put up with him? He does not care about her or the children.'

I am introduced to Lata's sister, Rani, who is also taking refuge at the same place. She tells me that she has been married for fourteen years, but has lived with her parents for most of her married life. Her husband does seasonal work. 'When he earns money, we begin to live together again. But then he blows it on alcohol and we are left without money. It's been like this for a long time. The children have grown up in my *pihar*. Some time ago, my parents raised the subject of a second marriage (*doosri shaadi*). But if my *bihata* (spouse) has not kept me well, what guarantee is there that a new marriage will be better? I may end up worse off.'

Both Lata and Rani reflect: 'For how long can we both continue to live in our *pihar*? We will outlive our parents, and our brother and sister-in-law also live with them. Things remain uncertain in the future. Our mother and sister-in-law are both financially protected. Our father has an MCD job and our brother has a government job with the Bank of Baroda. They also drink heavily, but at least they fulfil their provider duties. Our husbands do not.' But Lata later tells me that she will return to her husband: 'He has come here many times to ask about me. He also loves me. At such times, it becomes difficult for the children. My parents keep asking why I put up with him . . . but eventually I may not inherit anything from them. And what if in the future Rajbir sells our *jhuggi* and absconds? I will be left in the lurch. Neither do I want to terminate my relationship with him.' Lata confides that Rani is somewhat at fault: 'She has made little effort to work on her marriage. She relies far too much on my parents' support.'

Lata's example shows that women like her do not conceal unhappy domestic relations from their natal families, but rather approach them for assistance. In turn, natal families reaffirm their daughters' expectations of support. The Mohini Nagar data on arranged marriages illustrate that natal families in both *bastis* and resettlement colonies offer shelter as well as emotional, financial, and practical support to their married daughters during periods of domestic distress. With marital relations being highly conflictual, a systematic and wide-ranging pattern of marriage emerges whereby married women, often sisters such as Lata and Rani, routinely leave their conjugal homes to seek shelter with their natal families. Amongst the urban poor in north India, refuge in the natal home is thus recognized as a 'right', a moral and social entitlement possessed by a woman in an arranged marriage, a right that remains even after her parents' death, albeit in an attenuated form.[21] It is not considered unusual or unconventional for women to seek refuge, for in situations of marital breakdown they are not expected to live alone, as this has connotations of grave immorality.

By honouring a moral and social obligation to a daughter in an arranged marriage, parental refuge places a married daughter in a powerful position for renegotiating her domestic arrangements and conjugal contract in the event of a dispute or conflict with her husband. From the safety of her parental home and, if necessary, by mobilizing the support of her brothers, a woman finds herself in a position from which she can strike a tough bargain to alter her husband's objectionable behaviour and curb his bad habits. A threat to not return to her conjugal home unless her husband agrees to resume provider responsibilities, or to cut down his drinking, or to refrain from domestic violence is taken seriously. This is in marked contrast to the position of a woman who may have entered the labour force and taken up wage work, but who is compelled to negotiate with her husband from within the walls of her conjugal home. As discussed, women affirm that taking up employment outside the home and financially supporting their husbands only deepens male insecurity and jealousy and leads to protracted violence, which is often associated with the insecurity,

---

[21] For divorced and widowed women, the right to refuge is also an absolute given. For example, a widow named Shanthi said that after her husband's death she resided in her natal home for twenty years. On the other hand, Preeti, a married woman, said that her husband's sisters (one older and one younger) had been taking refuge for five years after having separated from their respective husbands. Preeti said that her sisters-in-law (I had also met them) would never leave her conjugal home as their mother (Preeti's mother-in-law) was too emotionally attached to her daughters.

low self-esteem, and sense of failure among men who are unable to live up to breadwinner ideals and expectations.

While feminists and economists have sought to identify the determinants of female bargaining power within the household, the main emphasis has been on factors such as women's earnings[22] or women's control over assets that affect their fallback position within marriage and on women's perceived contributions to the household economy. While Sen's (1990) focus is on women's labour force participation, Agarwal (1994) has made a compelling case correlating women's welfare with land rights on par with those of men.[23] Similarly, it has been argued that access to micro-credit loans increases women's voice in intra-household negotiations and leads to decreased violence against them (Kabeer 2001). In terms of women's property and land rights, Mohini Nagar residents follow north Indian patrilineal customs whereby only sons are expected to inherit property. In resettlement colonies, parents partition plots of three or four storeys between married sons who will ultimately inherit the plots when the parents die. Conversely, *basti* residents, irrespective of their sex, have no legal entitlements to their *jhuggis*, which are illegally located on public land. When seen from this angle, it is startling that women in arranged marriages who belong to a resource-poor group and who are placed in a precarious economic position with no effective inheritance prospects and with low levels of education are nevertheless well placed to challenge male authority. They also have the power to renegotiate domestic arrangements that have become unacceptably unequal, violent, or

[22] Sen's (1990) 'cooperative conflicts model' demonstrates how cooperation and conflict characterize intra-household relations. Intra-household bargaining rests on the fallback position of spouses, and the strength of their negotiations is based on the position in which they are likely to find themselves during the event of marital breakdown. Sen argues that women's weaker economic power, poorer health status, and lower educational levels are barriers to effective bargaining. Hence, earnings through participation in the labour force are essential for improving women's fallback position, whilst enhancing the perception of their well-being and perceived contributions. See also Haddad et al. (1997) and McElroy (1990), who have conceptualized threat-points, bargaining, voice, and exit options amongst household members.

[23] In a substantive study, Panda and Agarwal (2005) extend this argument wherein, using the case of Kerala, they argue that women who own immovable property face a lower risk of marital violence than women without property. Property ownership by women is a significant deterrent against violence.

gone sour, by virtue of being morally entitled to parental refuge. The experience of married women in Mohini Nagar shows that income, property ownership, and access to credit are not necessary conditions for determining women's bargaining power within the household. Even in the absence of these economic assets, women succeed in negotiating with their spouses (cf. Hameed 2003).

The Shifting Nature of Residence

As women take frequent recourse to parental refuge in Delhi, they end up spending long periods of their married lives in the natal home. From Lata's account we observe how during periods of marital discord she has oscillated between her natal and conjugal homes. These movements of shuttling back and forth occur repeatedly in a woman's marital trajectory, producing what Rajni Palriwala (1991) has termed a phenomenon of 'transitory residence'. In Delhi, the residence of married women in their conjugal homes is indeed of a transient and shifting nature. I found that there was no agreement as to where children should reside during the period of the mother's refuge or which parent should have guardianship. Women stress that at times it is essential to leave children with their fathers so that the latter will not abdicate their parental responsibilities completely. On the other hand, it is noticeable that as a consequence of intermittent refuge, many children effectively grow up in the mother's natal home.

Do husbands initiate divorce when their wives refuse to cooperate during periods of refuge or fail to return to the conjugal home? The data indicates that marriage breakdowns are not irrevocable; rather, the 'door remains open' between husbands and wives, allowing for future reconciliation. Even during a prolonged period of refuge and uncertainty, spouses may continue to negotiate the terms of the marriage and to coordinate essential responsibilities for their children. Rani, who has remained with her parents for most of her married life, continues to maintain contact with her husband who has not yet initiated a divorce. Yet there are several incidents where during the period of parental refuge, husbands and wives enter into new relationships (Chapter 4). Husbands often lament that the affection between spouses cannot be sustained if wives continue to take parental refuge as a matter of course. There are cases where husbands have given up on their long absent wives and remarried.

Negotiating Refuge over the Life Course

Women describe how negotiating parental refuge can be complicated and claim that it is not as straightforward as it seems. The process of seeking refuge can lead to disruptions in their married lives. When discussing these disruptions, women juxtapose discourses about their individual rights in the natal and conjugal homes. Their natal families provide them with some form of dowry and the right to refuge. Yet, according to patrilineal norms, their actual rights lie in their conjugal home; the discourse is that in the long term they are to be supported by their sons and husbands.[24] As women emphasize, refuge does not permit them permanent shelter, as they are likely to have brothers who—at least in the resettlement colonies—are entitled to parental property. Women contend that although they make use of refuge, this is an arrangement requiring continual and intense negotiation. They outline the limitations of refuge through cautionary and critical discourses. They do not lay complete trust in their natal kin; a likely future is one in which they will outlive their parents, their brothers will thereafter withdraw their support and the protective space of the natal home, and, in the long term, their own marriages will weaken.

Yet I found that many brothers are sincere in supporting their sisters' right to refuge. Married brothers who reside with their parents habitually accommodate their sisters, empathizing with their lack of options. Rani and Lata's brother told me that as long as he is alive he has a duty towards his sisters. Long-term refuge is nonetheless never fully approved of by the brothers' wives, who often protest when their husbands' sisters stay on for too long. I witnessed women being pushed into seeking refuge because the periods of refuge of their sisters-in-law were aggravating stresses and conflicts in the extended family. These patterns suggest how easy access to refuge in urban poor neighbourhoods may unsettle

[24] In situations where women face recurrent marital conflict and their husbands fail to provide, parents also offer to arrange a second marriage for their daughters. Women respond with the concern that a second marriage may turn out to be even worse than the first (cf. Jeffery 2001).

and disrupt marriage and kinship relations. The occurrence of temporary or permanent break-ups on account of refuge contradicts the active discourse of arranged marriage as a stable institution. If we evaluate the merits of refuge for women over the course of the life cycle, we find that a woman gains from intermittent short-term refuge as parental shelter offers vital security and a functional exit option. However, by availing of very lengthy periods of refuge, a woman may in the long run abdicate her rights and entitlements in the conjugal home by ultimately forfeiting the position of a respected senior woman or a mother-in-law in her husband's patriline. The failure to establish a stronghold in her conjugal home means that she may also forfeit her son's protection in old age. At the same time, recourse to extended refuge may also exhaust the goodwill of brothers and their wives. Thus, frequent resort to natal refuge also raises critical concerns about a woman's future security. When children are of marriageable age, women assert that they are reluctant to take refuge since any indication of marital breakdown affects the family's chances of finding suitable brides and grooms. In the life cycle of older women, the option of refuge starts to diminish.

Mother–Daughter Bonds and Married Women's Labour

'Our lives have two clear boundaries—*pihar* (natal home) and *sasural* (conjugal and affinal home).'
—Asha, a woman in her early twenties

Irrespective of the support offered by friends, neighbours, and work-related networks, for women, their natal and conjugal homes remain the two most important structures in their lives. In Mohini Nagar, married daughters are permitted visits to the natal home (as distinct from seeking refuge) for childbirth, periods of rest, and to attend family rituals. These family visits demonstrate the closeness of post-marital bonds with natal kin, especially the ties between mother and daughter and the nature of intergenerational reliance in the city, aspects that are crucial in shaping women's trajectories of marriage. In this final section, I focus on the strong mutual dependence between mothers and daughters. The following example documents a mother-in-law's reaction to her daughter-in-law's interludes at her natal home in an arranged marriage.

Shakuntala and her Bahu's Family Interludes

Shakuntala is a widow of the Khatik caste (meat-cutters or butchers). She and her sons own two spacious resettlement plots that stand opposite each other in the resettlement colonies. Two of her sons live on one of her plots with their wives, a pair of sisters. Shakuntala lives on the opposite plot with her unmarried son. Shakuntala has recently remarried her daughters to a pair of brothers. She tells me that their first marriages (also to a pair of brothers) broke down as the marriage intermediary and the groom's kin had deceived her. The arrangement was that after her daughters were married, they would live in Delhi. However, the grooms' family took the brides to live in Rajasthan, and their marriages broke down as a result of the grooms' betrayal. Shakuntala was complaining not so much about the plight of her daughters but about her *bahu* (daughter-in-law): 'What have we not done for my elder *bahu*? She just wants to keep going back to her *pihar*. The last time she was going to visit her *pihar* for eight days; she remained there for almost two months. She goes away on all kinds of excuses and takes the children with her. Sometimes she does not even give us a reason. Then she gets really proud when we plead with her to return. We always have to visit her natal home a couple of times to ask for her to return. Her parents do not treat us with respect. What is the point of having a *bahu* who is never around? We are fed up of her going back and forth.'

Another time I meet Shakuntala with her son. They are both discussing the son's wife that is, her *bahu's* future. They feel that a time will come when she will be left with nothing. She will not have cultivated a proper relationship with her husband, and in time her parents will no longer be around. Will her husband have the same respect for her then? She will not inherit her parents' resettlement plot, even though her two brothers have moved away and established separate nuclear households. Shakuntala points out: 'My daughters will also inherit nothing. The fact remains that sons inherit. I do not encourage my daughters to keep coming here. My *bahu's* rights lie in this house, and not with her parents.' Shakuntala's Muslim neighbour, who walks in, says that she is facing similar problems with her *bahu*. The two women exchange their stories, express their frustrations, and lament that their *bahus* are ruining their lives: 'Sometimes it's my *bahu* who goes away for long stretches, and sometimes it's hers. Obviously, their parents keep them for their own selfish needs. A mother has complete rest when her daughter is around.' Shakuntala and her neighbour compare their lives to those of their *bahus:* 'When we were married, we were so poor.' Shakuntala's neighbour recalls: 'We came from our village and my husband set up a vegetable stall. Later on, he got a job as a cook in the Ashoka Hotel.' Shakuntala adds: 'I did construction work for many years. Then my husband got a job as a gardener to private homes. We moved from the Greater Kailash *jhuggis* to here.' Both women say: 'We stuck it out with our husbands. We helped them to build a home. *Bahus* of the younger generation know nothing about this. Not all mothers-in-laws are bad. Our *bahus* have nothing to complain about.' A week later, Shakuntala's son met his father-in-law on the street and told him: 'Is this some kind of a joke that my wife is never around? We will not come to collect her again.' The following day, his wife returned to her conjugal home.

Shakuntala's narrative indicates that married women's prolonged visits to their natal families cause resentment among the husband's agnates. Visits permitted for ten days can last for up to two months, or even longer.[25] Shakuntala's *bahu* had not articulated any marital dissatisfaction with her husband or her mother-in-law. When a husband's character is known to be good, a married woman's constant visits to her natal home are questioned.

[25] From Shakuntala's narrative it is not possible to observe a traditional mother-in-law–daughter-in-law relationship or hierarchical affinal relations. Shakuntala is frank about the lack of control she can exercise over her daughter-in-law's visits to her natal family. Vero-Sanso (1999), in an article titled 'Dominant daughters-in-law and submissive mothers-in-law?' documents how relations between mothers-in-law and daughters-in-law are not necessarily static. She argues that these relations are shaped by socio-economic factors and family demographics rather than by cultural expectations. The vulnerability of an aging widow or mother-in-law outliving her husband depends on how many sons she has or the amount of land she owns. While a daughter-in-law is initially dependent on her mother-in-law, she may have little long-term interest in cooperating with her, as the economic circumstances of the family are likely to change. Instead, mothers-in-law may have to use several strategies to appease their daughters-in-law. This explains why in Delhi elderly mothers-in-laws, who are usually more powerful in their later years, may not be in a position to curb either refuge or lengthy family visits.

For just as there are stories about women not being treated well, there are also stories of how particular husbands are good and reliable. In such situations, the belief is that a woman may not have her heart and mind in the marriage (*'uska man nahi hai'*) or that she is likely to be having an affair with someone who resides near her natal home. She has shown little interest in building her marriage (*'woh rahna nahi chahti'*) and is indifferent towards her husband. The bonds of affection cannot develop if she is not present, and if she is continually in her natal home, she is not interested in nourishing those bonds. Nonetheless, it is convenient for women like Shakuntala's *bahu* to keep slipping back to their natal homes, which are nearby and where they can enjoy ample freedom, support, and affection. Women also informally visit their parents to assist them with chores, to look after them when they are sick, to attend to other siblings, or simply to drop in on the way home from work. These regular casual visits are actively supported by natal kin and strengthen ties with them. Maintaining kinship ties becomes an everyday and immediate affair for Mohini Nagar women who enjoy considerable flexibility in their movements between their natal and conjugal homes.

In her richly detailed monograph on urban neighbourhoods in Meerut, in north India, Sylvia Vatuk (1972: 140) describes gradual but fundamental structural changes in the kinship system in a sample of middle-class white-collar migrants. Compared to earlier generations, married daughters in Meerut in the 1960s and 1970s frequently visited their parents; younger siblings spent longer periods with their married sisters; and sisters who used to be married off to distant places were found to be living closer to the natal home and keeping in touch more regularly after marriage.[26] Vatuk (1972: 147) attributed these changes to a bilateral shift in urban kinship in line with migration to the city: 'We see in urban India a trend towards lesser incorporation of a married woman into her husband's kin network and greater assertion of her ties with

[26] Oldenburg (2002: 223) makes an analogous observation. She delineates the changed realities of urban life in contemporary India: 'Daughters are in their natal homes for longer, particularly in cities, and virilocality often means changing neighbourhoods in the same town rather than moving to villages a difficult distance away; women sustain far closer ties with their natal kin through visits and telephone conversations.'

the natal family.' We note a similar bilateral emphasis amongst the poor in Delhi; as arranging marriages between families living close by is acceptable, women merely move from one neighbourhood to another after marriage. The close post-marital natal bonds amongst the urban poor ease women's isolation in a city, allowing natal kin to continue to exercise a substantial influence in their daughters' lives. Urban poor women's habitual and frequent contact with their natal kin clearly contradicts kinship paradigms (Dyson and Moore 1983; Karve 1993 [1953]) that present a homogeneous picture of north Indian women as estranged from their natal kin. In an attempt to provide a corrective to the standard literature, Raheja and Gold (1994) have made an important contribution by depicting the diversity of natal kin ties as opposed to static and unitary conceptions of north Indian kinship, which assume that after marriage parents invariably, distance themselves from daughters. They show how women from rural Uttar Pradesh and Rajasthan regularly visit their natal homes and nurture their ties with their brothers, challenging the patrilineal ideology that mandates their complete assimilation into the conjugal family and identification with affinal kin.

Close post-marital bonds with natal kin can nonetheless lead to friction between married women and their affines. In this regard, Vatuk writes:

> However, residence near the wife's parents in the city does cause strains in the traditional affinal relationship. The woman who lives in her natal *mohalla* [neighbourhood] – or whose parents have moved nearby after her marriage, as many have done – cannot sharply separate her statuses as daughter and bride as she could in the traditional setting. The strong emotional ties between parents and daughters, which would have been compartmentalized by traditional residence rules and clear role definitions, are allowed active expression when a daughter lives within easy walking distance of her parents. Instead of periodic extended visits to the natal home gradually diminishing in frequency, the

married women in this situation can make almost
daily ones (Vatuk 1972: 142).

Husbands in Mohini Nagar complain incessantly that their wives
spend an unnecessary amount of time with their mothers.[27]
This grievance often creates frequent conflict between couples,
arousing intense jealousy and provoking violence. It also leads
to arguments about women's future rights in the conjugal home.
Local residents explain that parents frequently give refuge and
allow married daughters to visit them because the latter's labour
benefits the natal kin. This creates a conflict of interest between
the conjugal home and the natal home, and is a constant source of
friction between women, their husbands, and their in-laws. The
next case study, featuring Amit and Sunita, explores this aspect
of the conflict between natal and affinal kin. Amit and Sunita's
marital estrangement came to my notice when I was documenting
cases at the mahila panchayat (see Chapter 5). While it is usually
women who register complaints of ill-treatment against their
spouses, mahila panchayats also receive a small number of cases
from men like Amit who want to negotiate the return of their wives
from the natal home.

*Amit, Sunita, and Their Families: 'Those cows are ruining
my marriage'*

Amit and Sunita, who had an arranged marriage, are Kumhars
(potters) by caste. They live in a joint family in a resettlement plot.
Their house is spacious with modern amenities. Amit's father holds
a senior post at the local police office. When I meet Amit, he frets
that Sunita has hardly been around since they married: 'Look, I
provide for her well. I am employed in a photography shop and

---

[27] Jeffery and Jeffery (1993: 80) and Jeffery et al. (1988) note how being
married and residing within close range of a wife's natal home undermines a
husband's command. In order to retain their domestic authority, Bijnor men are
keen to maintain a distance with the wife's natal kin. Bijnor men and women also
express ambivalence about close-kin marriages because they believe that these
unions lead to excessive interference from the wife's natal kin. Interestingly,
women stress that being married distantly means that they will be treated more
generously when they visit their natal homes.

have studied up to Class 12 (education up to age 17). In our three years of marriage, she has only lived with me for six months. We have been trying constantly to get her back.' I hear that Amit's father is determined to confront Sunita's natal kin once again. They request some neutral arbitrators to accompany them to her house—members of the mahila panchayat team and myself. Sunita's natal home is only 45 minutes away from her conjugal home and is located in a newly built neighbourhood. On entering Sunita's house, Amit's father announces: 'Either you send Sunita back or we agree to a divorce. You have been evading us for too long.'

In the presence of the mahila panchayat members, Sunita speaks with us directly: 'Amit is not as good as he makes himself out to be. He and his mother never let me phone my parents.' Her natal kin join in: 'She is our daughter. Should she not come to us if she is being ill-treated?' Amit denies the allegations: 'I want to work on my marriage. Why would I plead with her to return if I am going to ill-treat her?' The arbitrators ask Sunita whether she wants to return to her conjugal home: 'Do you expect your marriage to work if you are always sitting in your *pihar*? Your parents are not always going to be around. It is better that you make your home than break it.' Sunita's mother remains obdurate, but after three hours of exchanges she agrees to send her daughter back. The mahila panchayat counsellors finally persuade both families to give a written undertaking in the presence of their neighbours that Sunita will return to her conjugal home.

A week later, when Sunita is in her conjugal home, her mother arrives with two local leaders from her neighbourhood and a policeman. They claim that Sunita was forcibly taken from her natal home while she was undertaking refuge. Sunita returns with her mother to her natal home. Amit files a case for marital reconciliation in the family courts at Patiala House where the Delhi Legal Service Authority provides counselling to low-income couples for a nominal fee. We meet Amit's parents in their house before the court proceedings. They discuss Sunita's mother's resistance: 'You have seen their house. They have a lot of housework. From the start, they have kept cows. Sunita's father's mental condition is deteriorating. Her two brothers leave in the morning for work and return home late. Her youngest sister-in-law does the other household chores.

But looking after the cows has always been Sunita's responsibility. Soon after they got married, Sunita's mother requested that we send her to her *pihar*. Her brother was getting married and they needed help. We allowed her to go. Two months passed and she did not return. Then her mother asked if they could keep her longer because of the cows. When she again failed to return, Amit told her we also needed her help at home. Within weeks of returning home, she went back to her *pihar*. For three years it has been her *pihar, pihar, pihar*. Those cows are ruining her marriage. Then when we raise objections, she claims that we ill-treat her.' We discuss Sunita's future. They show me around their house: 'Look, this is her house and this is where her rights lie. One day, she will realize what she has missed out on.' Amit's father cynically adds: 'Or she may just run away with another man when her *pihar* no longer needs her.' In 2003, Sunita and Amit's case was before the courts, with the outcome of reconciliation attempts remaining uncertain. Sunita's family did not appear at the Patiala House courts despite the judge's orders.

Amit and Sunita's marital estrangement reveals that the husband's kin perceive the excessive involvement of natal kin in a married woman's life as motivated by selfish interests; it is useful for them to have a daughter around the house. There is an element of truth in this explanation. Undeniably, the use of a daughter's domestic labour begins at an early age, when she might be kept away or even withdrawn from school. Adolescent girls accompany their mothers to work to help them, and, if the mothers fall ill, they take over domestic chores such as sweeping, cleaning, and cooking. In this dyad of mutual reliance, mothers and daughters routinely depend on each other for material support. Daughters and mothers stress that 'their lives are intertwined' and claim that they empathize with each other's predicaments, especially in cases where male family members neglect their responsibility as providers. Mothers are strong and loyal allies in difficult times, in sympathy with their daughters' problems. These strands of mutual dependence, where material help in the form of labour is intertwined with emotional support, create bonds that keep pulling women away from their conjugal home. The reluctance, and at times even active resistance, to letting a married daughter return to her conjugal home is most evident in the case of Sunita whose mother opposed mediation attempts for three years.[28]

The use of a married woman's labour by her natal kin appears to be a widespread phenomenon, yet its status seems to be in the nature of a public secret—recognized by all but not explicitly acknowledged by the parties directly involved. In her study of marriage residence patterns in a village in north-eastern Rajasthan, Palriwala (1991) shows that a married daughter's labour is used during *aoni-jaoni*, the adjustment phase between the wedding and the consummation ceremony (*muklawa*) when women shuttle back and forth between their conjugal and natal homes to facilitate their gradual adjustment to the rigours of their conjugal home. Palriwala reveals how *aoni-jaoni* is not only about visiting the family or about adjustment, but can also be related to a household's need for help in the fields, particularly when male family members have migrated in search of work. A married daughter's labour is preferred to that of an unmarried daughter or a daughter-in-law. She is considered a more experienced worker, is more familiar with the household, and, unlike a daughter-in-law, need not veil herself. Yet natal kin will never acknowledge that a daughter's visits are linked with the demands of agricultural work. Instead, *aoni-jaoni* is legitimized by association with post-marital prestations to the married daughter and her husband's kin. One of Palriwala's most compelling findings is that while a daughter's labour is fully utilized, it is never valued as such, nor made visible. Moreover, during the phase of transitory marriage residence movements, daughters end up being fully accepted neither in their natal nor in their conjugal home.

Just as the phase of *aoni-jaoni* in Rajasthan allows for the manipulation and utilization of a married daughter's labour, in Delhi periods of refuge and family visits also give mothers

---

[28] Another instance of how married women's labour is exploited by natal kin was described to me by a man called Pumu Lal. He claimed that his wife, Kamla, had resided with him for only three months since they had married a year ago, spending the remaining months at her *pihar*. Kamla is the oldest of seven siblings, and her mother leaves all the housework to her. During one of Pumu Lal's attempts to negotiate his wife's return, Kamla's mother told him that she plans to keep Kamla for six months of the year; Pumu Lal could keep her for the remaining months. When he objected, Kamla's mother declared that she had the right to keep her daughter. See also Jeffery and Jeffery (1993) for examples of how women's labour is extensively utilized in their affinal homes.

opportunities for utilizing daughters' labour, but over a far more extended period. These continual attempts to gain access to daughters' labour illustrate the economic insecurities of urban low-income households. Parents rely on their daughters' labour and monetary contribution, especially when sons have evaded their filial duties by breaking away from their parents.[29] For parents, the added economic costs of accommodating daughters and grandchildren in overcrowded plots and *jhuggis* are compensated for by women's assistance to their parents in the upkeep of the household economy. While appreciating the significance of this economic aspect in explaining the phenomenon of parental refuge, it is important to not interpret it as the sole or overriding motive, since parents also assist their daughters and keep them without exploiting their labour. Daughters are believed to be more dependable than sons. Brothers are also vocal about fulfilling their fraternal responsibilities if their sisters face marital difficulties.

Durable Support Structures: A Double-edged Sword

This chapter has shown that the marital relationships of SC and Balmiki sweepers are conceptualized on the basis of hierarchical male breadwinner ideologies. While Searle-Chatterjee (1981) places great emphasis on the Benares sweepers' joint division of labour, the Delhi data present striking counter perspectives. While appreciating Searle-Chatterjee's useful observations, my objective has been to demonstrate the variations and shifting trajectories of low caste women's marital and working lives. Accordingly, all sweeper communities in India do not subscribe to a unified set of gender ideologies and practices even wherein MCD is a pivotal entity in their everyday lives. Consequently, in Delhi, we are not witnessing a shift in ideologies towards spousal equality or discourses that place more emphasis on the mutuality of gender roles. Giddens' (1999) hypothesis on global conjugal equality is not congruent to the reality of the lives of the urban poor or the upwardly mobile (e.g. Amit's family). Across age groups,

---

[29] Sons do separate from their parents after marriage, especially when they acquire government or secure private-sector jobs. See Parry's (1979: 193) account of how a man's interests and responsibilities begin to diverge from those of the joint family, while women are usually blamed for family break-ups.

women tend to underscore effective male providing as the basis for a model marriage. While this endorsement signals a rejection of female economic independence, the ideal arranged marriage nevertheless entails negotiations both over women's control over the management of household finances and over men's long-term devotion to their family.

By juxtaposing marital ideals against practices, arranged marriages, when seen through women's eyes, turn out to be highly conflictual. Ramesh and Shantha's domestic lives reveal extensive marital friction such as alcohol-related abuse, violence, and suspicion, all highlighting the asymmetry of the marital bond. However, Lata and Rani's trajectories suggest that women can find effective ways of redressing marital tensions by invoking a variety of support mechanisms from natal kin. This enables them to cease cooperating with their spouses. Women's preference for an arranged marriage is anchored in the knowledge that they are guaranteed a moral right to refuge in the natal home, which in turn strengthens their fallback position. Thus, married women spend a large proportion of their married lives in the natal unit. The frequent resort to natal refuge raises critical concerns about a woman's future role in her conjugal home. The Mohini Nagar material reveals the complexities of seeking refuge confronted by women. The easy access to refuge poses dilemmas, complications, and disruptions in women's married lives. I have highlighted the limitations of parental support for women in arranged marriages and argued that women do not always invest complete trust in their natal kin.

A substantive part of the discussion has described how virilocal marriage residence patterns are reconfiguring marital relations. In Delhi, mothers and daughters meet regularly. Yet the near presence of natal kin proves to be a double-edged sword; it offers durable support structures while simultaneously weakening the marital bond and thwarting women's prospects of 'adjustment'. The collusion of natal kin in destabilizing a daughter's marriage is clearly visible in Amit and Sunita's example. Their example shows the active role played by natal kin in making marital disputes more acrimonious by using manipulation, blame, and humiliation to prevent reconciliation. Mothers thereby destabilize the very marriages that they had arranged. This contradicts the local and pan-Indian belief echoed by scholars like Kishwar (1999) that arranged marriages are stable, lifelong unions and undercuts the claim that parents play a constructive role in preserving the institution of marriage. As I have shown, natal-kin support—whether on account of daughters' marital problems, or of their living nearby, or of their utility to the household economy—shapes marriage in diverse and unpredictable ways.

3

Courtships and Love Marriages

'We are childhood sweethearts.'

— Couples emphasizing their childhood love
('*bachpan se pyar*') that emerged while they
were growing up together in the same
neighbourhood

Subversive Practices in Love and Marriage

This chapter turns the attention away from the normative system of arranged marriage and towards subversive practices that are based on romantic love. It offers insights into how love marriages are perceived, defined, accommodated, contested, and lived. It examines three interconnected phases of the love marriage cycle: (1) premarital romance; (2) the period between courtship and marriage; and (3) the post-marital phase or experiences of 'married love'. In Delhi's *bastis* and resettlement colonies, representations of romance in popular cinema, awareness of modern state laws that permit inter-caste marriages, and metropolitan freedom combined with close-knit urban neighbourhoods are all rapidly enhancing courtship practices.

Given that courtship is a visible trend, a pivotal question is how families are reacting to the romantic choices of the younger generation, and to those unions that contravene the established structure of caste endogamy. To mark the levels of social change occurring in groups that live on the margins, issues of parental consent and the extent to which love marriages are being accepted in low-income neighbourhoods form a key part of the discussion. In addition, the post-marriage phase receives extensive analytical attention, as extant studies give us little ethnographic sense of how self-chosen marriages are lived out over the life course. The post-marriage phase of love marriages, the gender content of this phase, and substantive evidence of conjugal stability are issues that have remained critically under-studied in Indian anthropology. For a deeper understanding of contemporary love marriages and self-chosen marriages that are today being 'arranged', it is imperative that we grasp how relationships between couples, parents, affines, and neighbours unfold over time. Crucially, an examination of the married phase will allow me to extricate women's positioning in love marriages and their entitlements to natal kin support. The thematic focus on post-marital trajectories also provides the basis for challenging, and exercising caution towards current anthropological debates that stress the experiential continuum between arranged and love marriages.

Premarital Romance in Urban Neighbourhoods

In Mohini Nagar, although arranged marriages remain hegemonic, young people are often involved in long-lasting courtships.[1] The regular festive events and everyday exchanges amongst neighbours provide the social context for adolescents to spend time together. More so, the metropolitan topography offers numerous opportunities for younger (and older) people from diverse social backgrounds to meet and mix in public spaces, away from the surveillance of their kin and neighbours. Affordable public transport and the availability of spacious parks in Delhi facilitate and advance

---

[1] My analysis of courtship and love marriages focuses on couples in the age group of 15–40 years. My sample of love marriages primarily consists of twelve couples, the majority of whom have had inter-caste marriages. I am unable to offer information on the experiences of the older generations (50 years and above) premarital romance. However, based on individual biographies of people in this age bracket, I discerned that courtships did occur in their generation although love marriages were strongly opposed. I do not, therefore, wish to communicate the impression that courtship is a novel construct in Delhi's low-income neighbourhoods. My aim is to capture the current practice of courtship.

courtships that begin in the *bastis*. Hence, within a large city such as Delhi, the mobility of courting couples cannot be easily restricted through means of parental control. In her insightful book on social change in rural Nepal, Ahearn (2001: 4) discusses how arranged and 'capture' marriages are being widely replaced by courtship practices and love marriages. In the 1990s, due to the rise in literacy, especially among females, young Nepali couples resorted to love letters, which prolonged courtship. Letter exchanges have opened up novel ways of expressing emotions, marking courtships as 'developed' and 'modern'. Likewise, in her Kolkata study, Donner (2002) alerts us to the prevalence and acceptability of middle class love marriages, mainly intra-caste, or within one's own *jati*. She points out that co-educational schooling has contributed to an increase in the incidence of love marriages. Girls today have the opportunity to meet boys in school, unlike girls of their mothers' generation for whom such interaction was strictly supervised if not altogether prohibited. These particular markers of modernity construed by Ahearn and Donner are less prevalent in Mohini Nagar. There is little evidence of amorous letter writing,[2] and education levels have only minimally enhanced cross-gender interactions for adolescents in the resettlement colonies. On the other hand as I have explicated, a key factor that facilitates courtships in Mohini Nagar is the cohesiveness of the neighbourhood combined with the anonymity and freedom that metropolitan spaces confer on individuals. In densely populated urban settings, daily and close encounters intensify social interaction and give rise to romantic and sexual relations.[3]

Many romances in Mohini Nagar occur specifically between neighbours. These neighbourly courtships are framed in the idiom of *bachpan se pyar*, that is, love from or since childhood, a bond

[2] Beyond the convention of letter writing, the influx of new technologies, such as mobile phones has enhanced easy and accessible communication. In 2002, few residents possessed mobile phones. In 2006–09, I noted how young residents came to possess increasing numbers of cheap mobile phones that are being used to facilitate flirtations and courtships. Specifically, it is the prepaid mobile connection that facilitates this communication because couples can buy SIM cards without providing much paperwork and can top up the cards as and when required. This ensures anonymity and is also cheap and convenient.

[3] See also Donner (2002) for how the 'neighbourhood' facilitates courtship. The routine social and religious festivities in Kolkata's very ordinary middle class localities bring young people into close contact.

forged while growing up together in the same locality. By stressing the idiom of childhood love, couples also strive to distance their courtship from conceptions of sexual desire. Thus, reminiscing about her relationship with her partner, Sandeep, Rekha described themselves as 'childhood sweethearts', expressing the familiarity and trust accumulated over the numerous memorable encounters they shared as children growing up together in Raju Camp. In narratives of courtship, young people mainly evoke the Hindi term *pyar* (love). The English declaration 'I love you' features minimally in male and female courtship narratives. *Prem, muhabbat,* and *ishq,* other Hindi or Urdu words that connote romantic love, passion, and desire are also cited less often by young people in courtship narratives. Chapter 2 has conveyed how married women ascribe *pyar* to other kinds of love, such as family devotion and marital happiness. In Mohini Nagar, *pyar* is, therefore, used across age groups as a generic and overarching term that refers to different forms of love and emotional attachment.

The theme of childhood love and closeness has been dominant in acclaimed (both popularly and critically) Indian films such as *Devdas*, a film adapted from the epistolary novella by Sharat Chandra Chattopadhyay, a story of neighbours Devdas and Paro and their childhood love, which ends in tragedy. Bearing in mind the central role of romantic love in Indian films (see Dywer 2000; Uberoi 1996; 1998; 2006) and television serials, I noted how many television soaps being watched by *basti* residents featured premarital love in an exceedingly positive light. In 2002, Zee Television aired a serial called 'Love Marriage'. Similarly, the host of Star Channel's serial *Ek Main Aur Ek Tu* (There is me and there is you) brings together couples who have fallen in love, announcing at the end of the programme: 'If you have a love story you would like to share, send it to us.' It goes without saying that the popular romantic narratives of Hindi cinema, television serials, and media romances play a critical part in stimulating thoughts about love in the minds of their young audiences.

Theatre of Courtship

Narratives of courtship form a pivotal starting point for gaining insights into young people's romantic inclinations and premarital sexuality. Notably, girls and boys discuss the build-up to romantic relationships in quite different ways. Consider the following narratives told by Rekha and Amrita, two married women, recalling the trajectories of their respective courtships. Through these narratives I wish to unravel the gender dimension of courtship and examine how couples construe romantic love.

Rekha and Sandeep: 'Childhood love'

Rekha, a Balmiki girl, and Sandeep, a Rajput boy, grew up in Raju Camp. During the period of my fieldwork, they had a love marriage, which their parents accepted. Rekha informs me that Sandeep and she spent much of their childhood playing together. Her mother, who is present while we are talking, reiterates their early childhood fondness (*'bachpan se pyar'*) shared by Rekha and Sandeep: 'When we would go out of Delhi, I would request Sandeep to look after our *jhuggi* as he was such a regular visitor.' Rekha reflects on her courtship years, telling me that at the age of fifteen she began working in a cinema hall as a female security guard. Her mother relied on her for financial support. While she was working at Priya Cinema (in Vasant Vihar), several of her male colleagues showed an interest in her and would buy her presents: 'At that time, I had forgotten about Sandeep. Yet he would often badger me that if I did not marry him, he would kill himself. But I did not want to marry so soon. One day, he made a huge scene by eating something poisonous to show me that he could not live without me. On another occasion, we fought in front of everyone on the road because he was not happy about me meeting other boys.' I asked her what had prompted her to marry Sandeep. 'Once when we were at a movie, he told me how much he loved (*pyar*) me.' She says hesitantly: 'After that, I do not know what happened [emphasizing] . . . but ours was not a sexual relationship. Sandeep used to sing lovely songs, which I liked. I had many proposals from male friends, but what I shared with Sandeep since childhood . . . I could not have those feelings for other men.'

Amrita and Purujeet: 'Encounters on a school bus'

Amrita, a Punjabi girl, lives in the resettlement colonies. Some years ago, she had a love marriage. Amrita reminisces about how she met her Rajasthani husband, Purujeet, on a 'deluxe bus' that took her to school. The hem of her *salwar kameez* (Indian dress consisting of a pair of loose trousers and a long tunic) had come down and she felt self-conscious and embarrassed. Purujeet, who was also on the bus, offered her a safety pin. After this enchanting personal encounter, they met on the same deluxe bus every day. Amrita says:

> Our friendship grew from then on. But not once in those years did he touch me [clarifying that their relationship had been platonic]. Look, things have changed so much compared to our time. Have you ventured into Delhi's Nehru Park or the other parks? If you enter Nehru Park, you will see shameless men and women, especially the women, who will have their blouses wide open. It's so disrespectful! Do they even care if elders are passing by? In our time, men never touched us. Nowadays, boys and girls go to hotels to have sex. Women who work in export companies have a lot of affairs.

Seven months into my fieldwork, I have another conversation with Amrita about her courtship days, whereupon she admits to being involved in a non-platonic relationship: 'Yes, all that did happen between me and Purujeet.' Yet she reiterates that they never had sexual intercourse: 'Even men take note of how far we are willing to be pushed into sex. Purujeet and I were once at a friend's house and he hinted to his friend to leave us alone. I caught on and refused to give in.'

It can be seen from Rekha and Amrita's case studies that girls are reluctant to reveal their feelings. Most girls (married and unmarried) narrate their courtship accounts with haste, unease, and caution. Their narratives emphasize propriety and respectability. Girls highlight a refusal to comply with the sexual advances of boyfriends or their insistence on embarking on a non-platonic relationship. In a study on friendship and adolescent romance in Kerala, the Osellas (1998: 201) comment on how young Malayali boys tease and pursue girls as a call for attention, just like their Bollywood heroes. If girls indicate their interest in a romantic encounter in return, young men almost immediately drop their aggressive stance and adopt the role of humble and ardent suitor. An interesting point that emerges from the Osellas' ethnographic study is that while flirtations develop reciprocally, girls' participation in the thrall of romance is ambiguous compared to that of boys. The Osellas write: 'A girl, even if she agrees to romance, is expected to remain reluctant and reticent, so extreme behaviour is necessary on the boy's part' (1998: 200). In Delhi, as girls such as Rekha and Amrita do not wish to be seen as having initiated a relationship, they usually insinuate, as per the official version of events, vigorous pursuit (*'usne mera peechcha kiya'*) on the part of their male partners. In an environment where arranged marriage and parental matchmaking are the desired norm, it is understandable for Mohini Nagar girls to tread a careful line in the way they conduct and position themselves in their courtship narratives. For this reason, female courtship narratives are always characterized by ambiguity and a moralistic tone.

On the other hand, boys, like the impetuous Raj, are more vocal about their desires and feelings, as the narrative below shows.

Raj and Hema: 'Intense sexual attraction'

Raj, a Balmiki boy, met Hema, a Balmiki girl, in the resettlement colonies. He tells me in a forthright manner that their love grew during their childhood (*'hamara pyar bachpan se tha'*), when they spent much time together in their neighbourhood. This was possible as the mothers of both Raj and Hema were 'honorary sisters' (*dharam behen*) or fictive kin. At the age of sixteen, and during the height of their courtship, Raj's family decided to move to another Delhi neighbourhood. At that time, Raj was driving an auto-rickshaw, and he wanted to remain in the colony where he had grown up so that he could continue his relationship with Hema. According to Raj:

> I could not live without Hema for even a second. I was mad about her. I loved her (*pyar*) so much. We would meet alone whenever it was possible. Sometimes we met first thing in the morning behind the latrines [public toilets]. We were together all the time. After a while, our problems

began as she got pregnant . . . it happened at a
friend's house. I could have run away with her
. . . but I took my parents into my confidence. I
brought her to my family. Everyone in our *gali*
found out that she was pregnant. I filled the
parting of her hair with *sindoor* [red powder
that symbolizes the married status of a woman].
Thereafter our parents separated us.

Raj's narrative reveals uninhibited feelings of sexual attraction.
Boys like Raj stress the inability to resist love. Usually, male
courtship narratives are emotionally charged (cf. Parry 2001), while
inevitably they also tend to stress appropriate moral behaviour,
as seen through Raj's honouable act of saving Hema's reputation
through the symbolic act of filling the parting of her hair with
sindoor. As the Osellas (1998) have argued, boys are more aggressive
in their romantic gestures, declarations, and intentions. In Delhi,
male aggression in certain instances can take extreme forms, such
as stalking, emotional blackmail, consuming poison to 'win' a girl's
heart, and coercing a girl into marriage (see section 'Elopement and
Forced Marriage' further in this chapter). Accordingly, the Delhi
ethnography on courtships exemplifies that the character of male
and female romance differs vastly in approach, deportment, and
intensity. While both girls and boys are specifically uninhabited
and candid about their childhood feelings of love, the majority do
not construe their emotional attachments on the basis of modernist
definitions of a companionate relationship, a phenomenon that
Ahearn (2001) underscores with reference to rural Nepal.

Raj and Hema's case illustrates the fact that pregnancy before
marriage is not unusual in low-income urban neighbourhoods.
Parry (2001: 795–8) points to the salient demarcation between
premarital sexuality and extramarital lapses. In Chhattisgarh,
premarital affairs, especially across castes, are less approved of. In
certain parts of Chhattisgarh, prepubescent girls were subjected to
token marriages, but were permitted to transgress sexual norms
once the mock marriage was over. In contemporary Chhattisgarh,
there has been a collapse in the marital rituals of *shaadi* (wedding)
and *gauna* (consummation ceremony), and women are under
considerable pressure to keep their virginity intact until they marry.

The sharp separation between premarital and extramarital affairs is also applicable in Delhi, and once again provides the necessary framework for understanding why women's discourses on courtship always centre on respectability. The ideal bride should be a virgin, and if she were to become pregnant before marriage, she would risk censure and face problems in finding a groom. Nevertheless, as is evident, young people who are infatuated with members of the opposite sex start spending time together while their families are out working. Stories of premarital pregnancies and how a mother faced humiliation in having to take her daughter to a government hospital for an abortion do emerge. A Raju Camp resident stated that behind their *basti* is a desolate hillock that is littered with self-aborted foetuses. It emerges, then, that while the ideal Mohini Nagar bride should be a virgin, in practice, premarital sexual transgressions are not entirely uncommon, thus revealing degrees of unofficial tolerance.

'Love Marriage' and its Many Connotations

As the practice of courtship is an increasingly visible trend, it is important to understand the connotations of 'love marriage' in a low-income urban neighbourhood in north India, the variants of this term, and the socio-legal routes that courting couples resort to while consolidating their unions that may not have been 'sanctioned' by their kin and community members. The urban poor of Delhi have widely adopted the pan-Indian terms 'arranged marriage' and 'love marriage'. Across the social divide, metropolitan residents are widely familiar with these two distinctions that conjure different scenarios. Love marriage, locally pronounced 'luv marriaze' (in Hindi, *apni pasand* or own preference), connotes a self-chosen marriage, denoting the antithesis of a respectable arranged marriage. The courtship trajectory of falling in love is a diacritical marker of a love marriage. Donner (2002: 83) explicates that in Kolkata, a clear-cut definition of love marriage exists amongst the middle classes that does not depend on 'the period or mode of courtship'. Arranged marriages in Kolkata increasingly involve premarital contact, and hence the agency and choice that a couple exhibits are more symbolic of one's own marriage. As Donner notes:

Consequently, this definition of a proper love marriage does not depend on the period or mode of courtship, the consent of the candidates or the notion of emotional involvement because women are well aware of the fact that these factors may be present in modern arranged marriages. The *agency* of the partners in initiating a premarital relationship is the crucial marker and is indicated by the phrase 'one's own marriage' in colloquial Bengali, instead of a love marriage (2002: 83).

While the agency of a couple in Kolkata signifies 'one's own marriage', other progressive notions emphasizing consent, choice, and premarital acquaintance also seem to be of importance to the middle classes.[4] Fuller and Narasimhan (2008: 751) have recently contended that the dichotomy between arranged and love marriage is fluid. Amongst middle class urban Vattimas in Tamil Nadu, a companionate intra-caste marriage through 'arrangement' is a joint endeavour between parents and partners, and constitutes the contemporary ideal.[5] The Vattima evidence suggests that a couple's personal happiness or a companionate ideology has become an important criterion in both arranged and love marriages. However, amongst Delhi's urban poor, marital choice and a couple's happiness are not regarded as salient by parents. The ideology of choice in particular is of no relevance to the primary alliance as it is to the secondary union (cf. Parry 2001; Chapter 4). In the primary marriage, matchmaking continues to be dominated by considerations of caste endogamy and the groom's economic

[4] Research on the south Asian diaspora and the Indian middle classes (Prinjha 1999; Uberoi 1998) also suggests increased flexibility in the realm of marital choice. In her marriage ethnography of British Gujaratis living in London, Suman Bala Prinjha (1999) notes that the term arranged marriage is queried by the younger generation. Replacements such as 'kind of arranged', 'not that arranged', 'assistance marriage', and 'marriage by introduction' are indicative of mutations and of the ways in which British Gujaratis are experimenting with new labels. Many of these recent labels are blurring the normative distinction between an arranged marriage and a love marriage.

[5] See also Kalpagam (2008), who has examined the marriage norms and aspirations of rural women in Allahabad. In documenting changes, the author remarks that intra-caste marriage 'by choice' is gaining approval.

position. At the outset, then, the arranged marriage is based on a strict 'parental arrangement', while the 'love marriage' has to be assiduously negotiated. As regards Fuller and Narasimhan's recent claims, we must take note that there are vast economic and social differences between the urban middle classes and the urban poor. However, as I am about to discuss, even in a low-income neighbourhood such as Mohini Nagar, the ideal merger between parental arrangement and marital preference is not inconceivable if couples finally manage to win over their parents.

The 'Arranged Love Marriage' Ideal

To mark the different types of love marriages in Delhi, Mody (2002: 255) articulates four distinctions: 'love marriage'; 'court marriage'; 'love-cum-arranged marriage'; and 'elopement'. These labels veritably complicate the picture. Clearly, there are many routes and modes through which young couples attempt to formalize their romantic choices. Mohini Nagar inhabitants also deploy the distinctions demarcated by Mody, and I will specify what they denote for the local populace.[6] While the term 'love marriage' implies marriage by choice, it has also come to signify an elopement marriage (Mody 2002), resulting on account of staunch parental opposition. In addition, 'love marriage' is equated—and interchangeably used—with 'court marriage' as couples may now legally register their marriage through the courts (for details see Mody 2002 and 2008). The Special Marriage Act of 1954 permits what is popularly known as a court marriage. This act or state-sponsored civil marriage has been adopted in India to allow marriage across castes and communities, and thereby validates love marriage. In the main though, the 'court marriage' label has negative connotations for it is associated with couples who have defied their families. As it is more prestigious to marry with parental approval, thus gaining the long-term support of parents and natal kin, couples desperately try to gain parental consent. In my sample, recourse to the courts, which is not unusual, is, by and large, a means of last resort, evidence of the marriage having failed

---

[6] To add to these existing labels, 'forced love marriage' is another distinct category. I will examine this form of marriage later in this chapter.

to receive parental approval. Couples also approach the Arya Samaj temples located across the city, where it is possible to legalize a marriage through a ceremony. Compared with the courts, the latter proposition is less expensive for the urban poor, and is an easier and more convenient route to obtaining a marriage certificate.[7] I noted that couples in possession of an Arya Samaj temple certificate construe these certificates for the wider public as 'a court marriage certificate' so as to highlight that they are in possession of an official document. In turn, residents rarely question couples when they produce their certificates as there is limited awareness in the local community as to what constitutes the contents of a proper court marriage certificate. A number of couples I knew had obtained counterfeit marriage certificates from dishonest lawyers.

Couples may also refer to their self-chosen marriage as an 'arranged love marriage', a metaphor representing a more respectable image. Indeed, during the courtship phase, couples greatly hope that their parents will come around to socially accepting their love union, approval that is publicly signified through the act of hosting a wedding. If this happens, the couple has no need to resort to elopement or to legalizing the marriage through the courts, actions that bring dishonour to their families. Uberoi (1998; 1997) has examined the concept of an 'arranged love marriage' in some depth, outlining how this arrangement is a new south Asian marriage ideal.[8] Explaining the apparent oxymoron in the terms 'arranged' and 'love', Uberoi defines 'arranged love marriage' as 'a style of matchmaking where a romantic choice already made is endorsed, *post facto*, by parental approval and treated thereafter like an arranged marriage' (1998: 306).[9] This

[7] Chowdhry (2004) specifies that runaway couples in Haryana and Punjab are not known to take recourse to state-sponsored civil marriage. They usually opt for an Arya Samaj ceremony. Although this ceremony is not on a par with a court marriage, it is a much less complicated and quicker affair.

[8] See also Mody's (2002: 249) conception of a 'love-cum-arranged marriage'. She writes that 'in a love-cum-arranged marriage', the social order that has been disrupted by 'love' is seen to be restored through the arranged marriage'. Mody argues that love-cum-arranged marriage remains the ideal for young couples in Delhi.

[9] The unification between 'parental arrangement' and 'individual choice' features as part of a larger social debate on the binary oppositions between 'family obligation' and 'individual desire', a subject that Hart (2007) takes up

interesting pattern that Uberoi describes in relation to the middle classes, whereby courtship usually between those from the same social background is conveniently reworked into a conventional arranged marriage,[10] cannot be replicated that easily in densely populated neighbourhoods such as Mohini Nagar. Given the lack of privacy in *bastis*, residents are only too familiar with the domestic lives of their neighbours.[11] In Mohini Nagar, the phrase 'arranged love marriage' is adapted to refer to a situation where parents have overtly 'given in' to the couple's demands and have granted them a public wedding (*shaadi*) which includes ritual functions and presentation of dowry from the bride's side. Couples may use 'arranged' without 'love' to signify the clear stamp of parental approval when actually the marriage is the outcome of romantic love. In the vernacular, this is symbolized in the phrase *'arranged hi kar diya'* ('it was arranged somehow'). I noticed that some couples proceed to obtain marriage certificates with the active consent of their parents, even after the latter have 'arranged' their marriage. Here couples are pursuing multiple legal, religious, and social routes to strengthen their union against future impediments.

Between Courtship and Marriage: Caste, Community, and Religion

I proceed to give the reader a sense of how couples experience the phase between courtship and marriage. Couples approach their parents with the subject of marriage when their courtships have

---

in her essay on 'marriage by arrangement' in western Turkey, and one that Uberoi (2006) has engaged with in her thematic work on *'dharma* and destiny'.

[10] Accentuating how arranged marriages and love marriages are actually part of a continuum, Marsden (2008) discusses how families in northern Pakistan are complicit in encouraging their children to develop premarital relationships that are later arranged. Hart (2007) also notes that in rural Turkey, the definition of arranged marriage has been expanded to allow for premarital romance.

[11] Here I would like to point to Aditya Nigam's (2002: 26) brilliant essay on the everyday spaces of subaltern existence in Delhi. As Nigam rightly observes, in subaltern neighbourhoods, the networks of communication tend to be strong: 'The lanes and bylanes where people simply sit outside on cots and spend their free time provide another mode of exchange of information, gossip and rumours. Unlike the middle class and affluent colonies, where contact with the locality is

acquired a particular intensity. Many are faced with the difficult task of persuading their families to accept a bride or groom from a different caste or religious background. As I have stated, more often than not, couples first and foremost appeal for an 'arranged love marriage', which would mean that they do not have to elope to legalize their marriage through the court or the temple. The ethnography hereupon sheds light on how marriages across caste, region, and religion are being received in Delhi's low-income neighbourhoods. I examine the local discourses around inter-caste, inter-regional, and inter-religious love marriages. While my focus is on issues of parental consent, it must be noted that families in Mohini Nagar do not function as autonomous units. They belong to certain caste groups, kinship networks, and religious communities whose members exercise some measure of control over the families. Hence, I provide in-depth documentation of the negotiations surrounding love marriages and parental reactions by examining caste boundaries, social identities, the dynamics and relations between religious communities, and the role of the state and other institutions.

Inter-caste Matches: The Balmiki Conundrum

All social groups in Mohini Nagar try to observe the rule of caste endogamy, a norm that is prevalent across north India (Chowdhry 2007). It is important, then, to examine how the numerically dominant caste group in Mohini Nagar, the Balmikis, react to violations of caste endogamy. I followed two case studies on inter-caste love marriages, both focusing on the younger generation of Balmiki girls. My ethnography illustrates that although the Balmikis reside in close proximity with other castes in a heterogeneous neighbourhood endogamy is more pronounced in their caste group.

---

minimal and where the routine trips to the markets too are likely to be purely commercial transactions with minimal human interaction, in these subaltern spaces the rapidity with which information travels through informal channels can often be truly mind-boggling.' As we can detect from Nigam's account, middle class and affluent Delhi neighbourhoods remain private and isolated compared with the 'face-to-face settlements' that are a hallmark of subaltern existence. For a description of the opposite conditions, see Donner (2002), who portrays the easy sociability of Kolkata's middle class neighbourhoods.

Kalpana and Rahul: 'Forced separation'

Kalpana, a Balmiki girl, and Rahul, a Garhwali[12] boy, describe how their long-drawn courtship in Raju Camp began in childhood. When they wanted to marry, Kalpana's parents refused outright as they wanted to arrange her marriage with a Balmiki boy. Kalpana recalls: 'My mother threatened to kill herself. Balmikis do not like us to go into the higher *jats*. They like us to stay in our *biradari*. Garhwalis will still take a girl from a lower *jat*.' Rahul says that when Kalpana's parents refused to let them marry, they eloped. Kalpana's parents immediately responded by filing a Missing Person's Application[13] at the local police station. Meanwhile, Rahul and Kalpana's elopement plan collapsed as they had been spotted by relatives in a nearby colony. Soon after this, Kalpana's parents forcibly arranged her marriage to a Balmiki boy. Rahul remembers that he could not stall Kalpana's arranged marriage as his mother was seriously ill at that time. The day after Kalpana got married she told her parents that she would never accept her arranged marriage. Her troubles began almost immediately after she moved to her conjugal home: 'I stayed in my *sasural* for two months. They started to harass me as they found out about my long-term relationship with Rahul. So I was sent back to my parents. Talk of a separation emerged as my *sasural* would not accept me back, and neither did I want to go back. I wanted to be with Rahul, and as he was my neighbour I started to see him again.'

During my fieldwork, Kalpana and Rahul's parents finally consented to their marriage, which they were 'arranging'. In the run-up to the ceremony, I noticed that several Balmikis in Raju Camp passed disparaging and reproachful remarks about their forthcoming wedding. Kalpana informs me that a neighbour of

[12] See the introductory chapter for a description of how people are not always identified along the lines of caste. Regional identity is often given more weight than caste identity, especially in the case of those from Garhwal, Bihar, and Rajasthan. Regional identity is also conflated with caste, and hence Garhwalis are not perceived as one of the lowest (*neech*) castes.

[13] A Missing Person's Application is a letter notifying the police that a family member is missing. Usually, in cases of love marriage (see Chowdhry 2004; Mody 2002), such letters provide lengthy accounts of how a daughter has been kidnapped while specifying that the girl is a minor, or under 18 years of age, so that immediate action can be taken.

to these castes want to marry, it would be less problematic. This suggests that for certain castes, the classification of 'good caste' has introduced an element of flexibility in marriage negotiations that allows the issue of endogamy to be sidelined. With Balmiki families, however, endogamy is a matter of acute sensitivity as internal loyalty and notions of betrayal are distinctive characteristics of their caste group. For this reason Balmiki youths, and especially girls, face far more difficulties in gaining parental acceptance. However, in many cases and across castes, opposition and attempts to separate the couple are initiated by the girl's parents who claim a greater loss of familial reputation (*badnami*) vis-à-vis the boy's kin. Rahul's Garhwali parents were willing to embrace a Balmiki bride who belonged in their view to a caste lower than their own. There was less objection and hostility from Rahul's parents who interpreted their son's marriage as hypergamous. Often the boy's parents are a little more willing to accept a bride from another caste. According to popular notions, women should take on the husband's caste identity and adjust to the customs of their conjugal home, such as in matters of dress code, ritual, and food practices. Specifically, when discussions of inter-caste love marriages came up with parents, I often encountered the widespread belief that in India, women do not have a caste identity ('*aurat ki to jat hoti hi nahi*').[17] As per the north Indian patrilineal ideology, women, irrespective of their caste, are ideally meant to assimilate themselves into their husband's kindred. Kalpana, formerly a Balmiki, now identifies herself as a Garhwali and has adopted Garhwali customs.

Gender Violence in Mohini Nagar

My findings vary somewhat from those of Chowdhry (1998; 2004; 2007) and Mody (2002; 2007; 2008), who emphasize that in north India and Delhi, violence, torture, and attempted murder often accompany love marriages.[18] I do not dispute that women and

[17] Marsden's (2008: 101) Pakistani informants told him that women have no religion; if they fall in love, they are willing to change their religion.
[18] Chowdhry (2007) offers a number of explanations as to why gender violence, honour killings, and the elimination of couples are recurring features in contemporary Haryana. She elucidates how Haryanvi society is in a state of rapid flux; caste and class divisions are being altered, new laws today permit

couples from Delhi's lower classes confront forms of violence. Girls encounter intense non-cooperation in being forcibly separated from a partner and then being married to another against their wishes; they receive various threats from parents, and in turn, counter-attack by threatening suicide. In one case that I followed up, a Sikh boy was made to separate from his Jat wife. He was warned never to see her again or he would be harmed. His Jat wife was then forced to marry someone from her own caste. In this case, violence was undeniably being forced on the couple. Yet it is noteworthy that over the period of my fieldwork, I did not witness incidents of extreme violence or instances where parents invariably resorted to the use of violence to separate or 'hound' a courting couple.[19]

Four factors may broadly explicate why extreme violence does not always manifest itself so prominently in Mohini Nagar. First, while families have the backing of their caste and kin members, the biradari panchayats (caste associations), as seen in the cases from rural Haryana detailed by Chowdhry (2007), do not play a significant role in facilitating honour killings and impeding love marriages in Delhi. The few biradari panchayats that operate in south Delhi do not in any measure exercise the same level of authority as their rural north Indian counterparts, and neither do they hand out judgments in cases of love marriage. Primarily, biradari panchayats, which are known for imposing social boycotts and fines and for conferring punishments, have lost much of their credibility in Delhi as many people find them to be untrustworthy. On matters pertaining to marriage and family, the residents of Delhi can also approach other institutions such as the mahila panchayats and human rights organizations that offer legal advice and assistance (see Chapter 5).

Second, crucial aspects such as family inter-generational reliance (see page 112), the economic status of the family, and the family composition of a household can influence the outcomes of love marriages. A girl who is eager to marry her partner may

---

women to inherit property, and the lower castes have become upwardly mobile. These new developments have engendered deep anxiety amongst the upper castes, who are resorting to violence in order to maintain the status quo.

[19] Violence is not always the central approach when it comes to separating couples. The case study of Suman and Dinesh (see page 102) illuminates this point.

belong to a family that consists only of her widowed mother and younger siblings. The absence of a father and older brothers alters the normative equation. It has to be said that the latter family composition where the father is deceased is not unusual in Mohini Nagar given the high mortality rate on account of poor health and alcoholism. In the case study of Rekha and Sandeep, Rekha's mother was a widow. Though Rekha and Sandeep faced obstacles in gaining the approval of their respective families for their marriage, the fact is that Rekha's mother did not want to collude in any violent opposition against her only daughter on whom she was (and is) financially dependent.

Third, while Mohini Nagar families use pressure tactics to terminate the courtships of their children, parental decisions are also being subverted by the young people themselves. Couples exercise their agency and assert their preferences for partners with whom they have had long-term attachments. In many instances, couples like Neetu and Mahesh go ahead and marry on their own, by eloping. A vast majority of Mohini Nagar inhabitants are aware that a 'court marriage' represents the right, authorized by modern state laws, to marry a spouse of one's own choice. In their negotiations with parents, couples use the term 'court marriage' rebelliously. Parents admit that if their decisions are disobeyed, the courts and temples offer an alternative route to marriage. One parent stated: 'What can we do these days? Our children will just leave the *basti* and marry elsewhere.' Although for Mohini Nagar couples the courts are a means of last resort and the court marriage procedure is generally difficult (Chowdhry 2007; Mody 2008), at a certain level the concept of 'court marriage' also undermines parental authority.

Fourth, the inter-caste unions that I came across are local love marriages, where families may have known each other for many years in a common neighbourhood. They may have interacted with the partner of a daughter or a son at a very personal level, as in the case of Rekha and Sandeep, who had formed a deep attachment since their adolescence and had signposted to others that they were a couple. Consequently, proximity and long-term association between families, such as those of Sandeep and Rekha's, significantly mitigates violence. In other instances, however, volatile relations between close neighbours and families may exist under certain conditions, and these strained relations are likely to have an adverse impact on inter-caste couples. In *galis* and residential areas where two dominant castes clash, the notion of caste identity and endogamy may assume heightened importance, resulting in tensions and rifts between inhabitants. In one *gali* in the resettlement colonies, I witnessed several ongoing clashes between the Balmikis and the upwardly mobile Khatiks (meat-cutters and butchers) who were asserting their superiority. Where antagonistic relations exist between two caste groups in surrounding *galis*, the situation will have perilous implications for inter-caste couples.

Inter-regional Matches: Place, Gender, and Culture

Regional communities in Delhi are evaluated on the basis of differing criteria, and hence certain inter-regional love matches are recognized as problematic. The next case study, which focuses on an elopement and love marriage—a Delhi girl eloped with a 'Bihari boy'—exemplifies the importance of place, culture, and gender in marriage. The case study throws light not only on elopements and their occurrence in a modern metropolis, but also shows how young women position themselves in elopement narratives.

Aarti and Rohit: 'An unsuitable match'?

Aarti, who belongs to the Bania caste, tells me that she has married Rohit, who grew up in Bihar, and then settled in Delhi two years ago. Aarti's father did not want her to marry a Bihari, as the local perception is that Bihari men ill-treat women. There were also rumours that Rohit had a wife in Bihar. Aarti recalls that during their courtship, Rohit kept insisting that her father was attempting to separate them. On Rohit's forceful insistence, they eloped and took shelter with a common friend, John Anthony, who lives in Savitri Nagar. John Anthony lent them money and put them in touch with a lawyer, who assisted them with both temple and court marriages. Neither Rohit nor Aarti's family is happy about their marriage. The couple currently lives in rented accommodation in the resettlement colonies, not too far from Aarti's father's house.

The resistance that Aarti faced from her father reveals how region and place of origin are also critical markers that signify the acceptability of a match. Aarti's father was against a 'Bihari'

highest-paid groups amongst the SCs (Searle-Chatterjee 1981).[15] Given the unique socio-political standing of the sweepers in Delhi, they are also resented on account of being perceived as an economically privileged group.

A Municipal Sweeper
A typical sight in early-morning Delhi, a municipal female employee sweeps her designated area.

Let us further examine how the Balmikis relate to their own caste. The younger and older generations of Balmikis interact with their fellow caste members in ambivalent ways. They feel constrained by the close-knit nature of their community. Balmikis like Neetu make critical comments such as: 'I strongly dislike my *biradari* because they are too interfering.' Many Balmikis profess a desire

[15] This striking aspect of how sweepers, the lowest social group in India's caste hierarchy, are able to command high salaries has been accentuated by Searle-Chatterjee (1981).

for friends from outside their caste. Despite the ambivalence they express about their own community, Balmikis, especially those of the older generation, exhibit an enduring loyalty towards their caste group. They proclaim that, unlike other castes, they never betray one another (*'hum sath kabhi nahi chhorte hain'*). This aspect of community loyalty seems to pervade the very fabric of their social relations, as they align themselves against everyday prejudice. Other castes endorse the fact that the Balmikis never betray each other. Consequently, such dissonances that mark the subjective experiences of Balmikis, such as extreme loyalty combined with a widespread critique of their caste, are not unusual given the exceptional circumstances in which the Balmikis find themselves in the social order. The caste loyalty that is the hallmark of their community identity has earned them a reputation of being formidable. The predominant view is that the Balmikis are a force to reckon with and are known to harass others. It is wise to avoid making enemies of them, given their numerical strength in Delhi, their unity, and the muscle power they command through their employment in large numbers in the MCD. The Balmikis are aware of their reputation as a strong and assertive community. As a Balmiki man in his forties explains: 'Look, in the whole of Delhi nobody can touch us! Our *biradari* is known for its strength. We have people (*hamare log*) who will shield us in every colony of Delhi.' The perceptions described above illustrate why Balmiki parents, chiefly those of a certain generation, are keen on retaining the internal cohesiveness of their caste. They are deeply wary of how others treat them, and their defensiveness leads them to preserve group boundaries. While all SCs in Mohini Nagar affirm the desire to remain endogamous, I was told that inter-caste love marriages between castes such as the Bania, Garhwali, Khatik, Koli, Kumhar, Rajput, Sunar, and Teli are likely to meet with less resistance. Although I did not find a large number of inter-caste love matches between these castes,[16] I was told that these groups fall within the 'good caste' category (*achchi jat*) and that if couples belonging

---

[16] Neither did I encounter many intra-caste love marriages in Mohini Nagar. Brief particulars about Mala who had an intra-caste marriage are presented towards the end of this chapter. According to Mala, her parents were against her intra-caste love marriage as they wanted her to marry someone of their choice.

'coercion' and 'love'. The two women who had narrativized their elopements admitted to having had premarital relationships with their partners. Features of premarital intimacy seemed to have been latent in their narratives. Ahearn (2001) discusses the conundrums in disentangling women's agency and their complicity in coercion in situations of courtship and elopement. As she notes:

> Women in particular, but sometimes men also, depict themselves in their narratives of marriage as having resisted coercion before consenting to elope, even when they have been carrying on an intense courtship for months or years with their eventual spouse. Obtaining a woman's consent in an elopement therefore always requires "persuasion" of some sort (*phakaunu*, "to persuade, coax, flatter and seduce"). Thus, consent and coercion go hand in hand in narratives of elopement (2001: 109).

Mohini Nagar girls often reconfigure their motives for entering a love marriage by shifting the onus onto their partner's use of persuasion and force. I have formerly explicated that this endeavour is strategic on the part of women for it enables them to guard their reputations. My data echoes Ahearn's findings: for young girls of Mohini Nagar, elopement and forced marriage paradoxically evoke both consent and coercion. Yet such examples whereby girls highlight coercion in elopement narratives need to be sharply distinguished from those cases in which families have physically separated their daughters from a loved one. Chowdhry (2004) points that in the latter scenario, girls are coerced by their parents into making the claim that their partner had kidnapped them.

Inter-religious Love Marriages

Rumours were afloat in Raju Camp that a Christian boy and a Rajput girl were having a relationship. Their families admitted that a relationship was indeed in motion. In my encounters with the parents of the couple, who are from different religious communities,

I was struck by how little attention was being paid to 'religious difference'. Conversely, other substantial factors such as the salience of caste identity and the desire for a village bride seemed to be matters of pressing concern.

Dinesh and Suman: The Village Bride Syndrome

In Raju Camp, I meet Dinesh's mother, who informs me that after a short courtship her son wants to marry a girl called Suman, who lives in an adjoining *gali*. Dinesh's mother says that her family are Christians, and recent migrants to Delhi. She asserts that her eldest son wants to marry suddenly, as he is having an intense relationship with Suman: 'She roams around with all kinds of boys. She does it with all of them. No wonder my son got hooked on her. Why else would he get attached to a girl who has a skin disease?' Dinesh's mother is vehemently opposed to her son's marriage: 'I am not prepared to accept this marriage. If necessary, I will issue a police case against my son. I want a daughter-in-law from the village [she repeats this several times]. Neither are we sure about the girl's *jat*. Her family claims to be Rajputs, but on other occasions they call themselves Thakurs . . . People say they are Chamars. All her uncles have eloped and married.' Dinesh walks in, looking forlorn. He tells me that love has no boundaries; caste and religion should not matter. He is threatening to hang himself from the fan. His mother has told him that before he hangs himself, he should leave a letter for the police stating that his parents will not be held responsible for his suicide act. She has locked away valuable household items in case he elopes, and her relatives have been cautioned not to assist him if he approaches them for money or shelter.

On meeting Suman's family, I find that they are defensive about their reputation. Suman's grandmother asserts, without my asking, that they are Rajputs: 'Yes, three of my sons had love marriages. It was futile to oppose their marriages. Why should I waste my life running from one police station to another?' Concerning Suman's wish to marry Dinesh, she comments: 'If the boy is threatening suicide, we are prepared to give in.' A few weeks later, I discover that Dinesh and Suman's affair has not led to either elopement or marriage. Dinesh's mother has taken her son to their village and has found him a village bride. When I inquire about Suman, her grandmother says that they have arranged her marriage. Suman has succumbed and agreed to marry whoever the family chooses for her. Suman's grandmother says: 'My sons had love marriages, but they are boys. I want to give my granddaughter away with respect. We are not marrying her amongst 'Bhangis' [derogatory term for sweepers] or Chamars, but into a good caste. They are Rajput Khars [palanquin makers] and have accepted her despite her skin disease.'

Dinesh and Suman failed to win the approval of their respective families. Typically, their families wanted them to have respectable arranged marriages that were not based on ties between close neighbours. Dinesh's mother successfully stalled her son's love marriage by threatening him with a police case. In the drama that unfolded before me, she did not exhibit unease about how the pair was not of the same religion. The quest for a village daughter-in-law (*'gav ki bahu'*) dominated her narrative. Formerly, I have described how Mohini Nagar residents do not usually conform to the north Indian ideal of long-distance alliances. Daughters and sons born in Delhi are married off locally within the city. Nonetheless, Raju Camp migrants from the post-1984 period have a different way of arranging marriages. They make it a point to arrange the son's marriage with a village bride since such a match is deemed prestigious, as also a village alliance enables migrants to keep their wider social networks intact. Replacing a village bride with a Delhi bride through a love marriage leads to deep disappointment and considerable resistance by mothers-in-law. Potential mothers-in-law espouse the advantages of a 'poorer' village daughter-in-law, who may bring in less dowry but who will be more subservient and pliable than a Delhi bride. They compare village and urban brides, and as one mother put it, 'A Delhi bride will start ordering me around and controlling me.' Nonetheless, a popular joke amongst *basti* women contradicts some of the myths associated with supposedly servile village brides. The migrant parents of a Delhi boy wanted to arrange his alliance. The joke goes that the boy requested his parents to find a village bride as it was widely believed that in all probability she would be sexually inexperienced. On his wedding night, he decided to make things easier for his village bride by enacting a 'game' (i.e. the sexual act). While he was preparing the wedding bed and gradually telling her more about the game, she blurted out: 'I have played this game in our lush village fields!'

Conversations with the families of Suman and Dinesh reveal once again how the discourse of caste identity is highly elevated and conspicuous, even in inter-religious marriages. The exception is, of course, Hindu–Muslim marriages, where religious discourses about the 'other community' become the overriding factor. Dinesh's family seemed paranoid over Suman's caste; once again, the significance of a 'Hindu–Christian' alliance was inconsequential. It suffices that residents express deep-seated anxieties about whether certain families have a tainted reputation or a good caste background. Dinesh's mother was critical of how Suman's uncles went around employing different caste names. Suman's family history also conjured multiple elopements as many of her uncles had love marriages. Frequently, residents contest the identities of their neighbours on the pretext that the latter's caste status is highly dubious. So it emerges that while caste endogamy remains the quintessential ideal, other status distinctions such as an individual's education, and personal attributes do not seem to motivate or influence marital arrangements.[20] As I have consistently argued, caste remains a strong social marker and continues to play a central role in Delhi's low-income neighbourhoods.[21] What is more, it is possible to some extent and for some castes in Delhi to disguise caste identities, given that urban existence manifests anonymity, particularly the heterogeneous constitution of crowded, low-income neighbourhoods. In several encounters with some residents of Raju Camp, I observed that they would introduce themselves with incomprehensible and multiple caste names. I followed the trajectory of a young boy called Raju and his relatives who had been inconsistent all along about their caste identity. At one point, they were collectively identifying themselves as Rajputs. Their

[20] In contrast, Béteille (1993: 441) in his seminal essay on the 'reproduction of inequality' has argued persuasively that for Indian middle class professionals there has been a sweeping shift 'away from caste and sub-caste towards school, college and office'. Caste today does not actively shape modern life or middle class occupations. For a certain section of society, caste has ceased to play a pivotal role in the reproduction of inequality.

[21] See De Neve (2005) for how caste membership continues to influence and determine job opportunities for south Indian informal factory workers.

Rajput identity was being contested privately by another set of Rajputs, i.e. the Siklighar and Lohar Rajputs (locksmiths), a group claiming genuine Rajput status as per their ancestry and ties with Rajasthan. The Siklighar and Lohar Rajputs of Raju Camp were disputing Raju's family's claim that they are genuine Rajputs. Clearly, families like Raju's are seeking upward mobility in Delhi. Yet while Raju's family had been scathing in their criticism of the Balmikis at great length, towards the end of my fieldwork I noticed that Raju had found employment with the MCD, which is primarily associated with the Balmiki sweeper caste. The attractive municipality salaries usually do not lure other castes because, by and large, sweeping is a stigmatized profession. Raju's career detour of a 'Rajput' who acquires a municipality job marks the shifting and ambiguous character of caste in an urban setting; residents belie and concomitantly assert new identities to further their socio-economic position.[22]

Hindu-Muslim Love Marriages

In comparison with inter-caste unions, I came across far fewer Hindu-Muslim love marriages in Mohini Nagar. The next set of case studies depicts the secrecy around Hindu-Muslim love marriages. It also signals how one partner may resort to disguising his or her identity, thus deceiving the loved one.

Sharia and 'her parents' secret marriage'

Sharia, a Muslim girl from Raju Camp, had an arranged marriage with a Muslim boy. Six months into her marriage, she is unhappy. I have several conversations with Sharia, and stories of her past emerge. She had once been in love with a Hindu boy who had lived in a nearby *gali*: 'I was told by my parents that if I married a Hindu boy, they would break their ties with me.' Radha, my field assistant, who knows Sharia well, confides that she had taken rat

---

[22] Iversen and Raghavendra (2006), in their study of food, caste, and employability, note that in the large cities of Karnataka, Dalits are rarely employed in hotels and small eating joints. Disguising one's caste is a common strategy for gaining employment in eating places.

poison in reaction to her parents' non-compliance. Nevertheless, she was still forced into an arranged marriage. To my surprise, Radha further informs me that Sharia's parents are themselves a Hindu-Muslim couple. Sharia's father, who is apparently Hindu, had picked up her Muslim mother on a railway platform in Kolkata. Sharia's mother made him convert to Islam and Sharia's father now calls himself a Muslim.

Janaki: 'Deception concerning religious identity'

Janaki, a Rajasthani woman, met her husband on a bus. While they were courting, he told her that he was Hindu. They married without parental approval by exchanging garlands in a temple: 'My family was initially angry. But after our first child was born, they came round to accepting it.' Soon after they married, Janaki's husband revealed that he was Muslim. In the sixth year of their marriage, and with three children to take care of, she feels betrayed: 'I did not know he was Muslim when we first met. I have been deeply misled.' Janaki's conversations about her husband are full of contempt for his religion. She says that she has forced him to give up observing Muslim festivals. All their children have Hindu names. While expressing her anger at his deception, she complains that he is a heavy drinker, which leads to constant rows between them.

Sharia was forced to marry a Muslim man against her wishes, with the familiar threat that if she did not agree her family would disown her. As her parents' reactions make it clear, the patterns and modes of opposing courtships of Hindu-Muslim couples hardly differ from those of couples in inter-caste love marriages. I was unable, however, to probe the veracity of my field assistant's claim that Sharia's parents are a Hindu-Muslim couple. Their marriage was not a topic meant for discussion or interrogation, but was shrouded in secrecy. Nonetheless, Sharia's mother was adamant that her daughter retain her Muslim identity. Interestingly, the deception perpetrated by Janaki's husband could relate to the fierce opposition against Hindu-Muslim marriages. The reactions of Sharia's parents and Janaki's sense of betrayal suggest that the only way forward for these Hindu-Muslim couples is for one partner to either convert or to disguise his or her identity. A conspicuous feature of Hindu-Muslim alliances is the accentuated focus on religious difference. What comes through sharply in such cases is the notion that the boundaries between these two communities are clearly fixed and demarcated. The case studies reveal, predictably and not surprisingly, that alliances of Hindus with Muslims are the most detested. The resistance against these alliances has only intensified over time.[23] Muslim communities have faced recurrent communal violence in post-independence India, with the Gujarat riots of 2002 being the most recent and notorious attacks. The minority status of Muslims has been heightened since the rise of right-wing Hindu politics and the emergence of international terrorism. Although in Mohini Nagar there have been no incidents of communal clashes, Muslims are nevertheless continually subjected to derogatory stereotypes.[24] A Hindu woman marrying into a Muslim family is regarded as the worst possible union (Donner 2002: 92). Hindus perceive their religion and culture as superior, liberal, and tolerant towards women. One common notion is that Hindu women are likely to be misfits in Muslim households; their expected adherence to *purdah* and the daily consumption of non-vegetarian food are cited as highly unsatisfactory (ibid.). This is the theme that Janaki was playing upon when she expressed hatred for her husband's religion, defaming it as anachronistic and oppressive.

Married Love: The Post-marriage Phase

While many courtships and love marriages meet with resistance and inconclusive endings, there are couples who nonetheless manage to elope and marry, while others negotiate 'arranged love marriages'. This final part looks at the married lives of couples and examines the ways in which women reflect on and evaluate their own love marriages. Rekha's narrative indicates what is expected of women once they marry.

---

[23] See Chowdhry (2007) for a rise in cases pertaining to state interference in inter-community marriages.

[24] On sexual stereotypes pertaining to Muslims, see Srivastava (2007).

Rekha and Sandeep: 'From courtship to marriage'

Rekha and Sandeep had an 'arranged love marriage'. When I visit Rekha, she mentions how she is happy to be with the person she chose to marry. But in her view, married life is different from courtship. Sandeep has lost his job and they are struggling to make ends meet. She confides: 'Prior to marriage, you know how independent I was. Sandeep will not allow me to work now.' In response to his uncompromising unreasonableness, she says: 'He thinks that another man may captivate me if I were to start working. He is scared of losing me as we had to put up a real fight to marry. When we have fights, he threatens to end the marriage and tells me to stop nagging him. In love marriages, your husband can walk out on you; there is no guarantee. Nobody is willing to take responsibility . . . My mother will just reprimand me by saying how she had cautioned me against the marriage. So I tell Sandeep that if he were to leave me, where would I go? Before marriage he really loved me . . . It's me who loves him now.'

Rekha is complaining that since their marriage she has been unable to negotiate democratic agreements with Sandeep, who has taken charge of their household decisions. One dimension of Sandeep's dominance is that he does not allow Rekha to take up waged work. He is highly insecure over the prospect that if she were to work, she would meet other men. As it appears, like other men, Sandeep, too, is unwilling to diverge from the existing ideals of the male breadwinner ideology. Rekha is nevertheless reluctant to accept the status quo and settle for a life of domesticity. Crucially, Rekha describes how her relationship with Sandeep has been radically transformed after their marriage; she marks a disparity between her courtship days and her married life. The declarations of romantic love that characterized the courtship period have been replaced by discourses of male dominance and female deference in the post-marriage phase (e.g. husbands wanting respect and obedience and not wanting to be nagged and harried). Newly married women are expected to 'normalize' their marriages by appropriating the standard or customary marital roles of arranged marriages, which are governed by hierarchical norms (see Chapter 2). Thus, the friction between Rekha and Sandeep is inextricably linked to the asymmetrical relationship that has emerged after marriage.[25] Rekha's emotive complaint 'Before marriage he really loved me, but after marriage it is me who loves him' is suggestive of a shift in power relations.

Women often mention that after marriage men come to occupy a position of greater strength. This female perspective finds resonance in other cultural settings as well. Writing on romance, parenthood, and gender, Daniel Jordan Smith (2001) illustrates the critical break between courtship and actual married life amongst young Igbos in Nigeria. Young Nigerian Igbos insist on choosing their marital partners, thereby adopting a modern model of romantic love. New ideas and expectations of romance and love are shaping Igbo constructions of marriage. Smith explores the progression from 'romantic lover' to 'marriage partner', and in doing so he makes a valuable contribution by portraying how marriage reinstates a more patriarchal order compared with the egalitarian nature of courtship. He writes:

> Courtship most often privileges the nature of a couple's personal relationship and is negotiated through interpersonal intimacy and expressions of love. In contrast, marriage tends to be constructed within the framework of continuing ties and obligations to extended family and community, privileging fertility and the social roles of mother and father. While modern courtship fosters a more egalitarian gender dynamic, modern marriage reinforces a more patriarchal hierarchy (2001: 132).

Smith cogently shows that after couples marry, their marital lives come under the intense scrutiny of kin groups who exert a powerful influence over the couple, while men have enduring obligations towards their families. In the post-marriage phase, women are primarily evaluated as wives and mothers. My data chimes with Smith's, as women stress how during courtship they are pursued

[25] In a remarkably informative chapter on arranged and love marriages, one that has gone unnoticed in recent analyses of Indian love marriages, Liddle and Joshi (1986: 209) draw attention to this aspect of post-marital gender asymmetry in love marriages. Their sample is drawn from professional middle class women based in Delhi.

and cajoled by men, thereby indicating the females' sense of power. In line with Smith's analysis, the post-marital phase reinforces a more patriarchal gender dynamic, as the process of normalizing a marriage and adhering to hierarchical gender roles requires women to transform more radically than men.

The Parental Role and Kinship Support

Women underscore the lack of emotional support from their natal kin as significantly adding to their weaker position in marriage. Women's assessments of their love marriages present a uniform discourse about their sense of vulnerability. While parental acceptance makes Rekha's marriage fall within the socially acceptable paradigm of an 'arranged love marriage', women like her still remain hesitant about bringing their marital grievances to their natal kin, or seeking their support in times of marital distress, as they feel that they cannot hold their parents accountable for their current situation. In an arranged marriage, a woman can just walk out of her conjugal home as the responsibility for her conflicts and actions is displaced onto her parents. In a love marriage, the option of walking out is restricted as the daughter is frequently told to adopt a conciliatory approach, since she has chosen her own husband and life partner. The 'arranged love marriage', then, does not grant women like Rekha the same rights of access to natal kin as it does to women who enter arranged marriages. This is a noteworthy point as it can be easily assumed that the 'arranged love marriage' is a sort of perfect modern-day 'compromise' between parents and couples. This is, after all, the situation portrayed in Hindi films, which present these marriages as having happy endings. As previously discussed, Fuller and Narasimhan (2008) and Marsden (2008) make the shared point that the distinction between arranged and love marriages is overstated. I argue that in Mohini Nagar the new accretion of 'arranged love marriage' indicates formal parental acceptance and bestows social respectability on the couple. There remains, however, a clear demarcation between a 'conventional arranged marriage' and an 'arranged love marriage' in the levels of support that women are able to exact from their natal families, which in turn has implications for a woman's future happiness and her ability to bargain in her conjugal home. To reiterate, the intensity with which married daughters in arranged marriages interact with their parents, as seen in their repeated and prolonged periods of refuge, is not evident in 'arranged love marriages' or in other types of love marriages. Even when women do approach their mothers for support, they do not rely extensively on their natal kin, who play only a marginal role in the resolution of the daughters' domestic problems. It is only in conventional arranged marriages that women can avail of repeated refuge, and not in love marriages that have been 'arranged'. Hence, rather than a continuum, there appears to be a disjuncture between how women actually experience arranged and love marriages, one that can be discerned only through a gendered lens that privileges the post-marriage phase.

On the subject of elopement and runaway marriage, the existing literature (Chowdhry 2007; Mody 2002) notes that couples who face violent reprisals in north India are often compelled to escape from their homes and to break away from their families. In Mohini Nagar, couples who initially break away from their families often reunite with them. This suggests that relationships do not always remain static. I heard stories of close relatives, and especially a mother's sister (*maasi*), who have played an instrumental role in reuniting parents with daughters. Moreover, whether women marry with or without parental approval, they form households in the same neighbourhoods as their parents, or close by. So Meeta whose conjugal home is in Raju Camp showed me her natal household in the resettlement colonies. She had grown up in a large resettlement plot, but moved to a *jhuggi* on account of her love marriage. I know of at least two other couples from Mohini Nagar who married against their parents' wishes but who continue to live in the same area. For women, the proximity of the post-marital residence to the natal home mitigates physical and emotional isolation, affording the possibility of fruitful interactions that might repair previously ruptured family ties. Sometimes women who have married their neighbours also reside with the husband's agnatic family in the same neighbourhood as their parents. Four women from Raju Camp who married their neighbours with parental approval (including Rekha and Sandeep and Kalpana and Rahul) live in lanes adjoining those where their parents reside, suggesting that the rule of *basti* exogamy is often contravened in the case of love marriages. The families of these couples have not been boycotted or maligned. Raju Camp residents nonetheless do pass remarks such as: 'These love marriages have ruined the neighbourhood's reputation and all the girls have a loose character.' Furthermore, even when daughters elope, causing considerable embarrassment to their families, the natal kin do not always sever ties with them. The birth of a child often brings about reconciliation. Natal families may initially contest the love marriage of a daughter or a son, but the daughter–parent dynamic can also alter in the post-marriage phase as a result of other crucial factors. Mutual dependence between mothers and daughters in a context of poverty prevents a daughter's complete expulsion or a long-term detachment from her natal family. Intergenerational reliance dissipates family tensions and leads to the resumption of affective ties.

For example, Neetu's parents, who are Balmikis, fiercely opposed her marriage to a boy from a higher caste. Neetu responded by eloping and became estranged from her parents for some years. She currently lives two lanes away from her parents in Raju Camp; the daughter–parents rift was temporary. Neetu's parents tell me bitterly that they were unhappy with the way in which their daughter had eloped. In response, Neetu says that she assists her aging parents both materially and emotionally, while her brother, whose marriage was arranged at substantial expense, separated from the parents and formed an independent nuclear household. Neetu's statement alerts us to the discrepancy between the public show of parental disapproval and the actual manifestation of intergenerational reliance. Even so, Neetu acknowledges that if she were to face marital estrangement she would not expect sympathy from her natal kin. At the other end of the spectrum, couples in love marriages may remain financially dependent on their parents, as in the case of a Balmiki boy and a Koli girl, neighbours in adjoining lanes, who eloped and got married. The couple's parents accepted their marriage when they learnt that the girl was pregnant. The couple lives in a *jhuggi* near the boy's parents in Raju Camp. The boy is known to borrow money from his parents since he does not have a stable job.

Consequently, women in Mohini Nagar who have love marriages continue to remain connected with their natal kin, albeit with diminished access to their support. At least amongst

Delhi's urban poor, we see a different dynamic working in love marriages compared to the reported episodes of social and family excommunication in north India. Love marriages in Mohini Nagar do not necessarily result in permanent ruptures, and I observed few examples of daughters having to completely cut ties with their natal kin. However, as stated earlier, women cannot expect the same levels of care and support that they would usually receive in the case of arranged marriages. I have highlighted how women do not see themselves as having the right to parental refuge after choosing their partners independently. Mala, a woman in her forties, reflecting on her own intra-caste love marriage, elucidates this point:

> When you marry on your own, how can you walk out on the person? In an arranged marriage, your parents are answerable. Not in the type of marriage we had. You put up with things. In love marriages, women are most at risk. Society will forgive a man if he leaves his wife. After all, he will just marry again. What will happen to the woman?

Conjugal Stability in Love Marriages

The next case study on Aarti and Rohit illuminates how, after a period of intense courtship, married men may experience shifts in emotions and feelings. Nonetheless while in the Indian imagination, love marriages are allied with conjugal instability and particularly divorce, amongst Mohini Nagar's urban poor, especially the women, we see quite the opposite.

Aarti and Rohit: 'Desertions in love marriages'

Aarti and Rohit had an elopement love marriage. Aarti is now visiting the mahila panchayat office because Rohit has deserted her. She recalls that after they married, Rohit treated her well for the first two months. By the third month, he grew irritable and would say: 'Let me go back to Bihar to meet my family.' He never offered to take her along. Then he started coming home from work later than usual, and if she questioned him about his whereabouts, he would retort that she had no right to ask. As the arguments escalated, he began to beat her and threaten to leave her. She says: 'Before marriage, I would get angry with him. Since our marriage, he is the one who has started hitting me.' One day, Rohit's friend, Ajay, arrived from Bihar. Aarti was told that Ajay needed to be shown around Delhi. After that day, she did not hear from him again. Four months into their marriage, Rohit left, taking with him their marriage certificate and photos of their temple wedding ceremony. Aarti, who is in a fragile state, says: 'There were rumours that he had another wife in Bihar. He denied it. I have been betrayed.' According to Aarti, there is no point in asking her father for help as he had warned her not to marry Rohit. Whether Rohit's desertion will prove temporary or not remains inconclusive, as Aarti did not revisit the mahila panchayat office after confessing her story.

Rohit's desertion shows how male commitment may be lacking in some love marriages. Aarti noted that her husband no longer found her attractive and accused her of being 'too sharp-tongued'. Women such as Aarti single-handedly shoulder the consequences of desertion, marital instability, and failed marriage. Such occurrences have only deepened the ideological divide between love marriages and arranged marriages, along with the parental security afforded by the latter, the former being seen as a highly risky venture for women. Two sisters who had love marriages with their neighbours in Raju Camp told me how, over the years, their husbands had become heavy drinkers. As a result, the women who are still with their husbands are now the family providers. In a milieu marked by poverty, couples who have married for love may face numerous hardships once they settle down. Men facing the pressure to provide for their families may no longer feel consumed by the intense passion that motivated their love marriage. In situations of desertion, stressful marital relations, domestic violence, and volatile male emotions, women are reprimanded by neighbours, family members, and mahila panchayats and are urged to compromise or 'face the consequences', as they have 'chosen their own partners'. It is a matter of conjecture whether women endure very high levels of violence in love marriages. They are certainly unable to secure sympathy from others, who keep reminding them that they were wrong in the first place to have had a love marriage. In the love marriages that I studied, women rarely dissolved their marriages when experiencing major marital conflict. Mala, who I introduced earlier as having an intra-caste love marriage, told me that throughout her married life she has made attempts at 'winning over her husband's entire family'. Her powerful statement indicates that women need to actively cooperate with and appease their parents-in-law and to make extra efforts to make their marriages work. Women like Mala attest how they were never welcomed as 'real' daughters-in-law. Notwithstanding local beliefs about the short-lived nature of love marriages, by and large, it is love marriages that at present seem to generate greater conjugal stability than arranged marriages. Local residents do not seem aware that love marriages result in fewer break-ups, and neither would they wish to acknowledge this fact. Similarly, residents have not recognized the notably high numbers of cases of marital distress and break-ups in arranged marriages. Herein the problem also lies in the fact that given the widespread prejudice against love marriages, there are few alternative discourses about the merits of self-chosen marriages. Many women in this sample 'who have gone against the grain' seem themselves to underwrite the risks, sacrifices, and difficulties associated with love marriages, even though some simultaneously stress the strong emotional bonds manifested in such marriages.

As a counter example, consider the concluding narrative in which Amrita positively affirms her love marriage.

Amrita: 'A love marriage is an unbreakable bond'

Amrita talks about her love marriage, which was 'arranged'. She is the only woman in my sample who has passed her Class 12 (education up to age 17). Amrita gives private tuitions to children at her house. Her husband will not allow her to work outside the neighbourhod. Whenever we meet, there is mostly praise for her husband: 'In love marriages, men treat women more sensitively. They know the risks we have taken in marrying against our families. In arranged marriages, women are made to feel like slaves. Men keep telling them how grateful they should be.' Amrita tells me that a love marriage is an unbreakable bond between two human beings. Another time when I meet her, she admonishes me: 'Why are you only wearing bangles and a nose ring? What about your *bindi* (a red dot on the forehead to signify a married women's status) and toe rings?' She tells me that I should not roam around Mohini

Nagar without adorning myself with the full range of marriage symbols. I am also given a long exhortation on how I must keep a fast for my husband on the festival of *Karva Chauth.*

Amrita, the most educated woman in my sample, is forthright when discussing the merits of a love marriage. She argues that a love marriage is a better and more satisfying form of marriage based as it is on reciprocity, friendship, and shared responsibility. Husbands are equally accountable for making the marriage work and for supporting their wives, unlike arranged marriages 'where women are made to feel subordinate'. Amrita claims that men in love marriages are more sensitive and cognizant about the risks that their wives have taken in marrying them. She states that there are few love marriages in Delhi, but that these are more successful than arranged marriages. Apart from stating her liberal views openly, Amrita also discusses with great interest the ornaments that women should wear and the rituals that they should keep for their husband's well-being. Amrita wants to convey to me that she is a good traditional wife, as she is keen to counter the scathing criticism levelled against 'loose' women who have had love marriages. It goes without saying that women who are seen to have wilfully asserted their independence by violating the convention of arranged marriage are vilified in their immediate surroundings as sexually promiscuous (Mody 2002). Those who do not endorse conventional gender roles, lower-class norms of domesticity, and appropriate codes of conduct are subject to much gossip. Amrita says that her neighbours gossip 'about that woman [she] who had a love marriage'. Disparaging remarks have been made in her *gali* about her sleeping with boys before marriage, and she describes how people treat her with less respect. As Mody (2002: 256) rightfully stresses, love marriage couples have to adjust to the normative social order: 'Most couples try as far as possible to conceal the fact of their marriage through "adjustments" in names, personal dress and deportment, so that an image of social coherence is presented to the neighbourhood and the world.'

Dominant Discourses and the Right to Love

A close analysis reveals that women in love marriages do not transfer their marital grievances onto their parents. Consequently, they endure greater vulnerability over the life course, feeling the need to adjust to the marital status quo. The dominant discourse in Delhi's low-income neighbourhoods is that women should accept responsibility for their violent and unhappy love marriages because they have chosen their partners. Women's personal disappointments remain trivialized, and their rights in the natal home are considered insignificant. Concomitantly, love marriages produce conjugal stability. Another overt feature of love marriages is a woman's particularly weak positioning. After marriage, husbands resist a companionate form of marriage, as couples are expected to replicate mainstream gender roles. The post-marital phase, therefore, enhances a more patriarchal gender dynamic (Smith 2001). It is clear that women experience love unions in distinct and more difficult ways than those women who enter conventional arranged marriages.

Moreover, the majority of ordinary residents do not consider the freedom to choose marital partners a legitimate right or aspiration. The primary marriage based on love should be discouraged since it challenges endogamous norms and parental matchmaking practices that form the legitimate framework for marriage. A number of case studies in this chapter have established how love marriages based on a trajectory of courtship have yet to gain approval or acceptance amongst the urban lower classes in Delhi. A recurring feature in these case studies is how the arranged marriage remains a powerful ideal, being the preferred way of marrying and ensuring a family's prestige, status and reputation, whether through an alliance with a village-based bride or the conversion of a love match into an 'arranged love marriage'. I have illustrated the rigid endogamy practiced by the Balmikis. For Balmikis and Muslims, initiating love marriages across caste and communities is extremely difficult. Young people from these communities, therefore, engage in negotiation with, and even risk alienation from parents at the critical juncture between courtship and marriage. Many experience heartbreak when their families disrupt their love marriages. Nonetheless it is obvious that couples are subverting parental matchmaking and defying the pressures of intra-caste and intra-community marriages. In comparison with those who opt for a conventional arranged marriage, there are others on the other side of the spectrum who assert their preferences for marrying partners with whom they share feelings of emotional intimacy. Across India, feminist groups, human rights organizations, students and the media have begun to play a more palpable role in creating greater awareness on the right to love. The Pink *Chaddi* (panty) Campaign directed at the extreme Hindu right (a counterattack aimed at protecting personal liberties), the Right to Love Campaign (organized by the youth in Bangalore), and a new law that decriminalizes consensual homosexual acts are all challenging normative values and practices of compulsory arranged marriages. The growing wave of social and legal awareness will certainly have an impact on those living on the margins of modernity, in neighbourhoods that are marked by extreme heterogeneity.

4

Secondary Unions and Other Conjugal Arrangements

> 'A male partner in a secondary union may turn out to be worse than a *bihata* (husband from the primary arranged marriage). Then what will happen to a woman? A *bihata* is after all a *bihata*.'
>
> Cautionary evaluation of secondary unions

Mapping the Terrain of Post-marital Consensuality

Alongside love marriages in Mohini Nagar, there are other conspicuous and prominent conjugal unions that are consensual by nature. In this chapter, I extend my analysis beyond arranged and love marriages to examine other significant conjugal arrangements that merit separate and detailed attention. The ethnographic subject of exploration is the secondary union, a term that will be employed here to cover unions that may be the outcomes of marital breakdown, elopement, separation, or divorce. For urban north India, little research has been carried out that addresses the meaning of consensuality and the nature of consensual unions; the latter is typically consigned to the category 'frequent remarriage', which is accepted amongst the lower classes. This chapter will delineate how post-marital consensuality is a deeply complex terrain, especially as it is characterized by many desires, relationships, and constraints over the life course.

The secondary union offers an interesting framework for evaluating gender equality. Many anthropologists (Dumont 1964; Jankowiak 1993; Parry 2001) link secondary unions and remarriages with greater autonomy and the legitimate choice of a partner. The very inception of secondary unions lies in women's ability to initiate marital break-up, divorce, and serial monogamy. In my opinion, feminist anthropology can shed an altogether different light on the egalitarian potential of secondary unions and on their dynamics. A way forward is by coalescing the social, legal, material, emotional, sexual, and reproductive dimensions of these unions. This approach, combined with an analysis of extensive life stories, will enable us to understand the many constraining features of secondary unions in the lives of poor urban women.

For rich anthropological insights into secondary unions, I draw upon my data set consisting of varied pairings, as those between Balmiki women and upper caste men, between widows and married men, between married women and unmarried men, and intra-caste liaisons. The couples in my sample are in the age group of 18–60 years. There are no secondary unions where either partner had previously been in a love marriage. Secondary unions are primarily linked to the breakdown of arranged marriages. Hence, I use the terms 'primary marriage' and 'arranged marriage' interchangeably, as the first marriage of a man or a woman is likely to have been arranged.

Secondary Unions in a Metropolis

In the anthropology of India, remarriages and subsequent unions are often classified under the rubric 'secondary marriage'. Dumont (1964), in his classic studies of the marriage systems of north and south India, makes the distinction between primary and secondary marriages. In his authoritative paper 'Marriage in India: The Present State of the Question', he notes:

> A woman must be married, and can be married in the strict sense and with full ritual only once. This is marriage proper, which I shall call "proper marriage". In many groups, the woman once married may afterwards, loosely speaking,

"remarry", i.e. she can, following the death of her husband, or divorce, enter a conjugal union which although distinguished from the first in the language and considered as inferior is perfectly legitimate. I shall call this union "secondary marriage". Let us note immediately, regarding the groups where the woman may not remarry, that this case does not obliterate the distinction: here the woman has only the primary marriage, and the secondary marriage is absent (1964: 82).

Dumont's distinction between the primary marriage and the secondary marriage is germane here, for residents of Mohini Nagar draw upon aspects of this divide in both discourse and practice. In Chapter 2, I have demonstrated how the primary marriage remains a 'compulsion' for most people in Mohini Nagar. The latter should ideally be a caste-endogamous arranged marriage. Secondary unions have a different *raison d'être;* they are not governed by endogamous rules and thus caste identity does not impede the formation of relationships (Parry 2001).[1] For this reason, in Mohini Nagar diverse combinations of inter-caste secondary unions are widely tolerated. Moreover, a central aspect of secondary unions has been described in the anthropological literature. Implicit in Dumont's (1964: 82) definition of secondary marriage is the potent element of personal choice in post-marital deportment. Other anthropologists (Jankowiak 1993; Parry 2001) describe similar ethnographic instances whereby secondary unions and post-marital conduct permit greater sexual and emotional freedom. Parry (2001: 798) discusses the liberatory nature of *shaadi* in Chhattisgarh. Once a woman has taken the mandatory seven rounds of the fire (*sat phere*), she is free to make a 'new' man. The secondary union is, then, a more acceptable form of 'love marriage', as it permits consensuality and legitimate space for the exploration of romance, love, and desire. It allows men and women to engage in relationships beyond parental mate selection. While those who prefer love marriages need to negotiate persistently with their parents and the community, the secondary union, which is

---

[1] See Berreman's (1963) study.

also consonant with personal choice (i.e. post-marriage), is more permissible. Parry (2001; 2004) points towards a sharp decline in secondary unions that are being viewed as anachronistic in Chhattisgarh. Divorce and remarriage are especially less visible amongst the upwardly mobile younger generation and among those who have secure employment in the organized sector, for whom the meaning of marriage is being transmuted. These shifts in marriage ideals relate to organized-sector employment that is associated with prestige, thereby enhancing class and status distinctions. Similarly, Kriti Kapila's study of Gaddi kinship (2004) exemplifies how a 'modern marriage' no longer involves multiple unions. Gaddi kinship and marriage norms and practices are changing on account of a new political economy. Consequently, for women the incidence of serial monogamy has declined: sexuality and romantic love can only feature together in the primary marriage. In Mohini Nagar, we see a contrasting phenomenon whereby across generations arranged marriages, secondary unions, and love marriages coexist. In residential *galis*, one notices the interlacing of these conjugal practices, especially as women terminate their arranged marriages to enter into new unions. The Mohini Nagar neighbourhood in a modern metropolis exhibits a wide range of secondary arrangements that have not been radically curtailed by postcolonial legislation or codes of kinship morality. Informal unions also prevail amongst the upwardly mobile, those who have prestigious jobs in the private sector, and those employed in the lower rungs of government departments. For the latter, the effect of greater wealth, status, and class mobility does not enhance conjugal stability.

Role of Secondary Unions

Before the reader gets the impression that all secondary unions are characterized by romantic inclinations, a qualification must be made. In Mohini Nagar at least, secondary unions also serve as critical exit options for women who have availed their share of parental refuge, or whose parents are no longer alive, or for widows and deserted or abandoned women, or even for those seeking to escape a violent or unsatisfactory marriage. In short, secondary unions have a purposeful role in a setting where it is considered immoral for women to reside on their own. As the choice of living independently is limited, women are compelled to seek new relationships (cf. Kakar 1989). Secondary unions are thus tied with the exercise of personal choice as well as with the need to deal with desperate socio-economic conditions.[2] In negotiations over the formation of secondary unions, women usually bargain for a share of the partner's resettlement plot, inclusion in a Life Insurance Policy (LIC, pension scheme), or insist that they should be provided for. Bargaining and negotiation over money, residence, sexuality, and labour are crucial components of the secondary union contract. Women may move on to other relationships depending on the financial security on offer, and this exemplifies that while they have the freedom to terminate old relationships and enter new ones, their dependence on male support is critical and continues to influence their choices in life.

Consensuality and Commitment: Customary Processes

'If you come out in the open with your partner, it is unnecessary to involve courts, parents, NGOs, or temples.'
—Radha, articulating the essence of consensuality

I have so far alluded how secondary unions are often self-initiated without parental involvement.[3] I now proceed to describe at length the ways in which married women and widows initiate divorce and separation, how and under what circumstances they consolidate new relationships, and the contexts in which they meet male partners. I discuss here how the formation of secondary

[2] Elsewhere in India, secondary unions may have a different purpose. Jeffery and Jeffery (1996: 231) describe how they came across a handful of women who were 'bought brides'. These women are normally widows and divorced women who have been married to Bijnor men under anomalous circumstances. These brides have been sold either by relatives or by parents-in-law, and are not entirely welcome in Bijnor.

[3] The practice of 'secondary arranged marriage', a form of marriage initiated by parents, also exists in Mohini Nagar. Here parents and kin formally arrange an alliance for their daughters or sons for the second time which like the primary marriage is also a social and public affair. I shall not dwell on the secondary arranged marriage as my focus is on consensual unions that augment without family and kin involvement.

unions must go through a customary process of acquiring social legitimacy and official recognition, with commitment and trust the overriding concerns underpinning these relationships. Features of oral commitment and their gendered ramifications have hitherto been the subject of limited anthropological inquiry. The life stories of Radha and her sisters establish that skilful negotiation and bargaining over commitment are necessary accompaniments to the formation of consensual unions.

In the following extended life story of Radha, her Balmiki sisters, and their upper-caste partners, notions of commitment are explored through the popular local phrase 'we came out in the open' ('*hum khule mein aa gaye*'). The reader should note that this phrase is pivotal in comprehending the nature of consensuality.

The Love Stories of Radha and Her Sisters

Radha Telling her Story

My bold field assistant Radha, is narrating her *lambi* aur *chauri kahani* (long and complicated love story).

Radha and her sisters deploy the term 'story' (*kahani*) to indicate transformative events, transgressions, hardships, anomalies, and achievements in their lives. Their invocation of 'story' does not necessarily refer to past events, but also to their current life trajectories. Unlike women's hesitant revelations of their love marriages, secondary-union romances do not pose a conundrum.

So Radha, my field assistant who is married to Ramesh, is keen that the world should hear her long story (*'lambi aur chauri kahani'*). Radha has a large group of Balmiki friends, women who are in their forties, with whom I interacted intensively. Her three closest friends—whose stories I narrate here—consider each other 'sisters' (*behen*). Amongst these sisters, Radha is by far the poorest. Her other sisters have permanent municipal jobs. Radha has been made the group's elder sister because of her loyalty and reliability when others are in need of support. In the narrative that unfolds, parts of Radha's story are about her current problems with her husband Ramesh, which are connected with a relationship she had with a man called Subhash. The narrative shuttles between the present (Radha's relationship with Ramesh) and the past (Radha's earlier relationship with Subhash).

Since the early days of my fieldwork, Radha has expressed animosity against Ramesh while talking fondly but vaguely about a man called Subhash. Radha points out that Ramesh does not give her *kharcha-pani*. Eight years ago, in this connection she filed a complaint against him in the mahila panchayat. Despite their ongoing conflicts over *kharcha-pani*, Radha continues to live with Ramesh, albeit without having sexual relations with him. Radha says that since the age of fifteen, when her marriage was arranged with Ramesh, they have never got along (*'hamari kabhi banti nahi thi'*). She explains that her marriage is the outcome of a love affair between her father and her mother-in-law, for which she has had to 'pay the price'. Radha recalls that several years ago her father used to play drums and sing songs at weddings. Her father saw a woman, Bala at a festival in Haryana. During the ribald dancing, their bodies touched. Radha's father became aware that Bala was unhappy as her husband, Radha's father-in-law, was prone to drinking and would periodically gamble away his money. Unable to pay his gambling debts, he would offer his wife to other men. As Radha's father fell in love with Bala they arranged the marriage of their children, Radha and Ramesh, to keep their own affair going.

Radha reflects how she has been torn between her husband, Ramesh, and Subhash. She describes how she got to know Subhash: 'He was a neighbour from my caste who lived in an adjoining *gali*. His younger sister would spend time with me. I used to treat her as my daughter. When he would come to collect his sister, we would end up discussing our *sukh* (happiness) and *dukh* (sorrow). I gave him a lot of support because his wife had recently died, leaving him with no children. Then Ramesh began alleging an affair between us. He made several public allegations that we were having an affair. Ramesh deliberately disgraced Subhash and me, and so 'we came out in the open (*hum khule mein aa gaye*)'. After being discredited publicly, Radha says boldly that she and Subhash began living together in a nearby neighbourhood: 'When we came out in the open, we roamed around together everywhere and did everything that husbands and wives do.'

More information about Subhash emerges as Radha and Ramesh's fights over *kharcha-pani* intensify. Ramesh points out that no conflict is ever one-sided. Asking him about the 'Subhash incident' and eliciting pertinent information is a difficult task. He offers few details about Subhash: 'He was never a friend of mine. He was merely living in Raju Camp and was a neighbour, that too a distant neighbour.' I am told without further elaboration that before Radha's association with Subhash, he was regularly handing his salary to her. Ramesh also discloses that in a 'man-to-man chat' Subhash had admitted that he had started an affair with Radha only because she was sterilized[4] and could not get pregnant. After hearing this startling revelation, I ask Radha how long her relationship with Subhash had lasted.

Radha states that a few months after she and Subhash had 'come out in the open', he betrayed her: 'While we were living together, I became ill with tuberculosis and he looked after me well. Then his parents arrived from their village. They made him drink *sattu* [an alcoholic drink made of barley]. Suddenly, he started acting strangely towards me. One day, I wanted to meet a friend of mine who lived in the resettlement colonies. Subhash and I agreed to meet later at a nearby junction. While I was with my friend, the phone rang and Subhash told me that I should return to my husband. I could not believe it. I thought he was committed to me. I remember that on that day I hurried to catch an auto-rickshaw so I could go and find him. When I reached our home, there was a lock on the door. He

---

[4] Most women in the neighbourhood undergo sterilization to end childbirth, especially after having sons. Sterilization and abortion remain the most common methods of avoiding or terminating pregnancies.

had betrayed me. In my dishonoured state, I thought that at least he would stand by me.' After Subhash ended their relationship, he moved in with a woman who had three children and was expecting a fourth. Radha is unsure whether the fourth child is Subhash's, but he had kept this woman with the consent of his family as they, too, wanted him to have children. After Subhash's betrayal, Radha returned to Ramesh and their three teenage sons in Raju Camp. Her parents are dead, and she does not want to live as a single woman.

In 2007, Radha found a new partner, who she 'loves dearly'. Her husband has accepted the new relationship. Radha now shuttles between Raju Camp, where her children live, and the residence of her new partner.

'To come out in the open': The Power of Public Commitment

In Radha's story about Subhash, the phrase 'to come out in the open' struck me as being ambiguous. It suggests a clear division between the 'before' (daily neighbourly encounters based on friendship) and 'after' (an open relationship without denial) in a pattern of events. There is a series of allegations about an illicit affair here, whereby the disgraced couple is 'compelled' to start a new relationship. There is ambiguity as to whether the couple was having an illicit affair. On deeper probing, however, Radha clarifies that her interaction with Subhash began as neighbourly conviviality but grew into something emotionally deeper. Thus, the use of the phrase 'we came out in the open' may suggest that as a couple they could no longer conceal their affair, and as they found themselves in an ambiguous situation, it became necessary to explicate the nature of their close association. More so, they had reached a stage at which they wanted to make their relationship public.

The ambiguous phrase 'we came out in the open' is also employed in the following story about Radha's younger sister. Omvati, who, like Radha, narrates a story about her past (*purani baat*) that resonates with Radha's own life story. Omvati lived in the resettlement colonies with her husband and their son. In a nearby *gali* lived an unmarried man named Prem Singh, who belonged to a much higher caste but who was a friend of her husband's. Prem Singh had assisted Omvati's husband when he was unemployed, and I am told that such gestures are associated with true friendship irrespective of caste differences. Omvati's husband died suddenly due to his heavy drinking. Following the death of her husband, Omvati's parents-in-law began insinuating that she had been having an affair with Prem Singh all along (*'kunware admi ke sat lagavi hai'*). While her parents-in-law were making these furious allegations about an illicit affair, she and Prem Singh 'came out in the open' (*'hum khule mein aa gaye'*).

Radha and Her Two 'Younger' Sisters
A picture of camaraderie, friendship and female solidarity.

I am keen to hear Prem Singh's version of this old story. After all, he was unmarried when he met Omvati. Prem Singh remembers that in the days when he first knew Omvati, she was of unusual beauty. Omvati and Prem Singh recollect that after they 'came out in the open', no one ever taunted them again. Prem Singh had taken Omvati to his village, and although she belongs to the lowest caste (emphasis on this by Prem Singh) and was a widow at that time, his relatives welcomed her. Prem Singh has been committed to Omvati ever since. They tell me that their story is famous in Raju Camp as one of true love, for Prem Singh resisted all attempts at having an arranged marriage. They have been cohabiting for twenty-one years and have two children together. They have had neither a legal court marriage nor a symbolic wedding involving the exchange of garlands, both affirming that these gestures are not necessary.

Radha and Omvati introduce me to Basanti, the third sister in their group. Listening to Basanti's account of her secondary partner, I notice that the phrase 'to come out in the open' is no longer ambiguous. Basanti is a widow with three children, and is involved with Suraj, a man of the Khatik (meat cutter) caste. She reveals many facts about her emotionally absorbing but violent relationship with Suraj, but bitterly points out that he has not 'come out in the open' with her. I notice that Basanti employs this phrase without referral to being disgraced or compelled to enter a relationship. Basanti anxiously explains that as a widow she wants enduring companionship but Suraj does not acknowledge their relationship in public—'he does not want to come out in the open with me'—and hence she is apprehensive about his level of commitment. Even though Suraj has left his wife, he will still not introduce Basanti to his immediate kin. Neither does he assure her of his lifelong support nor does he treat her children like his own. Some years ago, after her husband died, she acquired his municipal job. Every month, she hands her municipal salary to Suraj. When I query why she does this, she says that Suraj is better at managing her household finances. Basanti confesses that her children have constant arguments with her, as they feel that Suraj is taking advantage of her generous salary and pension scheme. Equally, they disapprove of Suraj's violent behaviour.

During my first ever encounter with Suraj, he notifies me that he is not a 'Bhangi' or 'Jamadar' (the derogatory terms for Balmikis) like Basanti, but belongs to the superior Khatik caste. At our second meeting, this time at Basanti's house, a young Balmiki neighbour walks in. Suraj directly points to Basanti and the boy and laughingly says: 'These people are 'Bhangis.' They are from the lowest (*neech*) caste.' When the boy protests, saying: 'We are Balmikis, not "Bhangis" ', Suraj replies: 'Why do you people try to hide your caste identity?' Basanti privately tells me that this is not the first time that Suraj has humiliated her and says that she has challenged him over claims that his caste is superior to hers. She says that Suraj is ashamed to introduce her to his relatives because of her low caste status, while Prem Singh, who is of a much higher caste than Omvati, has never made her feel inferior. Her neighbours, who belong to her *biradari*, have also raised objections to Suraj's conduct. They pass comments such as: 'Are we [Balmiki men] not good enough for you? Are we all dead for you?' Basanti asserts that she is harassed by her *biradari*. My conversations with Suraj revolve around the deep apprehensions that Basanti has raised about his future commitment. Suraj insists that even though he does not introduce Basanti to his relatives, in actuality he does consider her his lifelong partner.

Basanti compares her plight to that of the group's fourth sister, Geeta, whose husband accidentally died by falling from a wall. After her husband died, Geeta wanted support and companionship. She is now involved with a man from a higher caste. Geeta and her partner have 'come out in the open', even though her secondary partner has a wife in his village from whom he does not want to separate. Irrespective of these restrictions (i.e. the implicit practice of polygyny),[5] Geeta's secondary partner has decided not to conceal their relationship. Geeta receives constant reassurance from her partner about his lifelong support. After having listened to Geeta's positive portrayal of her secondary partner, Basanti confesses that her own relationship with Suraj is one of convenience for him. Geeta urges Basanti to make sure that Suraj publicly acknowledges the relationship: 'If you "come out in the open", no one can trouble you. People will no longer be justified in raising objections and the matter can be put to rest.'

From these interrelated stories it is possible to frame the meaning of consensuality by engaging with the phrase 'coming out in the open'. In Radha's narrative of Subhash, the phrase has ambiguous undertones, but is associated with making a relationship public. In the stories concerning her sisters, the phrase is unequivocal. For example, Basanti admits that she and Suraj are deeply involved, but he has not formalized their relationship by making their union public and official. Indeed, 'coming out in the open' is a central customary act that formalizes secondary unions. Officially endorsing a relationship signifies a declaration of commitment, and is linked with social acceptance and approval. This is why couples attest that once they 'come out in the open', local interest in the nature of their relationship dissipates. Radha explicates the overwhelming power

---

[5] The term polygyny connotes that a man is married to two women (Uberoi 1993: 470). Here I am using polygyny to imply that a man is keeping both his first wife and a secondary partner.

of commitment: 'If you come out in the open, it is unnecessary to involve courts, parents, temples, and NGOs.' I read her statement as 'If you formalize a relationship publicly, it is consonant with consensuality'. Formalizing a relationship demonstrates that the concerned individuals are a couple. Consensuality is symbolically affirmed by a man through gestures such as displaying affection for his partner, introducing her to his wider kin, and taking on the social role of a father for any children involved. These multiple gestures indicate spousal 'relatedness' (Carsten 2000) and are metonyms for commitment even when the union involves polygyny (e.g. Geeta and her partner). In general, men are keen to commit mutually, as many have been left temporarily by their wives. We are aware of the high rates of marital break-ups in arranged marriages and of women's routine recourse to refuge. Men are emotional about being abandoned, and stress their need for household assistance and companionship. So at the outset, they, too, attempt to nurture and secure their relationships. For women, the validation of male commitment is highly critical, as many secondary unions are self-initiated. Secondary liaisons originate at the workplace, between neighbours, through introductions by friends, or when a woman falls in love with her husband's friend (*dost*). A couple may perform certain 'secondary union rituals'. Exchanging garlands in a temple is one such ritual, while another is to have a get together ('reception') in their *gali* to introduce a female partner to the neighbours. I did not find couples to be enacting the *sat phere* ritual (cf. primary marriage) or a version of this ritual, or more elaborate ceremonies than the ones that have been outlined. In the post-commitment phase, couples use multiple and overlapping expressions to address their secondary partners. A male partner is marked as a *ghar wala* (head of the household), *pati* (husband), or *mera admi* (my man); a female partner, a *biwi* or *patni* (wife), or *meri aurat* (my woman). Secondary unions are also called *shaadi*, chronologically demarcated as *pahli shaadi* (first marriage), *doosri shaadi* (second marriage), or *teesri shaadi* (third marriage). Though couples perform secondary-union rituals such as the garland exchange with gusto, Radha's story illuminates the prevalence of betrayal (*dhoka*) and male desertions. Accordingly, irrespective of the promise to remain together, many secondary relationships, like arranged marriages, are also fragile, or, as Parry (2004) notes, the former is a consequence of the latter being unstable. While women equally instigate break-ups, the betrayal by a male partner places them in a position of greater vulnerability. I will discuss the factors that enhance or impede the durability of commitment in secondary relationships later in this chapter. Before couples form secondary unions, they seldom obtain legal divorces. A formal process of legal divorce rarely accompanies the formation of new relationships; the symbolic acts of eloping, 'walking out' with personal items and jewellery, or moving in with another man are all strong indications that a woman wants to end her marriage. Despite the Hindu Marriage Act of 1955, which enforces the regulation of monogamy and the compulsory registration of marriage and divorce, the above customary modes of divorce and separation remain widely accepted amongst Delhi's urban poor. As pointed out by Kapila (2004: 380): 'It is quite possible in certain circumstances for state legal processes and legal reform to remain relatively independent of local practices and understandings.'[6] In instances where a husband initiates a new union, the wife can, if she is financially resourceful, file a complaint of bigamy. This complaint also connotes male desertion and indicates that the wife is being denied a maintenance allowance. In Mohini Nagar, awareness of bigamy laws is growing. The crime of bigamy is extremely difficult to prove in a court of law, as women are required to produce evidence, such as photographs, to prove that their husbands have remarried. My data concur with the findings of Parry (2001: 808), who remarks that in Chhattisgarh, while people routinely make the rounds of the courts and the police stations, legalized divorce remains rare (cf. Kapila 2004).

Serial Monogamy: The Search for Love

Distinguishable patterns of serial monogamy are apparent from Radha's marital history. Explicating her account of serial monogamy, Radha claims that Subhash was the first man with whom she had ever fallen in love. Radha candidly eschews expressions of fidelity. She asserts that the sexual attraction for her husband was wholly missing and that her heart (*man pasand*) had never been in her

---

[6] See also Livia Holdven's (2008: 159) important work on Hindu divorce in Madhya Pradesh and how women primarily make use of customary divorce.

arranged marriage. Subhash, on the other hand, was a *tagra ashik* (passionate lover). Clearly, Radha like other women is critical of her arranged marriage. She argues that her arranged marriage was a mismatch, contracted at an early age, as a matter of convenience. Kakar (1989: 83) argues that Delhi slum women cling to the notion of the indissolubility of the *jodi* (the pair, or the marital bond): 'I believe that there is a cultural image which comes through sharply in the woman's yearning for the couple'. In Kakar's view, the strength or permanence of the *jodi* is an overarching marriage ideal. Women of the lower classes idealize and covet the permanence of the pair throughout their life. Kakar also notes that in actuality female slum dwellers are compelled to form attachments with other men: 'Unlike the spouse of most women in the higher classes, the slum husband is apt to be shiftless. For all practical purposes, the lower-class woman frequently finds herself abandoned and in charge of the family. The imperatives of physical protection, economic support, and the quieter need for male companionship lead her to establish more or less permanent liaisons with other men' (Kakar 1989: 67). I have presented a modified version of Kakar's insight, showing how abject poverty does lead to the creation of secondary unions. However, with respect to the *jodi*, the several instances of women like Radha, who are attracted to other men and who are ready to sever the primary *jodi*, contradicts Kakar's argument. Women take the romantic initiative to enter into new relationships, and are often strategic, opportunistic, and practical in doing so. In their quest for more emotionally fulfilling relationships, they often develop multiple attachments and do not talk of companionship in a unitary voice. Their search for love leads them again and again to renegotiate male commitment. In Mohini Nagar, the construct of the *jodi* is absent, but, as I shall argue, the symbolism of the primary arranged marriage is not entirely so. It appears that women are quite willing to leave their primary husbands, even though they are aware that secondary relationships can be transient. Concomitantly, given the evanescent nature of many secondary unions, there are notable instances whereby women reconcile and reunite with their primary husbands.[7] Women may also periodically shuttle between

---

[7] For a comparative perspective on marital instability initiated by women, see Hala Hameed's (2003) work on the Maldives. Out of a sample of 62 women,

primary and secondary spouses, indicating the ebb and flow of complex and emotionally shifting trajectories over the life course.

Gender and Caste Hierarchies

In capturing Basanti's emotional trajectory, I witnessed the distinctive trajectories of Balmiki women, who, unlike other Scheduled Caste women, face different constraints in their secondary unions. Basanti's relationship with Suraj, is strained as he is reluctant to publicly acknowledge their alliance. She is not assured of his lifelong loyalty. Basanti alleges that Suraj is ashamed to formalize their union because she is a Balmiki. She concedes that were she from a higher Scheduled Caste, Suraj would not dare to beat her incessantly or make her feel inferior. Basanti's statement symbolizes her vulnerability, which is linked to her Balmiki status. Suraj also arrogantly makes scathing remarks about the Balmikis in their presence, and his conduct has aggravated the tension between the couple. Basanti professes that if Suraj were respectful to her children and her fellow caste members, that itself would signal his long-term commitment and would dissipate existing tensions in her *gali*. Basanti's situation shows that it is particularly urgent and imperative for Balmiki women to secure substantive spousal commitment when initiating relationships with higher-caste men. Interestingly, Basanti's Balmiki neighbours are also critically questioning her association with a man from 'another caste'. In Chapter 3, I described how intra-caste loyalties are distinctive characteristics of the Balmiki caste. Balmikis are defensive about the way they are perceived and treated by others. Basanti's account highlights, at various levels, the imbrications of gender and caste hierarchies, as Balmiki women's loyalties towards their own caste are also under surveillance. Balmiki men resent liaisons between 'their women' and men from other castes. If Basanti were in an intra-caste secondary union, her relationship would not be perceived as transgressive. Amongst the Balmikis, endogamy

---

22 women who had separated from their husbands later ended up remarrying them. According to Hameed, divorce in the Maldives is more like an extended argument, as several women who break up their marriages ultimately return to their former husbands.

extends somewhat to the secondary union, which is otherwise free of endogamous considerations.

Widows as Providers

Radha's sisters—Basanti, Geeta, and Omvati—fall under the widow category. Low caste widows are permitted to remarry and form secondary unions. Some widows explicate that they prefer not to exercise this option, because while widow remarriage is socially acceptable, an element of stigma is attached to the practice. Another reason for their reluctance, as the widows forthrightly state, is that their children are unlikely to be loved by a new partner. They prefer to live, as long as possible, with their natal kin, with their children, or with a married son. Often, however, widows themselves are sought after by those men whose wives have abandoned them. There is a demand for widows, who form a surplus category in the marriage market. Alternatively, depending on their circumstances, many widows like Radha's three sisters regard themselves as being effectively on their own. They eagerly desire companionship, while social dependency is another driving force leading widows to seek partners. The most compelling example of social dependency is that of a woman called Mamta who emphasized the everyday harassment she encountered when she was living alone with her two children. Because her natal family was no longer alive, she had no choice but to seek a secondary partner. As she could not find someone close to her in age, she is cohabiting with a man twenty-seven years older than her. He could easily be mistaken for her grandfather. Mamta has got her partner to sign a letter in the presence of the mahila panchayat (see Chapter 5) stating that he will keep her permanently. The more difficult task she is facing now is to get his assurance on matters of inheritance.

Ironically, widows may end up as providers for their partners, as in all likelihood they are economically self-sufficient following the death of their spouse. Widows are entitled to their deceased husband's municipality and government jobs. I came across quite a few widows like Basanti and Omvati who had 'inherited' the jobs of the deceased husband. We may query whether secondary partners exploit relationships with widows for their earning capabilities, recognizing their vulnerability and desperation for lifelong commitment. This is apparent in Basanti's case, as she hands over her monthly municipal salary to Suraj. Her municipality job and pension scheme have done little to free her of male dependence. Similarly, Radha would caution me that while Prem Singh and Omvati's story is widely known in Raju Camp as one of lasting love, the only reason that Prem Singh has remained with Omvati for so long is because she has a municipal job that substantially covers their daily needs. In the twenty-one years of their cohabitation, Prem Singh has never provided for the family.[8]

Neighbourhood Codes of Morality

Any visitor to Mohini Nagar will notice the regular social interactions between men and women. A prominent attribute of adult relationships is the relative ease of home visits, open flirtations, and the affective neighbourly exchanges of *sukh* and *dukh*. Ideally, marriage and secondary unions are prohibited between neighbours and residents of the same *basti*. When secondary unions are established between neighbours, there is gossip aplenty in local circles (e.g. 'You know, in *ristha* she was his sister'). Regardless of the notion that neighbours are 'family members' and not lovers, secondary unions still flourish between those who live in close proximity. Given the enormous social freedom in everyday life, flexibility in conjugal arrangements,

[8] Uchiyamada (1997) has brought to our notice the sexual affairs of 'untouchable' widows in Kerala and has examined the minutiae of their relations with higher caste men. He argues that low caste women experience an ambiguous relationship with higher caste men, as they experience a split between the whore/wife dichotomy. Uchiyamada makes a worthwhile contribution by asserting: 'We need to follow the trajectories of these becoming-women, who are inherently split, who cross the boundaries of family, caste, and social structure, in a passing moment, in a liminal space which is created by the over spilling and heterogeneous *bandham* relationships {*bandham* connotes sexual, conjugal, and kinship relationships}' (1997: 305). My Delhi data differ in many respects from those of Uchiyamada's. In the relationships that he describes, sex and prostitution are striking aspects of widow relationships, while he notes that the sexual transgressions that 'untouchable' women experience with higher caste men often give them a sense of self-worth. In Delhi, while widows may be involved in a certain amount of casual prostitution, their narratives accentuate social dependence, male commitment, and public morality.

and tolerance of marital instability, once women form extramarital liaisons their reputations are nonetheless openly and closely scrutinized. Paradoxically, sexual freedom in the post-marriage phase coexists along with a powerful discourse on public morality and appropriate female behaviour. Radha mentions that after her affair with Subhash, people call her a 'loose woman' and that many men express an interest in having sex with her. She bemoans that her 'light' friendships with men are always mistaken for sexual advances. On the whole, Radha, who is a long-term female resident of Raju Camp, is less likely to be harassed if she forms a secondary union than are female newcomers to a *basti*. Long-term inhabitants have established a rapport with neighbours, whereas new residents perceived to be in casual relationships are more likely to face harassment. Radha relates an anecdote about a woman named Neelu and her widowed mother who had moved to Raju Camp. Neelu was renting a *jhuggi* from a woman called Kamlesh. Kamlesh and her neighbours noticed that a man often visited Neelu. Gossip circulated that Neelu and her mother were encouraging casual relationships and were unable to establish permanent relationships. They were literally chased out of Kamlesh's *gali* for supposedly engaging in immoral activities. Kamlesh retorted that she did not want to spoil the *gali's* reputation: 'Both mother and daughter are whores.' This incident substantiates that for women, the importance of ascertaining commitment is indeed related to the wider concern of public morality, and explains why women in secondary unions retain symbols of marriage such as the toe ring, the nose ring, *sindoor*, bangles, and *mangalsutra*.

Generational Shifts: Marriage, Consensuality, Cohabitation

Until now I have discussed 'older forms' of consensuality by drawing on the stories of women who belong to the age group of 40 years and above. Let us now examine 'newer forms' of consensual arrangements. In Mohini Nagar, there is an unambiguous inter-generational split in the way in which secondary unions are being defined. The couples in Radha's story reject marriage terminologies, endorsing instead consensuality as signifying the couple's unity.

Conversely, young couples assert that their secondary unions are 'proper marriages'. It is worth exploring whether secondary unions are redefined in a discourse on marriage.

Asha and Surender's example will show how the younger generation is exhibiting their relationships as 'respectable marriages'.

Asha and Surender: 'We had a court marriage!'

Asha, a resident of Raju Camp, is 23 years old. She ended her two-year marriage and moved in with Surender, a neighbour. She enthusiastically informs me that she and Surender have got 'married' (*shaadi*) and have legalized their secondary union. They have had a court marriage. As the court marriage procedure is difficult in Delhi, they went to Surender's village in Bulandshahr Zilla (in the Meerut region of Uttar Pradesh), where it was easier to obtain a marriage certificate. Asha shows me the certificate. It is a plain piece of paper with a short paragraph stating that Surender (son of x parents) has married Asha (daughter of x parents). There is no date or official stamp on the certificate, and neither does it show the name of the court where it was ostensibly registered. According to Asha, the certificate protects them against harassment from neighbours and will ultimately encourage them to stay together.

Asha and Surender's delineation of a 'proper married couple' relates crucially to the personal circumstances of the concerned individuals. As aforementioned, where either partner is new to a *basti*, as Asha is, or where the union has been consolidated suddenly and in dubious circumstances, the couple wants to rule out the impression that the relationship is casual. Consequently, they will make it a point to emphasize that they 'got married', whilst organizing documentary proof significantly enhances this claim. In addition, obtaining proofs corresponds with the trend in love marriages; the consensual nature of the relationship receives legal validity and, as I am told, the certificate encourages conjugal stability. So while legalized divorce remains a rarity, the use of documentary evidence to secure secondary unions seems fairly standardized. Nevertheless, in most cases, it is highly questionable whether Mohini Nagar couples are in possession of authentic certificates (cf. love marriages). In Delhi certificates can be arranged by paying a sum of money to a corrupt lawyer. Asha's marriage certificate, which was obtained from Bulandshahr Zilla, does not appear authentic.

Asha and Surender's intense focus on marriage certificates is very different from the more relaxed attitude of the older generation. The domestic life of Dyal Singh and Lakshmi foregrounds diverse conjugal arrangements and cohabitation, and shows how these are perceived in light of the discourses on marriage and consensuality.

Lakshmi and Dyal Singh: 'Rituals and courts are of no consequence'

Lakshmi, who is 50 years old, is a long-term resident of Raju Camp. She has been in a relationship with Dyal Singh for twenty-one years. She left her primary husband because there was no love between them. When she got involved with Dyal Singh, they did not have any type of remarriage ritual: 'With all this court marriage stuff and going to the temple to get married, men still desert women. We promised never to leave each other.' Dyal Singh, who is a local politician, has not left his *sat phere wali* (first wife). He does not cohabit with Lakshmi, but visits her every day.

While the present generation attempts to acquire marriage certificates, older women like Lakshmi assert that personal commitment is more significant for the foundation of their secondary unions and replaces the need for proofs and rituals. Among the older generation, secondary unions are mainly defined by couples as permanent consensual unions with the promise of lifelong continuity. Furthermore, non-cohabitation arrangements such as those of Dyal Singh and Lakshmi's need not signify casual relationships. Residents and neighbours in Raju Camp have for years noted how Dyal Singh is committed to Lakshmi. As in Lakshmi and Dyal Singh's example, non-cohabitation arrangements accompanied by the practice of polygyny do not rule out long-term loyalty. While those who cohabit are generally referred to as couples, non-cohabitants like Dyal Singh and Lakshmi are also perceived as a dyad. When secondary partners are not cohabiting, their conjugal arrangements may be tied with the practice of polygyny, although this is mainly found among the older generation. Among the young generation, the changes in secondary unions can be additionally explained on the following grounds. Let me begin by saying that class mobility and modern notions of companionate marriage are not amplifying ideological shifts. Young women in Mohini Nagar are losing faith in customary forms of consensuality. They feel that it is important to muster proof and documentation that may well serve as a form of protection. Equally, the call for systemized documentation is being spearheaded by mahila panchayats and local police stations. In their advisory role, mahila panchayats and other Delhi NGOs direct women to go through a registered court marriage or to obtain a written statement from the partner endorsing the permanence of the union (see Chapter 5). They also brief women on bigamy laws. Women are urged to collate photos of their partner (and of children if they have any together). The mahila panchayat claims that this documentation can legally protect a woman if she were to be jilted by a secondary partner.[9] Overall, documentation has gained increased emphasis and import in low-income urban neighbourhoods because of the mahila panchayat's presence and activity, and the spread of legal information.

---

[9] In a significant ruling, a *lok adalat* (people's court organized by the Delhi Legal Services Authority) decreed that a second wife also has a right to maintenance for herself and her children (Rashtra Mahila, March 2009, p. 3). There are also legal provisions that protect female cohabitants and couples who choose to cohabit. A landmark judgment by the Allahabad High Court (Uttar Pradesh) in the Payal Sharma case decreed that it is perfectly legal for a man and a woman to live together without marriage (*New Women Magazine* July 2001 and *The Hindu*, 15 July 2001). Law experts call it a mere clarification of Article 21 of the Indian Constitution, which empowers citizens to live as they wish. Payal Sharma, the petitioner from the Kunauj district of Uttar Pradesh, had complained that her father had lodged a case against her live-in partner on the charge that he had abducted his daughter. The high court decreed that as Payal was an adult, she was allowed to cohabit with the man of her choice. This landmark judgment legally endorses the right of men and women to cohabit. Chapter 5 describes how the mahila panchayat assists those women who have been abandoned by their secondary partners; documentation sources serve as evidence and can be used to threaten men.

Women's Appraisals of their Secondary Partners

On many occasions, women candidly appraise their partners. In the anecdotes they recount, standard spousal expressions such as *mera admi* (my man) are exchanged for other insidious terms like *bahar wala admi* (complete outsider) that conjure entrenched cautionary discourses about informal remarriage. Vimlesh's narrative assists in the exploration of the gender dynamic in secondary unions.

Vimlesh and Ishvar: 'Complex adjustments'

Vimlesh, a Balmiki woman, has a complicated story to tell. It begins when she befriended Ishvar, a Balmiki man working for the MCD. She and Ishvar 'came out in the open'. She then left her primary husband and their two children, and Ishvar turned his wife out of the conjugal home. She lost contact with her two sons, but is now the 'mother' of Ishvar's five children. Vimlesh claims that Ishvar does not respect or treat her well. He keeps suspecting her: 'When I was sitting in the sun yesterday, he asked me whether I was waiting for a new lover. I always leave the Municipal Corporation in a hurry so he has no reason to suspect me.' On another occasion, Vimlesh and her neighbour compare notes about their partners:

'Our Balmiki men will never reform themselves. Unlike other men, they routinely drink, fight, and suspect us of having affairs. Our relationship with them does not get less conflictual, even when we are getting older.' Vimlesh says that Ishvar has told her many times to leave 'his' house: 'If I address him disrespectfully, he beats me.' She has brought up Ishvar's children as her own, but his children instigate fights against her: 'There are differences between one's own children and those of another man.' Neither can she approach her natal kin about their ongoing conflicts, as Ishvar is not her primary husband. They will say: 'Did we tell you to abandon your husband (*apni toh marzi se ki hai*)?' When I ask Vimlesh whether she can seek reconciliation with her primary husband, she says that he died a while ago, and was a good man.

Vimlesh's appraisal of Ishvar leads to a reflective discussion between her and her neighbour on the comparison between a husband from an arranged marriage (*bihata*) and a partner from a secondary union. They refer to a secondary partner as a *bahar wala admi* and *doosra admi* (another man), while informing me that these terms connote a partner who has not been chosen by one's parents. Vimlesh's neighbour underlines the merits of a husband chosen by one's parents: 'An outsider is never as reliable as a *bihata*. There are many benefits of staying on with a *bihata*. You can shout at a *bihata* and say what you like. He, too, will endure it. An 'outsider' will just walk out when he gets tired of a woman. An outsider may turn out to be worse than a *bihata*, and then what will happen? Whatever the case may be, a *bihata* is a *bihata*.'

Vimlesh acknowledges that her association with Ishvar is based on love. They became lovers while working for the MCD. She was under no compulsion to leave her primary husband. Vimlesh's core experience of consensuality suggests that male partners assert their authority over women almost immediately after they have formalized their secondary unions, a pattern that is uncannily similar to that of love marriages. Men monitor their female partner's movements, work hours, and sexuality. The same aspects of gender conflict that women emphasize in arranged and love marriages—suspicion, sexual jealousy, alcohol-related abuse, and violence—appear in secondary unions. In addition, women experience extensive conflict even at an age when they consider themselves to be 'growing old'. Where other women in secondary unions claim that their partners are supportive, I observed that their relationships are free neither from violence nor from dependency on males. It is obvious that secondary unions do not foster an egalitarian dynamic. Balmiki women stress intra-caste patriarchies, or how male domination and violence are caste specific. While the Balmikis are generally self-critical about their caste, the women are also highly critical about their men's conduct. Earlier chapters nevertheless have shown that men's conduct is the same across castes. The female assertion that Balmiki men are the worst is therefore an exaggeration.

Women like Vimlesh who forego their children from their primary marriage become stepmothers to the children of their secondary partners. Studies on the biological and social ties in parent–child relations offer some insight into why mothers may be willing to forgo their children to be in other relationships. Das (1993 [1976]: 209) reports that in extended families, the web of love often extends to other children at the expense of a mother's own. Trawick's (1992: 222) study on 'her Tamil family' directs us to the fact that children have multiple caretakers, who are often extended family members. Comparably, in Mohini Nagar, we know that married daughters share intense bonds with their natal kin and siblings. A woman named Lajvanti informed me that her sister had run away with a driver, leaving behind her only daughter: 'Somebody must have done black magic on my sister, so she lost her mind and ran away with him.' Although her sister's daughter has grown up in her father's house with a stepmother, Lajvanti has regular contact with her niece, whom she calls her 'daughter'. Following Lajvanti's example, children who have been abandoned may not be seen as being subjected to harsh or cruel abandonment, as there is a sense that other family members will step in and take on the responsibility of raising them. Conversely, the transition to being a stepmother requires women to negotiate a new set of relationships and to make emotive adjustments. If a secondary partner's children are small, the intensity of domestic adjustments is less severe compared to the scenario where they are older. Furthermore, if a couple decides to cohabit, the usual convention is for the woman to shift to the male partner's residence. This is exemplified through Ishvar's virilocal assertion that Vimlesh is living in 'his' house. Thus, the distinguishing characteristics of secondary unions are the complex adjustments, fragmented lives, and difficult renegotiations that women experience, as men are fundamentally rooted in terms of residence, agnates, and children. While the latter virilocal features are equally present in arranged and love marriages, in secondary unions women have to renegotiate both residence and their status as a stepmother. They may also have to adapt to a new environment, possibly with different morality codes, while their secondary partners do not have to experience this change.

Responses of Natal Kin

In a primary arranged marriage, women have strong claims to natal kin support. Once they form a secondary union of their choice, whereby they opt out of an arranged marriage, the support they can expect from their natal kin can vary considerably. Certain moral codes of comportment determine the reactions of natal families. If a married daughter has left a primary husband with a good reputation, natal kin may withdraw their support. At best, a daughter's actions will be deemed morally untenable. As in the case of the condemnation of love marriages, she will be told firmly to face the consequences, for it was her choice to leave her children and a sound provider. Given this indignation on the part of natal kin, daughters often lose vital support, which deepens their vulnerability and increases their dependence on male partners (cf. love marriages). Castigation from relatives and neighbours also reduces levels of natal kin support. The withdrawal of family support signals that while secondary unions have societal legitimacy, not all unions receive validation from the concerned natal families. Otherwise, there are instances where natal kin are both non-judgmental and practical about their daughters' secondary unions, sometimes even encouraging them to pursue new relationships. When Renu, a married woman, ran away with a younger unmarried man, her mother was complicit in her daughter's elopement. Renu's mother argued that as her daughter was being ill-treated, the time had come for her to terminate her marriage. Renu's mother was not in a position to offer her daughter refuge, for she, too, had recently formed a secondary union and was making adjustments in her new life. Renu and her mother remain in close contact.

Symbolism of the Primary Marriage

Despite the prevalence of secondary unions, cautionary discourses stress the need for women to remain for life with their primary husbands, as they may face disappointment in consensual unions. In many female circles, the emphasis is on the necessity of enduring difficulties that arise in arranged marriages and on availing the moral right to refuge. Here we observe a sharp local caveat, whereby arranged marriages are juxtaposed against all other types of marital unions. As per this caveat arranged marriages are the safest, most successful, and most robust of marriages. So while there are articulations critiquing arranged marriages (e.g. the views expressed by Radha), there are also competing discourses about parental matches being the best. In their turn, women like Vimlesh who face disappointment in secondary unions tend to revoke the merits of arranged marriages and the importance of parental choice, while in actuality marital grievances are highly prominent in arranged marriages. Mohini Nagar women also evoke the powerful celebratory rituals of the arranged marriage (*sat phere*) and employ idioms such as *bihata, and shaadi wala* to indicate the durability of marriages based on parental choice and the guarantee of parental support. Women exalt and elevate the status of a *bihata*. In contrast, a *bahar wala admi* (outsider or a secondary partner) signifies that respect, loyalty, and long-term happiness are not necessarily guaranteed in secondary unions. To paraphrase, the most common fear is that 'an outsider may turn out to be worse than a *bihata* . . . and then what will happen to a woman?' Cautionary comparisons between arranged and love marriages form only one element of marital discourses. Discourses about the divide between arranged marriages and secondary unions are also equally cautionary. Writing on women, caste, and secondary unions, Leela Dube (1996: 15) states: 'Her subsequent unions may have social sanction and she may continue to use all the signs of the married state, but she has permanently stepped outside the bounds of a primary marriage.' Dube's emphasis on 'stepping outside the bounds of a primary marriage' is portentous. From women's narratives it appears that once they establish secondary relationships, they have to renegotiate their new relationships in a drastic way and on a more unequal basis. The ethnographic explorations in this chapter have conveyed the complicated adjustments that women are required to make.

Married Women and Unmarried Men

Married women often form liaisons with unmarried men. The final set of case studies offers a close look at the long-term durability of this specific combination of partners. Through the life stories of Usha and Shahnaz I delineate the congruent features of Hindu and Muslim women's secondary unions respectively.

Usha: 'Casual abandonment'

Usha, a distraught Balmiki woman, says that Ramu, her 'husband', has deserted her. She has to feed and take care of their five children on her own. Exactly a year ago, Ramu went to his village in Badaun

Usha with her Children

Usha and her two children are standing outside their decrepit
jhuggi. Usha was deserted by her 'unmarried' secondary partner
with whom she had five children.

(in north-central Uttar Pradesh) to assist in preparations for his
sister's wedding. When he did not return after several months,
she went in search of him, but without success. According to Usha,
he owed neighbours and moneylenders large sums of money, and
she believes that someone must have cast a black magic spell to
initiate his desertion. Usha's abandonment has attracted gossip
in Raju Camp. An auto-rickshaw driver remarks: 'Help her and
do something for her. She has been betrayed.' Others are less
sympathetic. Usha's affines state that Ramu is not her primary
husband. He is the unmarried cousin of her primary husband, with
whom she had eloped some years ago. Usha has left behind a son
from her primary marriage: 'Her *bihata* was a good man. He had

a government job and she was well provided for. So why did she leave him? This is what happens to women when they leave good husbands.' Usha's affines describe Ramu's character as devious. He acquired bad habits in Delhi and slowly started borrowing money that he could not repay.

On my next visit to Usha's decrepit *jhuggi*, I find her looking happy compared to her earlier anguished state. She reveals that she has found employment. Ramu had never allowed her to work, but now she is earning ` 1600 a month. Usha has some news for me. Word has reached her that Ramu had recently got married in his village. He was under pressure from his mother to do so. Usha shows me her court marriage certificate, which Ramu had torn to shreds some time ago on being taunted by his mother. He had told Usha to 'get out' of his house, to which she had replied: 'Where shall I go?' I try to reassemble Usha and Ramu's marriage certificate. Usha confesses that she no longer yearns for Ramu to return. She has mustered the strength to bring up the children on her own.

Shahnaz: 'Remarriage and family duress'

When I pass through a *gali* inhabited by Muslims, I witness an emotional scene. An amma (old lady) and her granddaughters are sitting with Shahnaz, a beautiful young woman, who is sobbing uncontrollably: 'My partner (*admi*) has told me that he is going to beat me to death (*jan se mar dalunga*). The abuses I am subjected to! I might be dead one morning. He says that he is going to hang me from the ceiling.' I conclude that Shahnaz is facing serious domestic violence, which needs immediate attention. I urge her to avail the services of the mahila panchayat.

Later, in private, Amma tells me Shahnaz's story: 'Look, Shahnaz had eloped with an unmarried man (the one from whom she was facing domestic violence). She had left behind her husband and five children. Her sisters were about to get married and she eloped just before their wedding. She has disgraced her mother and father so badly. Should a daughter not have respect for her parents? Her father has warned us that if she sets foot in her *pihar*, he will shoot her. We have stopped her from visiting us because we respect her father.' Amma offers me details about Shahnaz's primary marriage. Her former husband would also beat her, and for several years she had been taking refuge. She had received continual support from her *pihar*: 'Okay, her husband used to beat her, but men are men. If she had continued to take refuge, she would have got respect. Now who will bother about her?' Her unmarried partner was a carpenter who worked for her father. They became involved while she was taking refuge.

A few months later, Amma hears that Shahnaz's unmarried partner has been made to marry someone else by his parents. I am told that Shahnaz was sterilized and would have been unable to produce children for him: 'He would have left her anyway. A man wants his flesh and blood to carry forward his family name.' During my final meeting with Amma, she says: 'I am not sure whether Shahnaz is dead or alive or if she has married for the third time.' I am discouraged from asking further questions about Shahnaz. Earlier, a tearful Amma had told me how five members of her immediate family had died under dramatic circumstances in the last two years. As an elderly woman, she is now solely responsible for her grandchildren's future. She hints that the Shahnaz incident occupies little time and importance in their lives.

Usha and Shahnaz are from different religious communities, yet they faced cognate desertions. Jeffery (2001: 20) has argued that at the level of dominant religious discourses, Hindu and Muslim women in Bijnor are widely cited as being inherently different. This cogent polarization of Hindus and Muslims is found across Mohini Nagar as well. Jeffery enlightens us to the 'crucial parallels in the domestic lives of Hindu and Muslim women', who face similar experiences of marital breakdown and economic entitlements. Her data dispute right-wing assertions that Muslim women are more subordinated. Usha's court marriage certificate did not prevent marital desertion. The partners of Usha and Shahnaz could break away with impunity and embark on new marriages as they knew that they would not be reprimanded by any natal kin members. The women, in turn, received nominal sympathy from those around them for they were seen to get what they 'deserved'. Crucially, Usha and Shahnaz's secondary partners were unmarried (*kunvara admi*), and their casual abandonment raises questions about the durability of this frequent partnership between unmarried men and married women (and widows). At the outset, married women can quite easily form friendships with unmarried men; the distinctive norms between premarital and post-marital sexuality (see Chapter 3) permit this. Moreover, married women who are undertaking lengthy refuge often desire intimacy, as Shahnaz did with the man who was working for her father. On their part, unmarried men are liable to be attracted to a more 'sexually experienced' married woman. Having sex with a married woman is less perilous than with an unmarried woman, as the former may be sterilized and pregnancy can therefore be averted. From the perspective of unmarried men, these relationships may serve as 'flings' or sexual romances where 'available married women' are perceived as girlfriends rather than wives. Nevertheless, unmarried men are likely to encounter duress from their parents once they form liaisons with married women. For the sake of the family's reputation, they will urge sons to terminate these unions by insisting that they are jeopardizing their future for an older woman. Unmarried men are also likely to face constant rebukes from the wider community for cohabiting with a married woman, especially where there is a wide age gap. They may quickly terminate the union on account of the ridicule they face. There are, however, unmarried men who resist parental pressure and derision. I came across one who refused to terminate his union on the premise that his parents had not made efforts to find him a bride. He rebelliously argued that he has been unmarried for too long and that his secondary union was prompted by his parents' indolence in this matter of finding him a wife.

Fertility and Remarriage

The issue of fertility emerges as a major concern for women once they become sexually involved with unmarried men. As married women like Radha and Shahnaz normally undergo sterilization after giving birth to sons, they are unable to produce an offspring for their partners. Kapadia (1996) informs us that low caste discourses on sexuality are ambiguous, multiple, and contradictory. She separates sexuality from fertility.[10] In Tamil Nadu, low caste women have sexual freedom but are wholly responsible for controlling their fertility, as men take no responsibility for contraception. Kapadia

---

[10] See also Uchiyamada (1997: 301) for an analysis of how 'untouchable' women in Kerala experience the split between sexuality and fertility.

notes: 'With the lower castes the stress is on norms controlling fertility, but with the upper castes norms controlling sexuality are emphasized' (1996: 169). While Kapadia's observations on fertility and sexuality correspond to norms in Delhi, her ethnographic examples mainly relate to the predicament of older women in the event of pregnancy.[11] For older women, conceiving when they already have grown children and grandchildren is seen as being utterly shameful. My data suggest that once fertility is terminated through sterilization, women face dilemmas in their subsequent relationships since they cannot produce heirs. While initially affairs with married women are easy to initiate, this factor seems to have a contra effect in terms of sustaining the permanence of the union.

I now provide another instance of a union between an unmarried man and a widow older than him by fifteen years. The couple faced constant taunts and ridicule. In a chance encounter with the widow she told me that she was three months' pregnant. She told Radha that she was pregnant in spite of being sterilized. Radha and her sisters debated whether the widow was actually pregnant, since 'sterilizations are not always fool proof'.[12] Radha's sisters believed that the widow was deceiving them, as there were no physical signs of pregnancy. Radha told me: 'I checked her stomach and I am sure that there is no child in there. She should tell her partner the truth, because if he discovers she is lying, the consequences will be bad.' A few months later, there were no further allusions to the widow's phantom pregnancy. Radha kept telling me that the widow's partner would not keep her for long as she was much too old for him. Comparably, a male informant narrated how his unmarried nephew had run away with a married woman who was sterilized. After some months of cohabitation with her, his nephew started talking about wanting to be a father. She pleaded with him, saying: 'I will try to open up my operation–mine will open.' As her sterilization could not be reversed, his nephew gave her financial compensation and asked her to leave his house. Both

---

[11] See 'Thangamma's story' in Kapadia (1996: 169).

[12] The belief is that sterilizations are not always reliable. Radha tells me that things often go wrong in government hospitals: 'Given the mishaps that occur, chances are that women may still be able to conceive even after they have been operated upon.'

these anecdotes underline how fertility or its absence leads to major anxiety and represents a strong bargaining tool for sustaining conjugal stability in secondary unions. The pairing between unmarried men and married women is thus particularly fragile and to the disadvantage of women, the long-term sustainability of these relationships depending on familial and societal approval and on the fertility of the woman concerned.

Giddens (1999) has argued that in modern societies, the fissure between reproduction and sexuality has expanded women's lifestyle choices and led to greater emancipation. In his view women no longer need to worry about repeated pregnancies as contraception and new reproductive technologies allow them to control their fertility and sexuality in effective ways. Mohini Nagar women's contraception methods and lived experiences of sexuality differ drastically from Giddens' interpretation. Sterilization and abortion are indeed their main forms of contraception, and while sterilization per se may end childbirth, it also hampers women's reproductive choices with regard to future relationships. The Mohini Nagar data highlight how the dialectic between sexuality, fertility, and sterilization weakens women's reproductive autonomy in secondary relationships, and hence this finding is not in line with Giddens' assumptions.

Conclusion

This chapter establishes that women face extensive conflict in their secondary unions. So while these unions provide the space for women like Radha to explore their romantic longings and desires, and the freedom to terminate their primary unions and embark on such new relationships, which is suggestive of greater autonomy, this does not necessarily translate into egalitarian relationships. What's more, in particular relationships (those between Balmiki women and upper-caste men, and between widows and married men), the need for validation of male dependence and commitment is thrown into sharper relief. That women have to renegotiate the terms and conditions of their domestic lives in more drastic, complicated, and unequal ways is clearly evident. Notably, secondary unions may also weaken or undermine women's ties with their natal kin, as seen through the life stories of Usha, Vimlesh, and Shahnaz. The examples of these women show that natal kin can react adversely to secondary unions. That's why the cautionary discourse of remaining with a 'familiar' primary husband and not having to face disappointment in a new relationship underscores the importance of enduring an arranged marriage, even though the latter is equally marked by fragility, uncertainty, and asymmetry.

5

Informal Dispute Settlement
The Mahila Panchayats

'Have you seen the embittered disputes at the mahila panchayat? We do not want to get caught in this mess when we get married.'
— Young girls witnessing raucous scenes between spouses as they pass the mahila panchayat office

Legal and Non-legal Pluralisms in Everyday Life

In *A Remembered Village*, Srinivas (1976: 42) noted that disputes are a rich mine of data for the anthropologist. In Rampura, a village in Mysore district of Karnataka, Srinivas witnessed a gamut of marital and property disputes, and the eclectic nature of the settlement of these disputes through local panchayats, traditional courts, or influential arbitrators. Disputes, he remarked, 'were going on all the time'. This chapter focuses on disputes that also take place all the time, albeit not in rural south India but in contemporary urban north India. These are major breakdowns in relationships between husbands and wives, resulting in the loss of mutual trust and respect. This chapter examines how women file 'cases' with the mahila panchayat or 'women's court' in Mohini Nagar. As complaints are filed by women from distant and nearby neighbourhoods, we are presented in this chapter with a 'cross section' of the urban poor. In Delhi's urban landscape, the researcher is struck by how various legal and non-legal institutions coexist alongside and complement each other. Men and women approach the police, including women's 'grievance cells' in police stations, the legal system (courts and family courts), biradari panchayats (caste associations), influential mediators (neighbourhood leaders), and human rights organizations. These constitute the plurality of resources that they make use of in addressing their marital disputes. The mahila panchayat represents a significant addition to an already diverse array of institutions present on the scene that offers personalized services to women. As such, it is of heuristic value to assess the nature and content of their interventions in instances of conflict resolution and to see how they regulate incidents of marital discord, as their procedures are being replicated by other NGOs in Delhi. Indeed, many women's NGOs that have adopted the mahila panchayat concept and model have sprung up to resolve marital complaints, and their concerted efforts are directed towards helping poor women.

As a prelude to the documentation of the activities of the Mohini Nagar mahila panchayat, I explore briefly the efficacy of urban biradari panchayats in relation to dispute settlement as well as their general involvement in matters pertaining to marriage. This introductory exercise will help to establish distinctions between male-dominated biradari panchayats and women-oriented NGO initiatives that are grass-roots and community-based bodies. My main interest, however, lies in foregrounding the transformatory character of mahila panchayats, in examining whether their dispute settlement processes have the intended potential for democratizing marriage, and in assessing how empowering these informal women's courts turn out to be for low-income urban women. I study the mahila panchayat's dispute settlement processes from multiple angles: by examining who files complaints and how they do so, the various events or factors surrounding the resolution or non-resolution of cases, the aftermath of agreed settlements, and the spontaneous and open conversations and exchanges that take place between counsellors and clients. I endeavour to present an in-depth ethnography of the intimate, complex, and intricate inner workings of a marriage counselling centre. The arbitration procedures of the mahila panchayat, its success in resolving marital disputes, the discourses it articulates on marriage(s), and its ideological orientation are also other central concerns that I address.

Biradari Panchayats

Studies of village India have highlighted how informal modes of dispute settlement predate, and have survived, the advent of legal and formal institutions.[1] One such village institution is the biradari (caste) panchayat, which was set up for hearing local complaints and adjudicating conflicts. In rural and semi-urban Haryana, Chowdhry (2007) reports how caste panchayats dominated by upper caste landowning men play an intrusive role in the domain of marriage. They nullify inter-caste love marriages and even intra-caste arranged marriages that contravene the category of prohibited *got* through economic and other sanctions, including the use of violence (see Grover 2007). The latter includes executing couples and expelling their families from the ancestral village, as well as destroying their property, crops and household goods. Brutal violence also takes the form of burning couples' alive, and administering poison. Chowdhry accentuates the absence of functional democratic institutions able to effectively challenge traditional powers. Panchayats that have unrestrained powers are still prominent and widely utilized, as the courts are out of reach for a large proportion of the rural population. Given the resilience and dominance of caste panchayats in rural north India, it is of interest to see whether urban biradari panchayats are as interventionist and whether they have an effective presence in the metropolis. I observed few biradari panchayats in and around the vicinity of Mohini Nagar. Urban ethnographies, both recent and earlier, suggest a decline in the relevance of caste associations. With regard to Agra (Uttar Pradesh), Lynch (1969) writes: 'The courts, political parties and politics, the politicians, movies, schools, shoe factories and market, and the Neo-Buddist movement now perform for the Jatavs many of the functions that their own caste once did. In sociological terms, these new secular institutions are functional alternatives to the traditional caste institutions' (1969: 201). In Chhattisgarh, Parry (2001) remarks that the caste panchayats have lost their strength, while the state in general, and the courts

---

[1] Cohn (1987) depicts the persistent dominance of traditional caste associations. He observed that in Madhopur village (Uttar Pradesh), the Chamars came to depend more on their own caste group for dispute settlement.

in particular, have become increasingly intrusive in regulating domestic life.

In Mohini Nagar the Khatik Samaj Mahapanchayat is well-known. This biradari panchayat assembles in Mohini Nagar, and across South Delhi localities dominated by Khatiks, such as Mangolpuri, Kotla, and mainly Lajpat Nagar. In September 2001, I interviewed a senior male member of the Khatik Samaj Mahapanchayat,[2] but was refused permission to observe how the body imparts justice, as birdari panchayats do not permit women to participate in deliberations or in dispute settlements.[3] Some tentative conclusions may nevertheless be drawn from the interview about the current position of urban biradari panchayats. Biradari panchayats are caste-specific, close-knit organizations operated by men. There appears to be a link between the evolution of the biradari panchayat and the status of the caste group in terms of upward mobility and ritual upgradation. Many Delhi Khatiks have given up their ancestral/caste profession of meat trading and have risen in wealth, rank, and education. The founding members of this Khatik Samaj Mahapanchayat have prestigious jobs and wield considerable political clout. For instance, my interviewee was a retired sub-division magistrate residing in a modern three-storeyed house in the resettlement colonies. A board at the entrance of his house boldly displays his designation and he speaks fluent English. As biradari panchayat representatives have social capital, they are well placed for performing the tasks of collecting donations and accumulating funds. Notwithstanding the latter function, the Khatik Samaj Mahapanchayat is not a registered body, nor does it have legal standing.

I was informed that the Khatik Samaj Mahapanchayat does not pass injunctions against inter-caste love marriages, and neither does it (nor can it) regulate the marital preferences and alliances of youngsters: 'The courts handle inter-caste marriages. We cannot stop someone from marrying someone else.' Nonetheless, the Mahapanchayat assists couples in pursuing formal separation (i.e. in arranged marriages) and does intervene in disputes concerning

---

[2] See Annexure for the full interview.

[3] Bairy (2009: 100) examines the gendering of caste space in modern articulations, practices, and associations, and notes how Brahmin caste associations are overwhelmingly male dominated.

child marriage. Another key referent is that biradari panchayats prioritize particular modes of dispute resolution that the courts and women's NGOs do not. The nature of their dispute redressal system may be gauged from the following excerpt from the interview with the representative of the Khatik Samaj Mahapanchayat, B.L. Pachouri on 14.9.2001:

> Sometimes parents have arranged their son's and daughter's marriages during infancy. When they grow up, if either party, especially the boy, wants to marry someone of his own choice, then the parents of the girl feel betrayed. We usually ask for a fine. For example, if a boy does not want to marry his childhood bride, we ask him to compensate the girl's family. We also put it in writing. We also resolve property fights between brothers and neighbourly disputes. The police are not effective, and people face a lot of harassment from them. The courts are expensive and time consuming. We take decisions and solve matters quickly. That is why people come to us.

Hence, biradari panchayats deal with property and neighbourhood disputes and tackle urban miscreant-related problems of a perilous nature, which women's NGOs do not handle. To this extent, they are helpful to people who require urgent mediation and who cannot afford to approach the courts. The few biradari panchayats that exist in South Delhi therefore fill an important void for poor urban citizens. On the other hand, biradari panchayat do not observe democratic principles, and, as this chapter shows later, mahila panchayats follow more transparent and participatory methods of dispute settlement. Biradari panchayats impose fines and suspend membership, steps that may discourage their own caste members from approaching them. Individuals are deliberately humiliated in front of fellow caste members by the panchayat. In this regard, biradari panchayats have lost some of their credibility; a forceful local critique exists about the ways in which they operate. There is also little information or evidence to confirm whether biradari panchayat injunctions or judgments are ultimately effective. To further investigate the clout of urban biradari panchayats, I present data on a second biradari panchayat, namely the Kumhar Biradari Panchayat, who as per their professional ancestry, are potters.

I came into close contact with the Kumhar Biradari Panchayat while researching the marital problems of Amit and Sunita, as detailed in Chapter 2. I return here to their case, adding observations on the role of the Kumhar Biradari Panchayat in negotiating the couple's marital agreements.

Sunita and Amit: Biradari Panchayat Interventions

Sunita has lived with Amit for six months of her three-year marriage, taking refuge in her natal home for the remaining time. Several mediation attempts initiated by Amit's family have failed. Amit's father sends a message to Sunita's natal kin, requesting them to appear at the conjugal home (located in a resettlement colony) on a particular day, so that the Kumhar Biradari Panchayat can negotiate a settlement. At the same time, Amit's mother requests that the mahila panchayat caseworkers (including myself) join them on the selected day, to be present but not to intervene. Amit's father makes it clear that his son's marital problems must only be resolved through the biradari panchayat. On the appointed day, we wait at Amit's house for Sunita's natal kin to arrive. Meanwhile, ten men in white *kurta pyjamas* (Indian men's dress) ascend to the top floor of Amit's house. I am told they are members of the Kumhar Biradari Panchayat. The mahila panchayat caseworkers and the rest of the women sit downstairs, well secluded from the men. We wait for Sunita's natal kin to arrive, but she, and they, fail to turn up. Apparently, this is the third time that the biradari panchayat has gathered at Amit's house and Sunita's natal kin have failed to appear.

Amit's father asks the mahila panchayat caseworkers to accompany him to Sunita's natal home to confront her family. Two biradari panchayat members come with us. When we arrive at Sunita's natal home, the caseworkers formally introduce themselves as intermediaries 'whose job it is to mend homes'. Sunita's mother emphatically claims that her daughter has been ill-treated and that they will not send her back to the conjugal home. Meanwhile, the two members of the Kumhar Biradari Panchayat try to convince the men folk of Sunita's family to effect a reconciliation. In turn, the caseworkers use their skills to settle matters. Sunita's mother gives in on the condition that the mahila panchayat will take responsibility for Sunita's future welfare in her conjugal home. The caseworkers negotiate an agreement for the couple in the presence of Sunita's neighbours. Amit tells me privately that the biradari panchayat did not manage to assist them, and that it was the skill, persuasion, and arguments of the mahila panchayat caseworkers that ultimately prevailed.

Amit's father adopted an unyielding position, insisting that the Kumhar Biradari Panchayat should settle his son's dispute, while Amit's mother placed substantive faith in the mahila panchayat. There is a gender divide here regarding the mobilization and enlistment of resources and networks. Overall, the material is suggestive of the ineffectiveness of biradari panchayats, as Sunita's family discredited them on several occasions, and it was the mahila panchayat caseworkers who finally brought this prolonged impasse to an end. Clearly, the biradari panchayat's role was auxiliary to that of the mahila panchayat. Ultimately, Sunita and Amit's case ended up being dragged before the family courts at Patiala House (see Chapter 2 for details). At this stage, we need to reiterate how the modern legal system is impacting on the urban poor. In Chapter 3, I discussed how residents are aware of the notion of a court marriage, which represents the right to marry a person of one's own choice. The courts symbolize an alternative route to marriage, and although court marriage procedures are arduous (Mody 2008), couples confronted by trenchant parental opposition use the courts as a last resort. Chapter 4 indicated that there is no trend towards legal divorce, despite the high rate of secondary unions and marital break-ups. Yet in other domains, the courts are proving to be more relevant. In cases of marital breakdown, such as that of Amit and Sunita's, upwardly mobile parents often seek the intervention of the family courts. A clearer trend is for women to file cases, to retrieve dowry, and secure long-term maintenance. Though the success rate for resolving cases through formal courts is low, and though people complain of procedural delays, the few examples discussed here illustrate how, in a low-income urban setting, recourse to the legal system is sought only by those who can afford it. On the other hand, while the mahila panchayats are informal bodies, they have acquired tremendous influence in the field of dispute settlement.

The outright rejection by urban biradari panchayats of women in caste spaces had led women's groups to invent novel structures and to adopt different modes of conflict resolution. Against this backdrop, the mahila panchayat model evolved in Delhi so as to also provide alternatives to the male-dominated state apparatus.

The Mahila Panchayat in Mohini Nagar

The mahila panchayat established in 1997 in the neighbourhood of Mohini Nagar works systematically and full time on marital disputes. It is part of Action India, a women's NGO founded in 1974, as most women's organizations engaged in dispute settlement are affiliated to larger women's networks.[4] Action India is most renowned for its long-term engagement with *basti* women, who they have mobilized over civic struggles and in collective resistance against particular forms of gender inequality. Unlike some other women's groups in India, Action India, has no affiliation with state or political bodies.[5] Action India has introduced the concept of mahila panchayats,[6] or women's arbitration courts, in resettlement colonies.[7] Consider how these women's courts[8] advertise their services in their widely circulated pamphlet in Hindi:

[4] Since the 1970s, 1980s and 1990s, groups such as the All India Women's Education Fund Association (AIWEFA), Janwadi Mahila Samiti (JMS), National Commission for Women (NCW), Human Rights Law Network, Saheli, and Jagori have also been addressing marital conflict as part of their ongoing work.

[5] In contrast, the Janwadi Mahila Samiti (JMS), an ally of the Communist Party of India-Marxist Party, overtly encourages women clients who approach them for mediation to join the Marxist party.

[6] Action India has three other mahila panchayat branches in Delhi.

[7] Under a Delhi Commission for Women project, Action India took the lead in training thirty NGOs in Delhi to start their own mahila panchayats. As a result, there are now 54 new mahila panchayats run by different NGOs in the city's low-income neighbourhoods. Between January and July 2001, 650 cases were successfully resolved by these 54 new mahila panchayats (source: Action India).

[8] Merry (2006: 46–8) maps the historical trajectory of nari adalats (informal women's courts) whose genesis was the Mahila Samakhya empowerment programme and village-level processes and mobilization. In a vivid account, Bhatla and Rajan (2003: 1659) trace how women's arbitration fora evolved at the village level in Gujarat, West Bengal, and Tehri Garhwal. Both Merry and Bhatla and Rajan stress that although nari adalats are an adaptation of the

Sister
Do you need our help?
Are you unhappy in your home?
Is any type of violence being inflicted on you?
Do you need legal advice on family matters?

In my role as ethnographer, I captured the cultural orientation and organizational structure of the mahila panchayat. While Action India is supervised by a middle class woman (and by a team of middle class advisors), the responsibility for managing the mahila panchayats is delegated to SC and low-income women. Action India's middle class leadership believes that female residents of resettlement colonies should exclusively operate mahila panchayats as they not only have greater local knowledge about marital disputes but are also familiar with the caste and religious structures, customs, and realities of the lives of poor women. The Mohini Nagar mahila panchayat's main clientele also hails from Delhi's low-income neighbourhoods. Middle class women rarely ever file complaints or visit the mahila panchayat. The organization's arbitration procedures are not analogous with private and face-to-face counselling, a trend that is visible amongst the middle classes. The management of the mahila panchayat is in the hands of four caseworkers or counsellors who are employed as permanent staff. These four key players belong to the higher SC groups. The eldest is in her forties, the youngest is 27 years old, while the other two are in their late thirties. The organization also comprises twenty to thirty women in the age group 40–55 years, who are committed volunteer members from the resettlement colonies. These volunteer members, who share similar socio-economic backgrounds, and cultural practices, are assigned the title 'panchayat members'. The panchayat members add to the mahila panchayat's image of a community-based organization with local roots and one that is markedly distinguishable from state institutions. Their presence at and their role in the arbitration process fortifies the mahila panchayat assemblage and sends out the strong message that

---

existing caste panchayats, they specifically prioritize women's grievances and their subjectivities.

the mahila panchayat does not operate in isolation, but enjoys the vital support of local women. Given the mahila panchayat's self-positioning as a community-based organization, in actuality low-income communities, and the Mohini Nagar community, are neither homogeneous nor egalitarian, as they exhibit hierarchies of caste, income, and gender. While members of the mahila panchayat belong to their local community, their decisions, as I show later, may often conflict with community norms; in other instances, their judgements reproduce existing inequalities in the community.

Most of the volunteer panchayat members are illiterate. As a panchayat member put it: '*Behen*, your readers should know that we are unlettered women, but we play a role in mending homes.' The salaried caseworkers, on the other hand, have passed the tenth class (school education up to fifteen years of age) and have also received legal and gender empowerment training. A host of organizations, ranging from lower middle class feminist groups to middle class lawyers, have shaped their training. Caseworkers continue to participate in training sessions while receiving ongoing information from lawyers, human rights activists, and police officers. Nonetheless, it is difficult to gauge and comment upon how their acquired training may have shaped their ideological stance on marital dispute settlement. Their training has originated from various sources, and is thus shifting and complex in nature. Apart from providing training, Action India's middle class leadership has encouraged the mahila panchayat staff to build an indigenous grass-roots praxis with its own dynamic and character that specifically addresses the material needs of poor women. The mahila panchayat provides' an 'experiential space' (the Sabla Sangh) wherein their volunteer members and *basti* women can examine their lives and where women's political consciousness and solidarity are strengthened.[9] Consequently, the mahila panchayat has developed the ability to experiment with and refashion its own activism, which need not mirror a progressive feminist agenda. As I explicate later, at the mahila panchayat terms such as 'feminism' and 'equality' do not always configure at the forefront of their professional vocabulary.

[9] The Sabla Sangh forum was designed as an exclusive habitus for *basti* women: 'The Sabla Sangh is a women's space, free from subjugation to male domination. A space to give expression to thought and feelings, to share ideas, seek ways to resolve conflict, and negotiate.' Action India pamphlet, p. 2.

The mahila panchayat office in the resettlement colonies is housed in an unassuming four-storeyed building located at the junction of a main road. A large poster on the office wall conspicuously displays the scales of justice, identifying the organization as a women's court.[10] All the mahila panchayat members live close to the office, so that clients may easily have access to them in the event of an emergency or crisis. On a normal day, non-working and working women can be seen visiting the mahila panchayat, fervently asking how they can file a case against their spouse. They are usually accompanied by members of their natal family who offer these women support. So despite having the support of their parents and despite being entitled to shelter in the natal home (cf. arranged marriages), why do women choose to file complaints with mahila panchayats? Chapter 2 brought out how daughters recognize the limitations of refuge and do not always invest complete trust in their natal kin. Rather than taking the normative refuge route and recourse to parental intervention, many are looking for instantaneous solutions. Mahila panchayats offer women functional, alternative structures of support and a different platform from which they can re-evaluate and renegotiate the marital bond, and from which their marital tensions can be addressed. The *raison d'être* for harnessing mahila panchayats is that these are autonomous bodies, removed from the everyday politics, manipulation, and dictates of familial and kin networks. Furthermore, mahila panchayats located in a residential neighbourhood fill a critical void in the lives of women who are victims of extreme battering (Bhatla and Rajan 2003). Neighbours are often reluctant to interfere in cases of serious domestic conflict. Caseworkers will, however, resourcefully arrange for shelter and protection. Women can now register cases with the assistance of their natal kin, as they are aware that mahila panchayats may procure them longer-term solutions than the temporary mediation attempts activated through natal kin. By bypassing the natal kin

---

[10] Women also refer to the mahila panchayat as a *sanstha* (organization) and an NGO. For more on the mahila panchayat in Mohini Nagar (South Delhi), see Magar (2000). Magar examines mahila panchayat strategies for addressing domestic violence, while also assessing women's health status in Delhi's resettlement colonies. Her study offers useful insights into the activism of Action India.

route, women are also asserting their agency and are availing of new services that are on offer in their neighbourhoods.

Arbitration at the Mahila Panchayat

The Mahila Panchayat Office
The young woman sitting in the centre is narrating her complaint.
She is surrounded by members of her natal kin and the
volunteer panchayat members.

Ethnographically detailing the complaints filed by women will enable us to foreground the nature of their grievances, to understand the role of their accompanying marriage narratives, and to comprehend the importance of gender-based performance in an all-women's court. This ethnographic exercise will aid in tracing how the mahila panchayat members resolve disputes, what authority they exercise in an urban environment, and how credible and sustainable their solutions turn out to be. When a client registers a complaint, her grievance is first written up by a caseworker (cf. Magar 2000). Thereafter, a letter, written on the organization's letterhead paper along with its logo of the scales of justice, is sent to the spouse asking him to present himself at the mahila panchayat where the case will be arbitrated. The wife's natal kin and her affines must also present themselves, as in the context of marital discord they, too, will be closely questioned. Cases are arbitrated every Wednesday, from noon to 3:00 p.m., where, over several cups of tea, intense bargaining over marital solutions is carried out. The 'plaintiff' and the 'accused' sit face to face in the centre of an open space and narrate their accounts to a jury of caseworkers and panchayat members. The following personal testimonies are representative of cases that appeared before the panchayat throughout 2000–02. The first complaint centres on male suspicion and illustrates how women in arranged marriages file cases against their spouses.

Complaint of Suspicion

Case filed by Ramvati[11] on 17 January 2001

Duration of marriage: Twenty years; three children.

> *Ramvati (wife's account):* 'He kept me well for the first seven years of our marriage. After that, he would routinely suspect me (*sak karne laga*), but I continued to put up with him. Then he went to jail for ten years. I make paper envelopes for a living. Since he has come out of jail, he suspects me all the time. He asks me why I was roaming around in the park the other day. He keeps threatening that he will trouble my *pihar* members. I ask him on what basis is he always suspecting me. On Sunday, he hit me in front of my mother-in-law and my children. Well, that's it. I want to leave him and live with my children.'

> *Husband's account:* 'We loved each other so much when we got married. Even she used to really love me. Then we had

---

[11] I have anonymized women's names, as they are normally the ones who file cases. Permission was sought and received by the mahila panchayat to record all the cases in public. Clients often narrated their accounts in a manner that comes across as disjointed and fragmented. I have tried to truncate and reconstruct their accounts, while retaining the original flavour as far as possible. I would like to acknowledge my own complicity during the arbitration procedure, as I, too, questioned and interrogated couples.

children and they died. Then we had another daughter and after that I went to jail. When I came out on bail, we would go and buy vegetables together. I used to cry so much for her and she used to cry so much for me. After I went to jail, she began selling scrap. When I was in jail, I used to send her letters. Then I fell very ill and the jailers released me. The other day, I saw her with her *jeeja* (sister's husband). She told me that they had work. When I asked her *jeeja* what work they had, I was told that they were going to see a lawyer. Which lawyer, I asked them. The high court one, I was told. She said she had gone to Purana Kila [Old Fort, located in Old Delhi] to see the lawyer, but I saw her in the park. One day, she and the *jeeja* went to buy medicines together. She even went off alone to meet her *chacha* and *chachi* (father's younger brother and the brother's wife). But otherwise she is always making a fuss at home that she is not well.'

10 volunteer panchayat members were present at Ramvati and her husband's interrogation.

Panchayat members to husband: 'Why did you hit her the other day?'

Panchayat members to Ramvati: 'What's this between you and your *jeeja*? If you want to eliminate suspicion in your marriage, you should tell your mother-in-law exactly where you are going.'

Husband: 'I saw her going out the other day with her *jeeja*. But earlier she had told me that she was not well.'

Ramvati: 'I want to leave him.' *She starts threatening to end the marriage.*

Panchayat members to Ramvati: 'Think about whether you really want to leave him. The suspicion can be cleared up here and now. You have three children together.'
They urge Ramvati to think about it. Her husband starts to weep and begs for forgiveness. He remains very agitated.

Caseworker to husband: 'What do you expect? You have been in jail for ten years. She has brought up your children and has not left you. Then you accuse her of all kinds of things.'

Husband: 'I will never beat her again.'

The hearing of Ramvati's case resumes after a week. This delay is deliberate, to give the couple time to reflect on whether they really want to dissolve their marriage or not, and if not, then the type of solution they are interested in pursuing. At the next hearing, Ramvati confirms that she wants reconciliation, but insists that her husband must improve his behaviour. The mahila panchayat negotiates this agreement for her through a process of bargaining and brainstorming.

The conditions (*sart*) or requirements for the husband are that he should not beat Ramvati or suspect her again. The conditions for Ramvati are that she should not leave her conjugal house without informing her husband or her mother-in-law. She should be allowed to visit her *pihar,* but is cautioned that her visits should not be excessive.

After negotiating the agreement, the panchayat members engage in an animated discussion about the possibility of Ramvati being beaten to death by her husband's kin. Her husband is warned that if she is harmed in any way, he will be held responsible. Thereafter, Ramvati and her husband's family sign the official mahila panchayat document stipulating the conditions to which they have all agreed. Such a process of negotiation occurs in all cases where a final solution has been reached. Towards the closing of the case hearing, Ramvati's husband comments: 'I give credit to my sisters for looking after my wife when I was in jail. She would be dead without them. I used to write letters to my sisters from jail, asking them to look after my wife.' His sister responds: 'Yes, there is love between us and our sister-in-law.'

Reconciliation was achieved and the couple did not revisit the mahila panchayat office in 2001. According to the mahila panchayat's records, and in the wake of close monitoring during follow-up house visits, the couple's marital tensions have dissipated significantly.

As male suspicion is a frequent source of marital friction, women like Ramvati file a complaint exclusively about having to face protracted allegations of infidelity. Complaints follow specific narrative strategies. Before presenting their foremost complaint, women begin by evaluating how their husbands have treated them over the years: 'I was treated well for the first year of my marriage. Then he started to beat me.' Marriage narratives also tend to be strikingly gendered. Women in arranged marriages are vocal in narrating their problems, and the core of their narrative is centred on anger, betrayal, feelings of injustice, and frustration with the perceived lack of alternatives. Men's marriage narratives differ from those of women. Geetha (1998: 315, 326), who has worked as a marriage counsellor in Chennai, notes that male narratives overwhelmingly rest on scrutinizing, dramatizing, and moralizing about women's fidelity. Men in Delhi also speak in a language of unequivocal suspicion. By deploying the trope of suspicion, they question the paternity of their children. Oldenburg (2002: 216), who in the early 1980s worked with Saheli, a women's centre in Delhi, makes a notable point about marriage narratives. According to her, women's narratives begin with marriage but exhibit their 'discontinuous lives', while men's narratives exude virilocal confidence and revolve around continuity. Oldenburg (2002) and Geetha (1998) explain how marriage narratives are recast as life stories or allegories. Similarly, Catherine Kohler Reissman (2003), who has worked extensively on the topic of disruptive life events such as divorce, chronic illness, and infertility, states that she received 'long stories' in response to straightforward questions, which she interpreted as digressions. In the Delhi narratives, many digressions feature as stories about the couple's struggles in a city. For instance, Ramvati's husband described the dramatic deaths of their children and his jail sentence at considerable length. Reissman directs our attention to the fact that personal narratives contain performative features, such as appeals to the audience and gestures or body movements, which are evident in the open weeping that some men exhibit during the interrogation. Weeping also symbolizes powerlessness, for many men feel threatened, intimidated, and outnumbered in an all-women's forum. A particular form of men's comportment is revealed: the respondent is sceptical, defensive, insecure, and desires sympathy. To avoid being humiliated publicly, some men attend these case hearings alone or with only a brother, a father, or other relative. Women, on the other hand, will always bring an entourage of natal kin, relatives, neighbours, and friends.

The role of the mahila panchayat members in their official capacity is to reconcile couples. They offer reconciliation services to 'mend a home, rather than to break one' (*ghar basana*). Their policy is to assist women with legal divorce only if reconciliation attempts have failed completely. In the interim, they take great pride in fixing strained marriages. They are not strict advocates of monogamous marriage, because some of the members have themselves endured marital dissolution. Their contention is that the family courts have been established to deal with legal separation. It appears that many of their clients share their approach towards reconciliation since they are equally keen to avoid a formal break-up. A standard request by many women is for a settlement to the problem. Often women want a renegotiation of the status quo, or for their husbands to be berated publicly. Another common plea is for separation combined with the payment of a maintenance allowance. Bhatla and Rajan (2003) note that female clients approach the West Bengal and Tehri Garhwal arbitration forums with the intention of restoring their marriages. Rebecca Surtees (2003: 35) has explored how Cambodian women seek to repair their marriages: 'In seeking to change the relationship, getting advice from friends, finding temporary shelter, having someone intervene, or setting conditions for their return, women are acting out their resistance to domestic violence within the framework of staying'. Surtees, when discussing women's agency, points out that feminist debates tend to become narrowly dichotomized between 'victims' (those staying in the relationship) and 'agents' (those leaving the relationship), but in her view, women who decide to seek marital solutions are also expressing their choice and agency. Surtees's argument that women who wish to reconcile are not passive negotiators is a valid one. She is correct in that feminist debates are often fractured along the lines of 'reconciliation' and 'non-reconciliation'. Some Delhi women's groups believe that Action India needs to actively alter its policy that makes reconciliation the main focus. They are critical of Action India's project of restoring the patriarchal institution of marriage, and have limited faith in reconciliation attempts.

The final agreements, consisting of two or three sentences, that are drawn up by counsellors at the end of each case hearing constitute a significant part of the conflict-resolution system. How effective are these 'compromise pacts' (Magar 2000) or formulaic agreements in altering male behaviour? Women confirm that such agreements do have the effect of diminishing male violence and suspicion in particular. Bhatla and Rajan (2003), who evaluated the impact of similar agreements, verify that in a substantial number of cases the violence ceased. More importantly, they add: 'A very significant finding was that complete resolution of the problem was not a necessary precursor for a positive change in the women's self-image. Almost all the women in all sites reported an increase in confidence that can be attributed to the process of case resolution' (2003: 1663). Many Delhi couples whose cases were arbitrated in 2000–02 did not revisit the mahila panchayat. The caseworkers (including myself) visited couples in their homes over a three-month period to assess whether their marital tensions had dissipated significantly or not. After three months, if the couple did not contact a caseworker, the mahila panchayat established that they were not in need of further mediation. Over the course of 2000–02, I found that many of the mahila panchayat agreements were sustainable.[12] Mediation and counselling do stabilize ruptured marriages, although counsellers do not fully repudiate or challenge the existing patrilineal structures. Most of all, if the problem has not entirely resolved itself, women gain the strength, through counselling, to tackle domestic tensions and threats. It is, of course, impossible to predict what will happen to couples in the years to come or to determine whether continuity will always be maintained with regard to the agreements.[13]

Drop-in Visits and Letters

The role of the mahila panchayat extends beyond arbitration in cases of conflict resolution. One of their main activities is advising

[12] A detailed documentation of 25 case studies of arbitration in the period 2000–02 revealed that reconciliation was achieved in 15 of these cases.

[13] I was unable to follow up post-mediation trajectories beyond one year. Only more extensive and comparative research can shed light on whether mediation can have positive long-term effects on altering male behaviour.

and counselling women. They receive many 'drop-in visits' by women who inquire how they can secure consensual unions and if they have legal rights in the event of marital abandonment. The mahila panchayats offers women vital yet simplified legal and non-legal information. They inform clients about important and new applications (for example, missing person's application and widow's pension). From time to time, couples request counsellors to attend their secondary union rituals and ask that letters should be signed in their presence to secure the permanence of a secondary union. Battered women leave 'letters' with the organization that serve as a form of self-protection when they fear that their lives are in danger. Kalavati handed a letter to the mahila panchayat. Referring to her husband's violent behaviour, she wrote: 'In my nine years with him, all I have heard is that I am a whore. If I talk to anyone in my *gali,* he suspects me. He now thinks that I am having an affair with the barber. He is threatening that either he will commit suicide or he will kill me. I have come to you because my life is in danger.' Kalavati's letter, translated from Hindi, is reproduced below. The mahila panchayat keeps a record of such letters and follows up on battered women such as Kalavati.

> Dear Members,
>
> [The letter begins with details of her house number and *gali.*] I got married on the 5th of November 1993. After that he began beating me regularly. For years I have put up with it, but now I can no longer do so. Three days ago, on the night of 24.2.2001, he began abusing me. Then he began beating my children. After that he began threatening me that if I did not leave his house, he would commit suicide. As I did not leave, he took my *chunni* [scarf worn with the *salwar kameez*] and tied himself around the fan [that is, wrapped one end of the scarf around his neck and tied the other end to the ceiling fan]. I immediately managed to disentangle him from the fan and he was saved. I am informing you all that if he tries to commit suicide again, I should not be held responsible. If he tries to kill

me, he and his family should be held responsible
for I always live in fear of my life. Today he gave
me a warning that within three days he will throw
me out. I request you all to think about the future
of my children and me and tell us what we can
do. I am truly grateful.

The Mahila Panchayat's Framework of Resolution

Given the mahila panchayat's multifaceted services and self-imaging as a women's court, what authority does it exercise? Although its procedures and decisions have no legal backing, it nevertheless commands respect because it promotes a flexible and nuanced approach to conflict resolution. The police and courts are incapable of procuring solutions for complex gender grievances such as the complaint of suspicion (Bhatla and Rajan 2003). The mahila panchayat has local knowledge of male conduct, and hence is more suitably placed when it comes to addressing such grievances (ibid.). Its solutions are constructive and helpful, and these replace the judgments handed down by the law. Thus its greatest strength is precisely that it is not a law-enforcing body. For example, the caseworkers are engaged in unending dialogue and engagement with the couples that approach them. They are trained to handle the frequently volatile reactions of men. Marital negotiations at the mahila panchayat are open-ended; women and men are allowed a dissenting voice, and concerted efforts are made to arrive at effective and long-lasting solutions (cf. Bhatla and Rajan 2003). The mahila panchayat's mediation processes are also aimed at enhancing affection amongst couples, as counsellors make appeals based on the role of marriage in the couple's emotional life. Couples are advised to begin their marriage afresh, to talk lovingly to one another, and to not take their marriage for granted. What is noteworthy about the mahila panchayat's efforts in this context is that it propagates and works within a more democratic framework compared to the police and the courts; its procedures differ from the fixed settlements made by courts, biradari panchayats as well by the police, which some wives might not want husbands to endure (cf. Bhatla and Rajan 2003). As the counsellors point out, punishments and jail sentences should be measures of the last resort. Women claim that they are deterred from approaching courts and police stations, which are associated in the public mind with corrupt practices (bribes and muscle power) and complicated procedures. This stance explains the mahila panchayat's popularity, for though there are other legal and non-legal channels for grievance redressal available to low-income urban residents, the mahila panchayat offers accessible services. The absence of a conventional legal framework only serves to enhance the counsellors' ability to bargain solutions that involve day-to-day renegotiations of power and relationships within the household.

While mahila panchayats are not legal institutions, they convey the impression of following formal procedures (cf. Merry 2006), as caseworkers have legal knowledge and disputes are settled in a public forum. The constitution of a public forum, consisting of a body of elderly citizens, lends credibility and legitimacy to their procedures. Local leaders, the courts, and the police have come to recognize the mahila panchayat's procedures, and in some instances the latter collaborates with the judiciary and the state in dispensing justice.[14] In some instances, recourse to the mahila panchayat is a necessary first step in a longer-term exercise that might involve the police, the courts, and lawyers. As the mahila panchayat exerts considerable influence, the majority of men do appear at the Wednesday panchayat when cases are registered against them. If they do not comply, influential community leaders are requested to pressurize them to attend. It goes without saying that husbands and their families are deeply embarrassed and disgraced when cases are registered against them. Vanita, who lives in a *basti* in Khanpur, filed a case of extreme ill-treatment against her husband and mother-in-law. For weeks on end, Vanita's neighbours talked of how badly Vanita's affines had treated her and how a complaint lodged with the mahila panchayat would affect her husband's reputation. Vanita's husband, nevertheless, fully cooperated with the mahila panchayat. Overall, whereas some men defy the mahila

---

[14] On every Thursday of the week, the caseworkers meet to discuss whether some of their cases will benefit from judicial intervention. They liaison with middle class feminist lawyers who assist them pro bono.

panchayat, others are keen to seek solutions as they, too, experience the process of marital breakdown as tension ridden. The case studies in this chapter will illustrate how men cooperate with the mahila panchayat and how the organization's collective strength helps in pressurizing husbands to make concessions. The caseworkers use their skills and training not to antagonize the men, but rather to convince them that their narratives are given equal weight as those of the women.

Interestingly, in other milieus, different motivations prompt men to comply with agreements and to keep a marriage intact, as Parry's (2001) study shows. Parry reveals how the wives of the Bhilai Steel Plant (BSP) employees often approach the company's counselling cell with grievances about bigamy and strained conjugal relations. Marital reconciliation for BSP employees and their wives is achieved through compromises that are 'made to work' as male employees are keen not to relinquish prestigious and well-paid BSP jobs: 'Heavy hints about criminal cases and disciplinary proceedings generally ensure that love and understanding prevail' (2001: 811). The company ironically protects women and wives from its own employees by discouraging marital break-ups. Parry attributes this unusual responsibility on the part of BSP to the orthodox family values promoted by its middle class managers. Such values are an extension of BSP's modernization project wherein monogamous marriage constitutes the ideal: 'For them, I suspect it is a matter of reforming the morals of men, who must be encouraged to become new model citizens, as it is of providing succour to women and children' (2001: 812).

Frequently Reported Grievances

Women from different Delhi neighbourhoods approach the mahila panchayat with cognate-related conflicts that are reproduced across marriages (see Table 5.1). The highest number of reported grievances are *kharcha-pani* complaints. This grievance connotes ill-treatment and neglect on the part of a husband towards his family (see Chapter 2), and receives immediate attention from counsellors. Magar (2000: 131) points out that according to the Indian Penal Code, Section 125, men are required by law to provide maintenance to their wives.

Table 5.1: Marital grievances reported at the Mahila Panchayat

Primary (main) grievance	Number of cases	Secondary grievance	Number of cases
Kharcha-pani (accompanied by alcohol abuse, domestic violence, and suspicion of marital infidelity)	7		
Male infidelity	4		
Love marriage problems: violence and desertion	4		
Suspicion and violence	3		
Ill-treatment by affines	1		
Alcohol abuse	1		
Natal family not allowing wife to return to conjugal family (male grievance)	1		
Other (cases difficult to classify)	4		
		Dowry harassment	7
		Ill-treatment by affines	3
		Male infidelity	2
		'Wrong sex'	2
		Harassment over remarriage	1

Note: The information is based on 25 cases that were heard by the mahila panchayat in 2000–02.

When reporting the *kharcha-pani* grievance, women invariably stress three recurrent complaints: domestic violence, suspicion, and alcoholism (see Chapter 2). Domestic violence seems to be the common determinant. Women report male infidelity as both primary and secondary complaints. Mahila panchayat members normally react to alleged male infidelity with moral outrage.

Another grievance that appeared twice in 2001 concerns 'wrong sex' (sexual perversion). Here women claim that they are coerced into having anal intercourse and are coaxed to perform degrading acts based on the use of pornographic material. The mahila panchayat considers these sexual activities to be humiliating for women. Magar (2000: 64) reports that for the mahila panchayat, 'coercive sex' is akin to an act of murder: 'Sex in the wrong way, or anal/oral sex, was rated slightly more serious than kill/attempts to kill. Caseworkers frequently reported that sex in the wrong way was degrading and that it positions a woman lower than even an animal. A few claimed that it was worse than death'. Men are, therefore, strongly condemned if their wives complain of sexual perversion. This stance demonstrates that the mahila panchayat has a rigid conception of what constitutes appropriate sexual behaviour.

Women who choose love marriages also avail of the mahila panchayat's services with the hope that a women's court will employ different approaches to solving their problems *vis-à-vis* the conciliatory approaches adopted by natal kin and the local community.

Next, a commonly reported secondary grievance is the complaint of dowry harassment. In 2000–02, I did, however, encounter a single case where a woman's complaint centred exclusively on dowry-related violence. As a caseworker confirms: 'Everyone these days gives dowry, and women do get troubled over it. But when specific dowry harassment cases come to us, we find that the problem is more complex and other issues invariably arise.' Oldenburg (2002) noted that marital disputes in the 1980s were being framed primarily under the label of dowry violence, when in reality the nature of the problem was irrelevant to dowry. Related to Oldenburg's observation, we note today a concerted shift in the theory and practice of urban counselling. Caseworkers will monitor women's motivations for filing dowry-related complaints as they are now more aware of the complexity of marital problems.

Another grievance is collective ill-treatment by affines. Women claim that the latter abuse them verbally and overburden them with household tasks. Other complex grievances that are also articulated are difficult to classify, as the marital relationship is strained by a multitude of factors[15] (categorized in Table 5.1 as 'difficult to classify').

The mahila panchayat also receives a small number of complaints from men whose principal grievance relates to the wife's refusal to return from the natal home. As a matter of fact, the most common accusation made by men is alleged interference from the wife's natal kin. Men also complain about the wife's non-conformity to appropriate gender roles, such as not cooking food on time.

Bargaining for Solutions: The Mahila Panchayat's Articulations of Marriage(s)

Failed Cases of Arbitration

The types of discourses articulated by the mahila panchayat on marriage and its normative views on what constitutes a proper marriage are subjects that deserve more detailed attention. I elicit the organization's interpretation of the validity and importance of arranged marriages through the critical issue of how agreements are negotiated. The case studies described below illustrate how agreements are negotiated, but, more importantly, show that arbitration need not always be successful or workable even in a women's forum.

Domestic Violence, Infidelity, and Dowry

Case filed by Kajal on 11 July 2001

Duration of marriage: Over a year

> *Kajal (wife's account):* 'He kept me well for the first week of our arranged marriage. Then he got a transfer to Mumbai

---

[15] The mahila panchayat classifies its cases into the specific categories of *kharcha-pani,* violence, suspicion, alcoholism, dowry harassment, ill-treatment by affines, remarriage without divorce, sexual perversion, rape, sexual harassment, deserting the wife, marriage through deception, divorce, property disputes, and wives not wishing to return to their conjugal homes.

with the Mahanagar Telephone Nigam Limited (MTNL).
My parents live in the resettlement colonies. We lived in
Mumbai for eight months. Then he began beating me. I put
up with it. Then I got pregnant, but he went on beating me.
Then my *chachi* (father's younger brother's wife) brought
me back to Delhi. I have not had a day's happiness since I
got married. He demands dowry from me. He is also having
an affair with a widow.'

Kajal's chacha (father's younger brother) intervenes: 'Kajal's
mother-in-law has been spreading news in the village that
her son is having an affair with a widow.'

Kajal: 'Yes, I have seen the connection between him and this
widow. I have seen the love between them. When I tell him
that we should live in Delhi, he turns around and accuses
me of having lovers in Delhi. Not once has he given me
kharcha-pani.'

*Husband remains silent and refrains from giving his own account
of events.*

Panchayat members to husband: 'Wives do not come here
and tell lies. She has filed a case against you in Delhi for
particular reasons. Why would your mother alert people in
your village to the fact that you are involved with a widow?'

Husband: 'I am not involved with a widow.'

Husband's younger brother intervenes: 'Look, my mother just
said that if there is another woman involved, bring her in
front of a panchayat so that things can be sorted out.'

Husband: 'Kajal keeps badgering me about getting
transferred back to Delhi.'

Panchayat members to Kajal: 'After marriage, a woman resides
with her husband. You cannot demand that he shifts back
to Delhi.' *(They are very insistent on this point.)*

Husband: 'We men do not have a voice in your forum. You only take up cases for women here.'

Panchayat members respond: 'We listen to both sides of the story. At least a hundred cases come up here every year. And we do not break homes; we join them. What do you not like about our organization? Are we not settling cases properly here?'

Panchayat members: 'What solution do you both want?'

Husband: 'Members, I do not want to break up my home.'
Caseworker to Kajal (in a challenging tone): 'The truth is that you want to live near your *pihar* in Delhi. You want him to be transferred from Mumbai.'

Kajal: 'Yes, I want him to be transferred. If we live in Delhi, my *pihar* is there to protect me. I was never beaten while we were living in Delhi because he is afraid of my *pihar*.'

Panchayat members are outraged by Kajal's demand: 'How can you expect him to transfer to Delhi? This is an unreasonable demand. We can settle this case for you here. He will never misbehave again.' *The anger continues on both sides. Kajal's natal kin constantly intervene, taking her side.*

Panchayat members to Kajal: 'Your *pihar* does not want your happiness. They will not let you remain married. Pampered daughters who make the slightest fuss get parental support.'

Panchayat members: 'These days, filing cases has become a joke. Filing cases is a full-time occupation for people like you. Try and deal with the courts.'

Kajal's husband, who is agitated during the hearing, abuses his father-in-law, who reacts by throwing a shoe at him. They engage in hand-to-hand fighting. The members try to stop the violence. Kajal's natal kin immediately flee when the mahila panchayat threatens to call the police.

Outcome: Kajal is living with her natal kin in Delhi. The mahila panchayat asserts that she is not 'cooperating' with them as she still wants her husband to be transferred to Delhi. The husband is 'cooperating' with them. They have transferred his case to an NGO in Mumbai where he is living currently. Reconciliation was not possible in this case.

Kajal's case demonstrates how attempts at bargaining can be unsuccessful, and may even further disrupt the status quo. Preceding the violent scenes at the mahila panchayat, the couple, who had been married for just over a year, are no longer in dialogue; their case is at an impasse and an NGO in Mumbai has been given the task of reviving it. Hence, not all cases end happily or satisfactorily despite intervention by the mahila panchayat. Arbitration may lead to a completely and unexpectedly different turn of events, as in Kajal's case. To understand what went wrong in this particular case, we need to take a step back and scrutinize how solutions are negotiated or bargained. To negotiate a solution with counsellors, couples must state the preferences, conditions, and circumstances that they believe can improve, mend, or stabilize their relationship. A woman's preference may be that she should never be beaten again. A man may want his wife to spend less time in the natal unit. The process of articulating preferences by both wife and husband leads to a thorough review of marital rights and obligations. As Bhatla and Rajan observe: 'In the arbitration process, the fabric of relationships is often laid threadbare on what is right and wrong in relationships, what are its boundaries, responsibilities and duties' (2003: 1662). In endorsing the preferences stated by both husband and wife, the four caseworkers involved in Kajal's case are nonetheless the final arbitrators. Kajal's preference was for her husband to be transferred from Mumbai to Delhi as a preventive measure against domestic violence. She believed that close contact with her natal kin in Delhi would place her in a favourable position. The mahila panchayat deemed her preference unreasonable as this would necessitate her husband's relocation after he had just taken up a new job. Instead, a solution was proposed that would eliminate—or at least reduce—their marital tensions without a major relocation.

The mahila panchayat emphatically states that its clients have to 'cooperate' with the team in seeking solutions. Kajal was ostensibly not cooperating with the members as she had brazenly rejected their recommendations. This irked the mahila panchayat members, who began to turn their attention away from the central problem of domestic violence. On questioning a caseworker about this deviation in focus, I was informed that they had a right to challenge Kajal: 'The possibility of an ulterior motive must be eliminated. Natal kin can manipulate the process.' In Chapter 2, we saw that it is not unusual for a mother to thwart her daughter's efforts at marital adjustment. In the same way, the process and aftermath of reconciliation, as caseworkers emphasize, can also be obstructed by parental interference and near residence. Overall, reconciliation was hampered in Kajal's case as her aim was to bargain for stronger preferences. She felt that the mahila panchayat's solution would not carry weight in Mumbai. She had a strong fallback position for in the eventuality of non-resolution, her natal kin were willing to keep her. Other factors may also impede reconciliation, as seen in Chanda's complicated case study, described below.

Violence and Harassment from Affines over Paternity and the First Marriage

Case filed by Chanda on 29 August 2001

Duration of marriage: Four and a half years

> *Chanda (wife's account):* 'This is my second marriage arranged by my parents. After marriage, he [the husband] looked after me well for the first fifteen days. Then my mother-in-law and sister-in-law began troubling me. When I became pregnant, he alleged that the child was not his. According to him, I was carrying another man's child. They keep harassing me over my first marriage (*pahli shaadi*). I had to have the baby aborted because he hit me when I was two months' pregnant. I do not want to leave him, but I want us to live separately from his family.'

Husband's account: 'She does not make tea for me in the morning. She behaves like a queen. She claims her first husband was a *hijra* [transvestite], but he was not. She has two children by him. The child she aborted was not mine. The dates do not add up. *(He encourages the members to calculate the dates of their wedding, Chanda's last period, and the abortion.)* How can an abortion take place without a father's name? That's why she had it done in a private clinic, because in a government hospital they need the father's name. I do not want a divorce either. If she wants to live with me, her *pihar* should not turn up every day and make a fuss.'

Panchayat members: 'Yes, we will ensure in the agreement that her *pihar* does not turn up every day.'

Panchayat members to husband: 'Can you live separately from your parents? That is what she wants.'

Husband: 'I have just got a new job as a driver. I do not earn enough.'

Chanda and her husband agree to a reconciliation based on the following conditions:

Chanda's husband should stop troubling her over her first marriage (*'pahli shaadi ke tane nehi dena'*). Chanda should be allowed to visit her *pihar,* but her visits should not be excessive. To avoid conflict, they should live separately from the husband's kindred (he accepts this condition). Chanda should perform her household duties properly.

On 24 September 2001, less than a month later, the couple returned. The members had negotiated earlier, on behalf of Chanda, that her husband should establish a nuclear household. This time it is Chanda's husband who has brought his wife to the mahila panchayat. He claimed that he had spent an entire week searching for a new house, but now Chanda does not want to move out.

Caseworkers to Chanda: 'You specifically told us that you do not want to live in a joint family. What do you want now?'

Chanda: 'I want our own floor in his four-storeyed plot. His brother and wife have their own floor, so why can't we? We can get the couple who are renting it to move out.'

Caseworkers: 'How many times have you changed your mind? Your husband has spent a week trying to arrange a new home for you. Now you say that you do not want to move out. Do you not want to make this marriage work?'

Husband: 'She never wants to have sexual relations with me. I had to force her on our wedding night. This is the main problem.'

Panchayat member to Chanda: 'Chanda, are your mind and heart not in this marriage?'

Panchayat members to Chanda: 'This is your second marriage. How long can you stay with your parents? You cannot refuse your husband sexual relations.'

Panchayat members ask Chanda privately why she refuses sexual relations.

Chanda: 'He does not behave properly. He is like an animal. Once when I refused him, he hit me badly. Since the time I have filed this complaint, his family has begun to trouble me even more.'

To satisfy Chanda's needs, her husband is told to make arrangements for a separate floor in his four-storeyed plot. On 29 September 2001, he reappeared at the mahila panchayat. He told us that Chanda's parents had come to visit her. After they left, she locked herself in the kitchen and turned on the gas in an attempt to commit suicide. The police were called and they broke the door down. The police saw that Chanda was fully responsible for trying to harm herself. The next day, Chanda collected all her dowry items and left for her natal home.

Outcome: Chanda has withdrawn her case and ceased all cooperation. Reconciliation was not possible.

Despite the mahila panchayat's painstaking efforts at reconciliation, there are many examples, like the cases of Chanda and Kajal, where the client main party remains dissatisfied with the bargaining outcomes, and their next step will be to approach a different organization, grievance cell, or mediator. Moreover, women may lose faith in the mahila panchayat process and they may decide not to visit or cooperate with the organization again. Cases such as Chanda's are also too problematic and difficult to reconcile, as they are shaped in complex ways by other emotions and household dynamics. In the case of Chanda, the sequence of events and changing circumstances led to delaying and digressive tactics. The caseworkers concluded that Chanda was not keen on working to save her marriage. As she refused to turn up for some of the hearings, it became clear that other factors were straining her marriage. Her husband revealed that she was refusing him sexual relations, while Chanda confided that sexual relations with him were accompanied by coercion. Furthermore, reconciliation agreements, like the elaborate one drawn up for Chanda, can backfire and be inimical for a woman if her parents-in-law insist that she has disgraced them by filing a complaint. So even after a solution has been obtained, a woman may face increased harassment from her husband and parents-in-law, who fear loss of respect in their *gali*.

It should be clarified that women from the neighbourhood may not always avail of the services offered by their local mahila panchayat. Kabeer's (2001) analysis shows that women from the same social class may not respond identically to the services that are on offer. She separates women into a socially subordinate category and a highly diverse group of individuals: 'There are always some women who will not or are not permitted to take up the possibilities on offer' (2001: 82). This explains why not all women contact the mahila panchayat when they face adversity and nor do they give into the counsellors' demands as their agentival capacity plays an important role. It needs to be specified that the multiplication of mahila panchayats has not led to a significant elimination of domestic violence in low-income localities or to a fundamental shift in attitudes. The mahila panchayat concept is a salient addition to the array of non-legal institutions that are attempting to carve out a niche for themselves and to eliminate violence in the conjugal home. These institutions are making an impact, but given their limited resources they cannot by themselves bring about rapid change. To achieve far-reaching change, better laws,[16] more effective and gender-sensitive legal systems, and extensive material transformations are needed to accompany the efforts of women's groups.

Significantly, it is the mahila panchayat that regulates and determines the outcomes of bargaining. While couples voice their views openly, it is the mahila panchayat that ultimately makes the final decision. What are the ideologies and discourses that guide its decisions? The mahila panchayat validates the male breadwinner ideology. In their discourses there is an overwhelming emphasis on the need for men to assume or resume provider obligations. As it stands, the mahila panchayat's comprehension of the institution of arranged marriage is analogous with the local community's conception of marital relations. According to this local exegesis, marital duties, economic arrangements, and the breadwinner– housewife model form the core of marital relations (Chapter 2). Mirroring the views of the local community, the mahila panchayat does not embrace the notion of companionate marriage. Its agreements reinforce the understanding that women should subscribe to hierarchical gender roles. Mahila panchayat agreements thus actively revolve around bargaining with patriarchy (Kandiyoti 1988: 274). Kandiyoti calls this the 'patriarchal bargain', which, she argues, leads women to optimize their life options within a concrete set of constraints. These patriarchal bargains provide women with varying levels of potential for actively resisting or submitting in the face of oppression. In engendering patriarchal bargains, the mahila panchayat disavows forms of violence, yet it endorses the hegemonic discourse of the patrilineal ideology or the

---

[16] The Domestic Violence Act 2005, which has extensive provisions for women facing all kinds of violence, is a step in the right direction.

belief that a woman's place is in her husband's home. Women like Kajal are advised to compromise with and adjust to conditions in the place where their husbands work or live. The mahila panchayat holds the position that after marriage women should be entitled to certain rights in their natal home, yet their actual rights lie in their conjugal home, and this institutional separation characterizes marriage. To stabilize marriage, women are cautioned against becoming over-assimilated into their natal kin network, as they may unduly abdicate their marital rights, while over-assimilation also creates conflict for men. This key bargaining adjustment that cautions against over-assimilation is commonly voiced, and receives inordinate attention at the mahila panchayat. A more textured analysis of why the mahila panchayat, as a women's assemblage, chooses not to contest patriarchal bargains or why urban activists do not question the patrilineal social structure is yet to ensue.

Discourses on Romantic Love and Love Marriages

The counsellors' ideological position on romantic love and their attitude towards love marriages are other important indicators of how the mahila panchayat members understand a proper marriage. The following two case studies examine complaints filed by young women in love marriages.

Ill-treatment and Violence

Case filed by Shazia on 4 July 2001

Duration of marriage: Two years

Before describing her problem, Shazia says apologetically that hers is a love marriage.

> *Two panchayat members respond:* 'See, this is what happens when people have love marriages. From the start you were wrong in having a love marriage. Did you not think about the consequences?'

> *Caseworker:* 'Yes, only one in a hundred love marriages works.' *(Other members click their tongues in disapproval.)*

The youngest caseworker reacts: 'Do arranged marriages last? Most of the couples who face marital breakdown have had arranged marriages.'

Shazia (wife's account): 'I grew up in Delhi. My husband and I lived in the same neighbourhood, and we wanted to marry. When both our families objected, we married by ourselves. A year after we married, his mother came to Delhi and took him away to Bihar. He told me that he would return to Delhi soon. As he did not return, I decided to track him down in Bihar with the help of one of my neighbours. Our problems began after that. His mother kept me well for a few weeks. Then she started beating me. He also started beating me. I felt that things had become unbearable, so I returned to Delhi. That's why I have filed a case here.'

Panchayat member to Shazia: 'Why did his mother start beating you?'

Shazia: 'She would say that I was not of her choice.'

Husband's account (In the same apologetic tone, he, too, states that theirs is a love marriage): 'Yes, we married according to our own choice, and nobody was ready for it. I told her that after marriage we might have to live in Bihar. Then I got a message from my mother that the rains had destroyed our house in Bihar. When I was in Bihar, I explained to her that I could not return to Delhi right away. But she did not understand this. She demanded that I return immediately. She came to Bihar with a boy who she calls a neighbour. They were together for the night, and his character is not good. Then they went to the police station to track me down.'

Panchayat members comment: 'Men seem to sleep, dream, and eat with thoughts of suspicion. . . It never leaves their mind.'

Husband: 'I could not leave my mother alone in Bihar in the state we were in. I blame Shazia for all the problems with my mother. In Bihar, she was roaming around without veiling her face. My mother veils her face, so why can't she? She was spoiling our family's reputation. She wanted to be in the *bazaar* (market) every day or to see a film. Bihar is not Delhi. If she wants to live in Bihar, she had better do it properly, like a Bihari women, with respect.'

Panchayat members to Shazia: 'You have to adjust to the environment in which you live.'

Panchayat member to husband: 'The rules are not that strict in Bihar, are they? Son, you have to see that the world has changed.'

Author to the husband: 'Why did you marry her in the first place? You married according to your own choice.'

Husband: 'I married to take her out of poverty. I have given her respect. I pitied her because she was poor.'

Panchayat members: 'Is this the way to talk? The way these Bihari men treat their wives!'
(Members make critical comments about Bihari men.)

Panchayat members to husband: 'Tell us why you beat her.'

Husband: 'If she is in the wrong, I will beat her. In Bihar, we beat people. And if need be, I will beat her in Bihar. Women in Bihar are scared of even looking us in the eye. She does not get scared when I beat her.'

Panchayat members are outraged: 'Bihari men are the worst type of men. This man's character is not all right.'

Caseworker: 'You will not beat her again. Do you understand? We will have you arrested.'

Husband: 'Go ahead. I am not frightened of going to jail. You cannot touch me when I am in Bihar.'

Caseworker: 'Yes, we can. We have our contacts everywhere.' *(Fiery exchanges take place between the caseworker and the husband. The caseworker presses for a guarantee that the husband will not beat Shazia again.)*

Husband: 'Look, I am willing to keep her, but my mother comes first for me. Then it's me and then it's her. She should get used to that order. My mother has a right to tell her off every now and then.'

Members: 'Have you married her or your mother? Once you marry, you have a responsibility towards your wife. Who will look after you when your mother is not alive?'

Husband: 'You members do not understand a mother's plight. You do not listen to men's voices.'

Panchayat members: 'Yes, we do. We ourselves are mothers.' Shazia and her husband settle for reconciliation based on the following conditions:

Shazia's husband will not beat her again. From now on, he must take care of his wife and not just his mother. Shazia should adjust to life in Bihar and stop demanding that they live in Delhi. She should realize that her husband has obligations towards his family.

Panchayat member to Shazia: 'Look, you have to adjust to things in this marriage [referring to living in Bihar]. You married according to your own choice.'

Other members echo similar sentiments: 'If she married according to her own choice, she should adjust to life in Bihar. A wife adjusts to wherever her husband works and lives.' At the same time, the members sternly warn Shazia's husband never to beat her again.

Outcome: Reconciliation was achieved. The couple, who commute between Bihar and Delhi, did not express dissatisfaction over the agreement nor did they revisit the mahila panchayat in 2001–02.

Ill-treatment and Violence

Case filed by Reena on 17 October 2001

Duration of marriage: Two years; one child

Reena's husband is not present at the hearing.

> *Reena's account:* 'My husband took me to the Arya Samaj Mandir in Khan Market and forced me (*zabardasti*) into marriage. He told me that my father had filed a case against me at the police station. He married me through deception.'
>
> *Caseworker to Reena:* 'Where did you first meet your husband?'
>
> *Reena:* 'At a relative's house.'
>
> *Author asks for clarification:* 'Did you not know each other before the marriage took place?'
>
> *Reena (very hesitantly):* 'We were neighbours. Yes, he was always around.'
>
> *Reena's mother:* 'They did know each other and there was love between them before the marriage.'
>
> Reena reluctantly admits to this.
>
> *A caseworker reacts to her claim of being forced into marriage:* 'In love everything happens.'
>
> *Reena's mother:* 'But the actual wedding did take place through deception. He took her to the temple on some excuse and married her. His mother was there, but I was not informed. Before Reena was married through deception, his

mother came to see me. She wanted Reena as her daughter-in-law. I told his mother that the *gotras* [prohibited degrees of kinship] of our families match and hence we do not approve. She did not understand that the *gotra* matter was important to us. Okay, he married her by force, but now at least he should keep her properly.'

Panchayat members are astounded: 'How can you marry when the *gotras* match!'

Caseworker: 'What problem are you facing now?'

Reena: 'They beat me very badly, especially his mother and my sister-in-law. They beat me over small things. They even troubled me over dowry. I have one brother who is much younger, and my father is mentally disturbed.'

Panchayat members express sympathy about Reena's father. They lament that Reena's mother is in a vulnerable position.

Reena: 'He hits me with his belt. *She shows us several marks on her lower back.* Before marriage, he was the one who came after me. Now he says things like I am no longer beautiful. How can I look good when he beats me all the time?'

Caseworker: 'Reena's husband is not here. We will track him down in South Extension where he is a driver.'

I did not meet Reena's husband, but the caseworkers told me this version of the story:

Caseworker: 'We met Reena and her husband privately. He clarified that theirs was a love marriage and said that 'they had done everything' before marriage. He told us that Reena asks for trouble as her tongue is too sharp. That is why he beats her. After he returns home from his work, which is very stressful, she nags him endlessly. We settled their case. We told him that he should not beat her again.

If there are disagreements, he can explain things to her. We told her not to trouble him after work. We observed that she does nag him a lot.'

On 31 October 2001, Reena's mother revisits the mahila panchayat. The interchange between Reena's mother and a caseworker is given below.

Reena's mother: 'I know that Reena's husband will continue to ill-treat her. What if he kills her? I want a guarantee that he will not kill her. They treat her like a slave. I give her food to take to her conjugal home. Her husband has made it clear that from now on Reena can only visit me on important occasions. If he is with his mother every day, why can she not visit me more often? I live just around the corner.'

Caseworker interrupts: 'You want to break up your daughter's marriage, don't you? No story or situation is one-sided. Your daughter has many faults. She is sharp-tongued. We saw it the other day. You are too interfering. If you know the minute details of her household, then you are also to blame for your excessive interference. Let her learn to live with her husband, while we are there to protect her.'

Author to caseworker: 'Reena's mother is worried. Are you not being unreasonable?'

Caseworker to author: 'No marital problem is ever one-sided. We are expressing irritation because of Reena's mother's repeated visits. Everyday casework is extremely time-consuming, and once clients decide to arbitrate cases with us, our judgments and post-meditation procedures should be trusted.'

Outcome: The mahila panchayat claims to have 'settled' this case, but it appears that Reena's mother is not happy with the negotiated agreement. The couple do not revisit the mahila panchayat.

Chapter 2 analysed the post-wedding phase of love marriages and the problems faced by couples in combining 'premarital love' and 'marriage'. It portrayed some of the disconnections between courtship and actual married life; it examined how husbands start to enforce their domestic authority and how they may experience shifts in their emotions; and it looked at how women are expected to conform to the patriarchal joint family. It is notable how after marriage, Shazia's husband's affections shifted rapidly; his mother now occupies the central place in his narrative. So while men opt for a love marriage, this does little to dissipate the affections and loyalties of the mother–son bond. Men justify a shift in their loyalties and behaviour by eliciting discourses of filial obligations. Correspondingly, Reena's admission that her husband no longer finds her beautiful—and her question how she can remain beautiful if he unremittingly beats her—indicates a rupture from his previous romantic behaviour. I have shown earlier that women rarely initiate marital dissolution in love marriages. Shazia and Reena had the courage to file cases against their spouses, and it is noteworthy that they are reluctant to admit that their marriages are the outcome of courtship and self-choice. Fearing that they will be judged harshly or unsympathetically, they either frame their narratives apologetically or assert that they were forced to marry. In a forum where women are emboldened to discuss marriage and relationships openly, it becomes clear that the older panchayat members are wholly unsympathetic to love marriages. Echoing the dominant discourse, they argue that the primary alliance should be caste endogamous and based on respectful parental matchmaking norms. Only the youngest 27-year-old caseworker endorses inter-caste love marriages, and her articulations on marriage by choice are not well received. The mahila panchayat as an influential women's collective has not reflected seriously on notions of premarital romantic love or the right to choose marital partners, despite the fact that in their *galis* and neighbourhood, young people assert their emotional and romantic preferences. Although the caseworkers have been trained by a human rights activist to aid couples who may be facing violence and opposition from their families, the mahila panchayat still does not separate itself from the wider social view that regards love marriages as an anathema, and nor do they express a more progressive view on marital choice. Like their neighbourhood residents, they, too, reinforce stereotypes about love marriages as short-lived unions, while in reality the majority of the disputes they arbitrate actually involve the breakdown of arranged marriages. This highlights the fact that the mahila panchayat powerfully advocates conservative discourses on the subject of compulsory arranged marriage, while subscribing to a particular notion of marital relations that is recalcitrant and unresponsive to interrogation.

When love marriage grievances do surface at the mahila panchayat case hearings, the team applies the same patriarchal bargains and methods of reconciliation as they would to arranged marriage grievances, without understanding or identifying the disadvantages that women in love marriages may face. As counsellors, they attempt to normalize the love marriage with preconceived notions and implicit evaluations of what a marriage should be. There is no attempt to recognize the fact that women experience greater vulnerability in such unions. The mahila panchayat also supports the widespread notion that women should take responsibility and put up with a self-chosen spouse. However, it needs pointing out that irrespective of whether a woman's marriage is arranged or self-chosen, the mahila panchayat has an unshakeable stand on domestic violence. While husbands validate the use of violence in their conjugal lives, the mahila panchayat contends that irrespective of the mode of marriage, violence and ill-treatment are always misdemeanours. Despite exhibiting a less sensitive attitude towards love marriages, the mahila panchayat issued several warnings to the husbands of Shazia and Reena, with no compromise on their prescriptive behaviour. Reconciliation worked in their cases precisely because domestic violence and ill-treatment from affinal kin constituted the principal grievances.

Conceptions of 'Nagging' and Post-marital Consensual Unions

Using Shanti's grievance as a case study, I show that in contrast to cases pertaining to love marriages, the mahila panchayat is more sympathetic and non-judgemental in cases involving secondary unions. The analysis of Shanti's complaint leads me to engage with the mahila panchayat's view of nagging, shouting, and verbal arguments, which are perceived by the members as undesirable feminine attributes.

Kharcha-pani and Violence

Case filed by Shanti on 23 August 2001

Duration of marriage: Seven years; three children

> *Shanti (wife's account):* 'This is my second marriage. After my first husband died, I lived with my mother for twenty years. One day, I was walking on a hill and an old lady approached me. She asked me my caste. Initially, I deceived her. Then slowly I confided that I was a Khatik. She told me that she knew a man who was looking for a new wife. She gave me her guarantee that I would be well provided for. But after I began living with him, he started to beat me. And he does not provide me with *kharcha-pani*. If my husband from my primary marriage (*sat phere admi*) were alive, I would not be going through this.'

> *Husband's account:* 'I break stones in the quarry all day long. She never listens to me. She is so quarrelsome with my daughter [from his primary marriage]. She just walks out of the house whenever she wants to go to her *pihar*. She never informs me or asks me.'

> *Shanti constantly tries to interject and is told not to interfere.*

> *Panchayat members to husband:* 'What happened to your first wife?'

> *Husband:* 'She went on the wrong path. She would roam around with other men and so I left her.'

> *Panchayat members:* 'You do not just leave a wife like that.'

> *Husband continues:* 'I find it impossible to deal with Shanti. She never lets me open my mouth.'

Husband's daughter: 'My stepmother verbally abuses me. When I cook food for my father, she says I am behaving like his wife. Then when relatives visit, she instigates fights between us. She never respects them. She takes off her *pallu* (veil) in front of them. Our relatives do not visit us any more.' *She starts to cry.*

Panchayat member: 'Having a stepmother is so difficult. Very few love their stepchildren as their own flesh and blood.'

Caseworker to Shanti: 'Look, Shanti. You know how important the custom of *pallu* is for Rajasthani people. Why do you not respect his relatives? We have seen today that you do not give others a chance to talk. How do you expect there to be any peace in your house if you are not going to talk lovingly to others?'

The couple settles for the typical compromise pact based on the following conditions:
Shanti's husband should not beat Shanti again. He should give her regular *kharcha-pani*. Shanti should not go to her *pihar* without her husband's permission. She should respect his relatives and follow their household customs (keeping the *pallu*). She should speak properly to others, treat the husband's daughter well, and not instigate family fights.

Outcome: Reconciliation was achieved. According to the mahila panchayat's records and the observations made during follow-up house visits, the couple is getting along fine and has not revisited the mahila panchayat.

The narrative opening 'this is my second marriage' used by Shanti invokes particular discourses, meanings, and expectations within which the interrogation proceeds. Women and men tell their audience why and how they formed a secondary union, and panchayat members consequently make in-depth inquiries about the dissolution of their primary marriage. In the process, metaphorical juxtapositions are drawn between primary husbands and secondary partners, and extended kin step in to offer information about kinship arrangements. While Shanti highlighted the issues of violence and *kharcha-pani,* her husband and stepdaughter drew out another set of problematics. A central problem in this triangular relationship is the tense interaction between a stepmother and an elder stepdaughter and the dynamics of this close family connection. In secondary relationships, women and children have to make complex adjustments, which may not always work. Nonetheless, in comparison with their attitude to love marriages, the mahila panchayat members do not, in the first place, condemn the formation of secondary unions. They accept post-marital consensuality, for they validate the local practice of primary arranged marriages followed by permissible subsequent unions. More than the quest for post-marital emotional freedom, the members equate secondary unions with widowhood and the consequent narrowing down of options for women. They also discuss with concern how women in secondary relationships are harassed about their first marriage. If they slip up on housework, they are reprimanded by their spouses and affines, who say things such as: 'That is why her first marriage failed.' Furthermore, notice how the caseworkers berate women (as they do in the case of all marriages) for not conforming to mainstream gender roles. Shanti was urged not to be quarrelsome at home. Caseworkers assert that women are responsible for provoking and exacerbating marital conflict by nagging, arguing, and shouting, and state that 'no marital problem can be totally one-sided.' Leaving aside the alleged cantankerous temperaments of individuals, the members do not seem to consider the fact that shouting and 'nagging' might be connected with violence, lack of care, and women's frustration at not receiving *kharcha-pani*. It seems that their assertion of 'no marital problem is ever one-sided' (*'tali dono hath se bajti hai'*, it takes both hands to clap), a phrase that is also commonly employed by husbands, is a metaphor for compromise. The mahila panchayat delivers its judgments in a performative language of obedience, rectitude, docility, and restraint. The members prefer that their clients' exhibit these quintessentially feminine attributes, traits that they firmly believe will make a marriage work better.

The Mahila Panchayat's Transformatory Character
New Spaces of Symmetry for Women: Contradictory Outcomes

I have outlined how the mahila panchayat oversees patriarchal bargains and how it propagates conservative discourses on marriage, domesticity, and family life. Its covenants perpetuate the patrilineal ideology and reinforce the validity of mainstream gender roles. At the same time, the organization boosts women's confidence as their agreements are designed to achieve reconciliation based on eliminating or reducing marital violence, suspicion, and friction. The mahila panchayat opposes prescriptive norms such as violence, while simultaneously its judgments reproduce the inequalities existing in the communities of the clients. Mahila panchayats are transforming the institution of marriage in contemporary urban India in contradictory ways. They are creating new spaces of symmetries for women without disrupting the status quo, or, to quote Bhatla and Rajan (2003: 1663), 'agreements are a fusion of forward movement and necessary compromise'. We have observed the emergence and influence of this fusion as the mahila panchayat covenants have the intended effect of reviving marriages and increasing cooperation while also re-establishing patrilineal norms.

Having indicated the contradictory outcomes of the mahila panchayat's judgments, I will now engage with cross-cultural studies on women's agency and empowerment. My findings fit well with Saba Mahmood's (2001) analysis of non-liberatory movements and traditions. Mahmood's remarkable study of a Cairo women's mosque movement that is part of the larger Islamic revival underscores how resistance to social norms need not be the only form of women's agency. Mahmood reveals how agency can be cultivated through traits such as modesty, shyness, docility, endurance, passivity, and persistence. In the women's mosque movement, shyness and modesty are aspirational values that can easily be identified with the subjugation of women. Mahmood points to the movement's latent liberatory potential and discusses how it can be empowering for women. As she notes:

Viewed in this way, what may appear to be a case of deplorable passivity and docility from a progressivist point of view, may very well be a form of agency-one that must be understood in the context of discourses and structures of subordination that create the conditions of its enactment. In this sense, agentival capacity is entitled not only to those acts that result in (progressive) change but also those aimed towards continuity, stasis, and stability (2001: 212).

In light of this, it is not surprising that the mahila panchayat encourages its clients to cultivate feminine virtues such as domestic obedience, verbal passivity, and endurance, which are aimed at ensuring marital continuity and stability. As Mahmood says, the liberatory goals of feminism should be 'reconsidered in light of other desires, aspirations, and capacities that inhere in a culturally and historically located subject' (2001: 223). Correspondingly, Kabeer (2001) examines women's empowerment and social agency by foregrounding women's perceptions and experiences. She argues against narrow and unilinear registers of empowerment that cast women into being 'either empowered or not': 'Even within the same context, empowerment is a complex rather than a simple phenomenon. It has multiple dimensions and can occur through a multiplicity of routes' (Kabeer 2001: 80). Kabeer's (2001) argument is that empowerment need not be unilinear, while Mahmood's contribution shows (2001) how non-liberal movements have the potential of bringing about change through the conscious employment of a 'docile agency'. The works of these scholars provide an effective framework for understanding the Delhi mahila panchayat movement and its role in empowering urban, lower-class women.

Does the mahila panchayat, after all, envisage alternatives to patriarchal bargains that can challenge the wider asymmetries of marriage? What is the mahila panchayat's comprehension of 'feminism'? Low-income activists have their own opinions about shaping feminist agendas in working-class cultures. On questioning the youngest caseworker about what a transformatory agenda might consist of, she cites various obstacles that would emerge if they were to adopt a radical stand: 'We *basti* women cannot always start taking drastic steps. Who will support us, Shalini *ji*? We do not have the same economic choices as you middle class women. In our resettlement colonies, change evolves gradually.' She alerts me on how they do enforce radical injunctions, albeit intermittently, compared with the drawing up of agreements whereby women are told to adjust to their conjugal and affinal homes (see the case studies of Chanda and Shazia where the husbands were admonished to build separate relationships with their wives and mothers). Yet, she and the caseworkers believe that taking an overt radical position on marriage will alienate them from the local community, resulting in a backlash. How will they get men to comply when the mahila panchayat is not a legal organization, they ask. Moreover, in their opinion low-income women have limited options. The majority are materially disadvantaged, have few alternatives to natal kin support and basic housing, and can rarely exercise the option of living alone. I am told that as long as poor women are economically provided for and are safe from violence, the mahila panchayat will have achieved its purpose of 'mending a home.' It suffices that while the panchayat members are deeply committed to improving women's status, their goals are not about seeking radical solutions, but about protecting women against marital abuse and restoring marriage within the framework of existing options. Their ideology is, therefore, rooted in a particular type of agency and pragmatism that does not embrace radical worldviews of equality or feminism. This is how they navigate between subaltern structure and feminist consciousness. Accordingly, this stance reinforces the prevailing view that the Indian women's movement is not homogeneous and that feminisms are shaped by class- and caste-specific conceptions of gender relations (Grover 1997). The idea of a one-nation Indian women's movement is today deeply contested by feminists. The mahila panchayat experiment only verifies how articulations and movements in impoverished settings are mediated by other concerns.

Although the mahila panchayat is a public arbitration forum, the panchayat members and caseworkers also engage in introspection about their own married lives and their relations with men. Many of their intra-group discussions, oscillating between traditional and modern issues, reveal vexed disagreements. These discussions centre on both critiques and endorsements of feminine roles and perceived shifts in family relations, such as the domination of daughters-in-law over mothers-in-law. Questions are raised as to whether festivals such as *Karva Chauth* and gender-based customs such as the keeping of *pallu* are regressive, and whether the wearing of western clothing (jeans in particular) is eroding Indian culture. Animated debates are also held about whether or not global media practices and current television serials are retrograde. Amongst panchayat members there are as yet no disagreements on the prevailing caste disparities in urban low-income neighbourhoods, such as the discriminatory attitude towards the Balmikis. Several panchayat members retain their caste identities and positions, and re-inscribe the caste system. The gendering of a public forum of arbitration is confined to preserving the caste system, rather than critically engaging with it. The need for transforming caste along with gender and class has, therefore, yet to emerge as a major theme in the public debates of the mahila panchayat. However, in their intersections with metropolitan modernity, globalization, and Delhi's middle classes, from which they are not entirely isolated, mahila panchayat members of different ages are currently flummoxed, and are caught in a significant way in questioning, debating, and grappling with gender issues, lower class domesticity, and transformations in their own community.

The Conservatism and Success of the Mahila Panchayat

When the working day ends at the mahila panchayat, after several cups of cardamom tea have been consumed, tired couples head back home, either separately or together, and the counsellors call it a day, what stands out are the wide-ranging negotiations and bargains that have been facilitated in a single day, the advice given, and the informal assistance extended. Undoubtedly, the mahila panchayat offers a varied range of services to the urban poor. Its agreements are often workable, sustainable, and open to renegotiation because the panchayat is not guided by preset legal diktats. Mahila panchayats also distinguish themselves from male-dominated biradari panchayats, whose dealings are very different. But mahila panchayats exhibit some congruencies with biradari panchayats, which cannot be denied or overlooked. A parallel endorsement of the role of caste in urban life is universal to both these male and female bodies.

Crucially, the mahila panchayat's principal strategy of reconciliation is the patriarchal bargain. Some women clients repudiate their patriarchal bargains while others are willing to give up their freedoms (for example, visits to the natal home) so as to gain something in other spheres (for example, the reduction or elimination of violence). Mahila panchayats are actively mediating between the genders and transforming marriage by ensuring better treatment for women. The organization does empower and instil confidence in women, albeit in highly contradictory ways. It does not deviate from local understandings of marriage. It embraces the male breadwinner ideology and the institution of arranged marriage based on patrilineal norms as the legitimate foundation of marriage. For a more fundamental transformation of marriage, the mahila panchayat will need to reflect more deeply on the eschewement of marriage and on the adoption of a more egalitarian notion of companionate marriage and its practical and ideological implications. It can be argued that mahila panchayats, at least at present, remain functional, successful, popular, and useful because they articulate conservative discourses on marriage and reject a radical approach. While feminist groups, scholars and activists may disregard some of their non-progressive ideologies (as Mahmood [2001] argues, typically such movements fit uncomfortably with liberal feminism), it suffices that in the current milieu their conservatism is an enabling factor for their male clients. The mahila panchayat's underlying strength is, therefore, its proximity rather than its alienation from local norms and values.

6

Towards the Democratization of Marriage and Relationships
Conclusion

This book has employed a contrastive mode of analysis to examine whether certain types of marriages are more democratic for women and whether the support systems that married women are entitled to vary across these marriages. Alongside, it has delineated how notions and ideologies of love may vary across conjugal arrangements. My hope is that the ethnographic findings that are summarized in this conclusion will enable scholars, activists and policy makers to initiate theoretical debate and reform in furthering democracy in intimate relationships.

Beyond the schema of the ways in which poor women with no resources enter into arranged alliances, love marriages, arranged love marriages, secondary unions, and other intimate bonds we have observed a common thread in all these relationships. This is that women face physical violence, alcohol-related abuse, sexual jealousy, and conflict over money and other matters, which are regular features of unequal marital relations. One of my objectives has been to contrast the Delhi ethnography with Giddens' (1999) overarching claim that the global trend is towards a model of marriage based on gender equality. My observations from Delhi unequivocally contradict Giddens' ethnocentric hypothesis. While women clearly voice a preference for relationships that are free of violence and maleficent conflict and are otherwise vociferous in their critique of irresponsible male behaviour, the expectations of emotional and sexual equality as envisaged by Giddens do not emanate from or feature as a theme in discussions amongst the younger or the older generations in my study area. If we ask which type of marriage in urban north India makes women stronger and more confident, my observations suggest that women are most favourably placed within arranged marriages. In Mohini Nagar, the system of arranged marriage has been resilient and not undergone fundamental transformations. Young people continue to have little say in choosing whom to marry and most face pressing compulsions to marry early. Matchmaking continues to be dominated not by a concern for the couple's happiness, but by factors that will supposedly augment post-marital happiness for instance, potential husbands being good providers while abstaining from alcohol, etc. I have shown why in a modern metropolis, the primary arranged marriage remains the ideal amongst the lower castes as does the hold on male breadwinner ideologies. With respect to women's more favourable position within arranged marriages, a noteworthy finding is that daughters who abide by parental choice in mate selection remain intimately linked to their natal kin. An arranged marriage guarantees post-marital support as well as a crucial moral entitlement to refuge. This book has uncovered the practice and strategic use of refuge as a distinct urban phenomenon.[1] The right to refuge places a woman in a strong position within the conjugal unit, thereby enhancing her self-confidence. It enables her to bargain effectively with a spouse, to challenge male authority, and to withdraw cooperation if and when she feels the need to. Thus, women's strength within arranged marriages is manifested in their ability to access vital emotional and material support from their natal kin. However, the data on arranged marriage also illustrates the limitations of parental intervention and natal kin support. A closer look at the politics of refuge reveals the manifold complications in negotiating repeated recourse to shelter. In

[1] As reported by Patricia Jeffery (2001), rural women in Bijnor who face marital difficulties also take shelter in their natal homes. Jeffery observes that although natal kin are the best and most reliable source of support, seeking their intervention on the part of married daughters is a form of last resort: 'Generally it is considered inappropriate for parents to become involved in their daughters' marital problems' (2001: 13).

addition, after a certain stage in the life cycle, older women are meant to fend for themselves.

It thus appears that women's strong fallback position in arranged marriages and their ability to terminate marriages does not depend on their economic situation or earning capabilities as emphasized by economists like Sen (1990). Radha, my very poor field assistant, who had walked out on her husband many times, has never worked for a wage prior to becoming my field assistant. Moreover, far from being an enabling factor in women's lives, taking up employment outside the house or the residential neighbourhood often exacerbates conjugal conflict (cf. Panda and Agarwal 2005). I have also substantiated that the marriages of the sweeper caste are not necessarily based on economic equality or on a joint division of labour, as suggested by the Benares case (Searle-Chatterjee 1981). The Delhi sweepers present a telling and interesting point of comparison to the Benares sweepers because of their otherwise similar socio-economic circumstances. Searle-Chatterjee links the autonomy of the Benares sweeper women to equal labour market opportunities, a circumstance that is paralleled among the sweeper women in Delhi, as seen by the availability of MCD jobs to both sweeper men and women. Yet, in my Delhi sample and across castes, women take up waged work only when confronted by financial constraints. The marriage stories of widows in secondary unions, such as Basanti and Omvati (Chapter 4), suggest moreover that secure MCD jobs, along with their pensions and benefits, do not free women of male dependence, nor do they alter the power dynamics of a low-caste and higher-caste pairing.

Urbanization and virilocal marriage residence patterns in Delhi also influence and shape the institution of marriage. In her ethnography of white-collar migrants in Meerut (Uttar Pradesh), Vatuk (1972) illustrates a gradual but fundamental shift in the kinship structures of the middle classes. She argues that urban migration has strengthened women's ties with their natal kin. This bilateral enhancement has led to unconventional patterns of interaction between married couples and their affines. My contribution in this context has been to show that in Delhi, kinship is an everyday and immediate affair for Delhi's urban poor. Close post-marital natal kin bonds in a city enable women to maintain and enjoy habitual and regular contact with their parents. I have highlighted how the strength of the mother–daughter dyad is tied to strands of mutual emotional dependence, to a married daughter's labour, and to the economic vulnerabilities of subaltern life. In the face of poverty, natal families and married daughters seek continual mutual support, which simultaneously strengthens women's position whilst also debilitating marriage. While there is much local emphasis given to the relative durability of arranged marriages, we have seen how mothers rupture their daughters' marriages that were arranged with dowry. In the context of north India, further research is needed for a greater understanding of how strong post-marital natal kin bonds affect the everyday conjugal lives of women and men. These data would supplement the dominant and extensive literature on how long-distance alliances engender vulnerability in women's lives.

Chapter 3 has illustrated that although there is no drastic shift away from arranged marriages, there is nonetheless an incipient trend towards courtships and love marriages. To explain the prevalence of local courtships, I have pointed to the close-knit nature of shanty settlements and resettlement colonies and shown how metropolitan spaces present opportunities for people to socialize and meet. Although courtships in Mohini Nagar and in other parts of Delhi often continue to be conducted in secrecy and the movements of adolescents are closely monitored, young urbanites can easily form attachments with neighbours, colleagues, or someone they may have accidentally met on a bus, park, or in a cinema hall. The Raju Camp love marriages are mainly liaisons between close neighbours. Couples such as Rahul and Kalpana and Rekha and Sandeep had managed with difficulty to negotiate an arranged love marriage with their families. These couples were candid about their intense feelings of childhood love and their desire to remain together. Accordingly, some aspects of Giddens' (1999) argument about the shift towards romantic love and the wider importance being given to the latter do apply to these couples. Amongst the urban poor there are individuals and couples who are now vocalizing and asserting a preference for marriage based on personal choice. For these couples, feelings and emotions are key precursors to marriage. However, where there has been no significant shift is in the actual acceptance of love marriages. While the local development of the 'good caste (*achhi jat*) and regional category' has engendered some flexibility in the acceptance of particular types of love marriages, it has also sharpened non-negotiable boundaries. The identitarian markers between 'Balmikis, Muslims, and all the rest' are most evident. Whether in the years to come we will see a waning of these boundaries depends upon the resilience of the caste ideology. I have illustrated that in Mohini Nagar, education, employment, and class mobility are given less importance than caste and religious identity (the opposite has been noted by Béteille [1993: 441] in the case of Indian middle class professionals). Consequently, prejudice against certain inter-caste and inter-religious unions remains intense. Yet, as my ethnography reveals, it is most desirable to marry with parental approval. Couples who have had arranged love marriages sometimes refer to their unions as 'arranged' without 'love' to signify explicit parental consent. It is certainly true that the younger generation does not want to outright repudiate their parents, but is keen to secure their active consent and involvement.

Crucially, it is in present-day love marriages that women have the weakest fallback position. Women state that they face vulnerability in self-chosen marriages, the main reason being that when it comes to tackling their domestic problems, the parental role of support is muted. Women cannot hold their parents accountable for their choice of a partner as the majority of natal families will implore their daughters to accept responsibility if their unions turn out to be unsatisfactory. Neighbours, local residents, community members, and mahila panchayats will do precisely the same. Reforming such prejudicial attitudes and confronting this unequal logic of conciliation and compromise are matters of urgent necessity, so women do not have to face a heavy burden of guilt, stigmatization, insecurity, and violence. Furthermore, the conciliatory approach of adjusting to the status quo is also evoked unanimously and frequently in the context of 'arranged love marriages'. This book has made the argument that the recent accretion of arranged love marriage should not necessarily be seen as a modern-day concession.

On conjugal stability, the ethnographic evidence confirms that the presumed fragility of love marriages does not hold for the Mohini Nagar setting. Given women's overall lack of exit options in love marriages, they rarely initiate marital break-up. Instead, they invest more emotion, energy, and effort into making their marriages work. A love marriage has come to signify indissolubility, as the language of 'marital adjustment' is a prominent feature. There is also another factor that contributes towards women's weaker voice in love marriages. In the post-marriage phase, husbands tend to be in a position of greater strength. I have highlighted the contrasts between the dynamics of courtship and those of married life; the former is a more egalitarian phase rooted in the vicissitudes of friendship and romance. After marriage, an asymmetrical relationship begins to develop, as husbands normalize relations with their kin, and wives are expected to conform to conventional hierarchical gender roles.

In love marriages there is a particular discourse adopted by women that stresses the sacrifices and risks they have undertaken in order to be in these unions. Women tend to evaluate their marriages by particularizing the hardships they have experienced. While the discourse of hardship is prominent in arranged marriages and in secondary unions as well, there is much less sympathy for women in love marriages. A question that emerges from this is whether these gendered discourses are specific to the lower classes. I suggest that more data are needed on how class, education, women's employment, and media exposure are shaping women's experiences of love marriages. It may be that more positive discourses and evaluations can be elicited in other cultural settings. For middle class professional women in Delhi, for instance, Liddle and Joshi's (1986) perceptive study on work, compromise, and marriage shows that women did emphasize their disappointments when after marriage their husbands vetoed their decision to work. Liddle and Joshi propose a democratizing strategy, i.e. irrespective of whether the marriage is arranged or based on love, women should outline their future demands and priorities before marriage when they are in a position of strength. In their sample, many middle class women had professional careers before they married, which gave them a strong position to negotiate from. The women in Liddle and Joshi's study decided to remain unmarried until they found a husband willing to accept their demands for more self-reliance after marriage. We must acknowledge that Liddle and Joshi's interpretations are based on middle class professional women who exhibit a different set of experiences and who enjoy greater economic security than the poor lower caste women who are the subject of this book.

My last point of comparison has been the secondary union. I have described how these unions provide an important space for people to openly explore their desires. In a patriarchal setting, they also serve and operate as exit options; serial monogamy and the fluidity of relationships have a meaningful and purposeful role in women's lives. Currently, in the local community, secondary unions are not being viewed as *passé* nor are they being curtailed by the state. Whether the practice of secondary unions will eventually decline (see Kapila 2004; Parry 2001) largely depends upon the endorsement of monogamous marriage by future generations. At present, the legality of these unions is not frequently contested, while residents rarely file for formal divorce. Nonetheless, the mahila panchayats are encouraging women to organize documentary proof and evidence of marriage, to ensure that they are better protected in these unions. Another noteworthy change is the younger generation's rendering of their unions as 'proper marriages', while the older generation, in contrast, evokes the symbolic importance of lifelong commitment, thereby rejecting the discourse of marriage, courts, and temples.

I have analysed whether secondary unions are inherently more democratic for women. While many women resort to secondary unions, the freedom to terminate the primary marriage and to enter unions over the life course is not necessarily suggestive of greater female autonomy. Secondary unions reproduce patriarchal relations, gender inequality, and domestic violence. They have more parallels with love marriages than with arranged marriages. In arranged marriages, certain rights, such as natal kin protection and economic provisioning by the husband, are guaranteed at the outset and are renegotiable. These rights may not be assured in secondary unions, and my evidence suggests that women are less able to bargain effectively. Another common feature of love marriages and secondary unions is the withdrawal of family support in certain instances. Hence, as the data has shown not all secondary unions receive validation. For this reason, consensual secondary unions are also perceived as being risky and to the disadvantage of women. Additionally, the general instability and fragility of secondary unions also manifest disparate combinations, such as those between unmarried men and middle-aged widows or sterilized women, and those between Balmiki women and higher caste men. How, then, are we to account for these skewed, transgressive, and anomalous unions and the chances women take when they enter into more 'meaningful relationships' with the promise of commitment? As it emerges, women often end up at the receiving end in these relationships when they are casually abandoned. The durability of these relationships depends critically on familial and societal acceptance, on whether the woman is still fertile and thus in a position to meet her partner's demand for his own offspring, and on the social dynamics between lower and higher castes.

The chapter on mahila panchayats (Chapter 5) vividly displays the contradictory ways in which a certain segment of the women's movement in Delhi is transforming marriage. The mahila panchayat concept is being replicated by many NGOs working in low-income neighbourhoods. Mahila panchayats have created alternative structures of dispute settlement and conflict resolution, and have adopted effective ways of negotiating on behalf of women without alienating men and members of the conjugal family. They are facilitating better treatment for women, especially by attempting to change attitudes towards domestic violence. The agreements negotiated by mahila panchayats repudiate prescriptive norms while increasing women's confidence. Yet mahila panchayat counsellors and their supporting team of panchayat members deliver judgments in a performative language and fail to dispute the caste system or combat deep-rooted biases against love marriages. They also disengage themselves from changing the wider asymmetries of marriage and the patrilineal social structure. Given these myriad incongruities, I have argued that nevertheless mahila panchayat spaces are still empowering for poor urban women.

It is significant that informal women's courts concentrate on reconciliation. Reconciliation is a contested feminist terrain. Many feminists in India and abroad do not concur with the ideology of reconciling couples. Rather than evolving functional agendas beyond reconciliation, mahila panchayats have put more of their energies into fixing troubled marriages, reforming male behaviour and bringing estranged couples together. In terms of their ideological orientation, mahila panchayats are unabashed in promoting male protection as the basis of marriage and family life.

They appear to be arguing that it is inconceivable for low-income populations to adopt a democratic ideology of marriage; the focus on democratic marriages is seen as impractical and unworkable in a setting where there is heightened concern about where the next meal will come from. Men, as they say, should be held accountable as providers. The mahila panchayats place emphasis on men and women making certain modifications in their conduct by deploying existing options. Consequently, these informal women's courts 'bargain with patriarchy' and do not advocate equality or radical shifts in marriage. Their conservative discourses and motivations are at variance with recent feminist articulations that propose egalitarian marriage and democratic family structures (see Hensman 2005 and John 2005 for a feminist perspective that advocates reform). Clearly, there is a disparity here within the Indian women's movement and amongst women's groups as to which ideologies, praxis, and agendas suit women's interests best.

Finally, this book has portrayed the social world of the dominant caste in Mohini Nagar, the Balmikis. The division and separation between the Balmikis and other SCs is a prominent part of everyday speech and life in Mohini Nagar. The Balmikis are associated with immoral vices and blamed for all the social problems in *bastis*. By capturing Balmiki constructions of self, I have shown how they exhibit both extreme loyalty and ambivalence towards their own caste. On account of their social isolation, Balmikis of all age groups feel constrained by their cloistered, inward-looking community. In a heterogeneous urban milieu, they have secure jobs and yet they face enduring discrimination and hostility, as their profession is considered deeply polluting and debasing. The Balmikis remain a despised urban group, and their self-defensiveness and caste loyalty have engendered a rigid ideology of endogamy. For this reason, Balmiki women will always be more vulnerable in their intimate relationships with upper caste men and Balmiki youths will have to mediate much harder to gain parental approval for inter-caste relationships.

7

Epilogue
Perspectives on Change and Continuity:
2000–16

The anthropological and feminist literature on marriage is undergoing an overhaul. Recent studies appraise conjugality against the backdrop of globalization, and more and more scholars are texturing intimacies. While these are welcome additions, marriage patterns have met with close media scrutiny in relation to actual and ostensible trends. These for example include the import of cross-regional brides in Haryana and the phenomenon of love-jihad conversion to Islam. Intimate relationships feature even more prominently in Indian films and television serials, with premarital sex and adultery occupying central leitmotifs. All these developments are evoking beliefs about a 'new India' that has rapidly changed in the post-liberalization years. The country's projection of a rising global economy has equally bolstered this perception, whereby marriage is being allied with portentous societal transitions.

New Delhi, as part of the National Capital Region (NCR) has also experienced concentrated economic expansion. Some low-income neighbourhoods have embraced new markers of modernity. In Mohini Nagar, noticeable are electronic outlets, retail shops with western attire, and the odd placard displaying 'Fitness Studio'. Girls who in 2000 would rarely be seen in jeans are no longer an anomaly. Conspicuous in this low-income setting are fragments of shifting aspirations. At the same time, through recurrent field visits, my understanding is that many sections of the urban poor and particularly my respondents have not gained from India's economic reforms. This is nowhere more apparent than from the calamitous events in Radha's life.

I have known Radha, my field assistant now for several years (see chapter 1). Since 2011 her immediate kin have all contacted tuberculosis (TB). Her younger son acquired Meningeal TB, a condition when the bacterium travels to the membranes surrounding the brain and spinal cord. His speech became impaired. Next, Radha was diagnosed with Pulmonary TB that affects the lungs. From 2011–13, she underwent treatment, in congested government hospitals. She and her husband, Ramesh, had reconciled following many years of hurtful conflict (see chapter 4). So I will never forget Ramesh's frail figure, as he stoically made the hospital excursions to assist Radha. Shortly after, Radha's eldest son, his wife (Radha's *bahu*), and Ramesh contacted TB. Tragically this resulted one by one in their demise. Irrespective of the financial assistance Radha received from me, including expenditures for private health care in the National Chest Institute, none of this prevented the deaths of her loved ones. Radha is a shadow of her former self, and blamed by her neighbours for 'spreading a disease'; she faces ostracization. The latter combined with her stigmatized sweeper caste identity means that in her quotidian environ, Radha faces extreme isolation. The only saving grace is her deceased husband's MCD pension. As Anirudh Krishna's apt title 'One Illness Away' (2010) implies, if one family member falls sick, this can lead to a succession of illnesses plunging the entire family into chronic poverty. Some of my other respondents have likewise neither survived beyond the age of forty-five. This coincides with their inability to recover from debilitating, yet treatable illnesses, along with their decent into poverty. So whereas India's market reform discourse accentuates the 'new India' of economic modernity, the state continues to fail its most vulnerable citizens.

What implications does Radha's narrative, one of enduring poverty, have for anthropological research that foregrounds the conjugal lives of India's lowest strata? I would argue that little has changed in terms of what has been documented in this book. To reinstate, while social transformations are transpiring, radical shifts in marital practices are not prominent. Chiefly, economic vulnerabilities continue to foster inter-generational dependencies. This observation is crucial for the book's over-arching theme i.e. the materiality of support structures central to the lives of poor women, young and old. Intrinsically, this explains the preference for family-arranged marriages that guarantee substantial post-marital entitlements during conjugal conflict and familial economic crisis. This is notwithstanding the fact that many more women have opted for labour market opportunities.[1] While their economic contributions are germane to the natal unit's overall survival, the arranged marriage still signposts a more protected future. A working mother of five adult children reiterated this to me in early 2016: 'My daughter said, "Mother! I completely trust your judgment over marriage decisions. I do not need to see the boy even once."'

Undeniably, the broader social and kinship order favours the time-honoured arranged alliance, hitherto the most common form of marriage in India. Chapter 3 has captured the parallel assertion of young people desiring love marriages in shanty settlements. A question I am habitually being invited to address is whether in globalized South Asia, the caste-endogamous marriage system is in decline. Southeast Asian countries often feature in these evaluations, with Singapore, Hong Kong, South Korea, and Japan having moved away from parental match-making. As is the case, in many of India's cities, the geography of romance and courtship has undergone modifications. At-least in certain layers of the urban middle classes, love marriages are becoming more common. Mixed-sex spaces are discernable in varied degrees across the social divide. The affection couples now and then display publicly, in universities, leisure sites and on social media make us ponder whether the rigid control over sexuality is a relic of the past. The backlash to this is evident in the moral policing of the Hindu right wing. As young people's emotional lives meet with disruption, certain permutations of love marriages continue to incur resistance.

More so, in terms of marriage research, chapter 3 underscores the importance of examining the 'post-marriage phase' of love marriages. The period after courtship when the couple settle

---

[1] New opportunities created by market reforms for working class women in Delhi include employment in beauty parlours, hospitals, shopping malls, pre-schools, the Delhi metro services, and the burgeoning care economy.

down (if they do at all) is essential for insights into whether a marriage by choice translates democratizing gains for women in shaping their post-marital lives. Rather what should remain of import to the anthropologist is whether the 'married life course' alienates a woman from her kin-community or affirms her choices without harsh indictment. For 2000–2, I have discussed the inter-generational bargain of coalescing 'love' with the socially sanctioned 'arranged'. The 'love arranged marriage' does not procure women the kind of kinship support that is available in conventional arranged marriages. This often comes as a surprise to readers and the important counter evidence is reinstated through my chapter on the Mahila Panchayats NGOs. Expanding this debate by inducting a more recent timeframe, my latest research (2010–12) investigates how women's choices, divorce, and kinship support are being viewed by new women-led institutions (see Grover 2006).

In 2009, the capital saw the setting-up of 12 Crime Against Women Cells (CAW cells) that commenced conflict resolution and legal aid services. Crime Against Women's Cells or 'Special Units' are situated across Delhi in all-women police stations. Lawyer-mediators from Delhi Legal Services Authorities, NGO personal, educators, psychologists, and female police officers are the typical specialists who run CAW cells. As such CAW cells have mixed state and non-state features. With their array of interlocutors, individual CAW cell counsellors are espousing liberal notions of 'accountability' in the realm of marriage. Consider this instance of a middle class female litigant stressing vulnerability in a mediation session: 'My husband and I had a love marriage…. it is not fair that he is ending the marriage. It will be harder for me to remarry.' Next, a working class woman echoes a similar narrative, but is candidly told by the counsellor: 'He does not have to put up with a marriage just because it is based on love.' While appealing for empathy both these litigants are informed: 'Today, any party—man or woman—can annul a marriage.' This is a slightly altered adaptation from the normative reprimand women receive in love marriages (i.e. 'you choose your marriage so deal with the consequences.'). These statements conjure how any person, in any marriage, is at liberty to dissolve a union. It suffices that given the current milieu of India's modernizing impulses, women are being viewed as new liberal subjects. But this ideology manifests once again an implicit form of gender-blame shifting, whereby society, institutions, and counsellors do not have to account for a woman's personal choices. This stance can have grave consequences for women who may be told by interlocutors to either fend for themselves or admonished to adjust to a difficult mother-in-law through a re-negotiation of domestic hierarchies. With liberal notions being espoused in state-run institutions, the irony is that the gender framings and reconciliation verdicts may converge with conservative ideologies. An underlying finding is that women's institutions are still unable to grasp the vulnerable relationship dynamic of love marriages. The first edition made a plea to scholars and activists for furthering democracy across the conjugal unions women enter. Despite a decade gap from erstwhile fieldwork, it is time once again to reinforce this plea.

ANNEXURE

An Interview with a Male Representative of the Khatik Samaj Mahapanchayat, September 2001

Q. What is the official name of your biradari panchayat?
A. Khatik Samaj Mahapanchayat.

Q. What is your ancestral profession?
A. We are known for selling and purchasing meat. But today we have moved into other professions.

Q. Do Khatiks fall under the SC [Scheduled Caste] or the OBC [Other Backward Classes] category?
A. SC.

Q. From where have the Khatiks come? When did they migrate to Delhi?
A. They migrated to Delhi from Haryana and Uttar Pradesh in 1965 and 1976.

Q. When was the Khatik Samaj Mahapanchayat founded?
A. There is no date as to when it started. It has been there all along. I cannot specify any date.

Q. Where do your meetings take place? How often do you meet? Do you have a central office?
A. It depends on where the problem takes place or arises. We meet only if there is a problem, not otherwise. Our meetings are held

in Mangolpuri, Kotla, and especially Lajpat Nagar [all colonies in South Delhi], where a lot of our Khatik people live.

Q. Can women sit in the Khatik biradari panchayat?
A. Absolutely not.

Q. Do women approach you with cases of domestic violence?
A. No. For that, you have the mahila panchayats. We do not deal with that sort of stuff.

Q. Is your biradari panchayat only for Khatiks? Do you deal with cross-caste problems?
A. Yes, it is only for Khatiks. If there is a problem that involves interaction with a different caste, they have to go to the courts.

Q. What is your stand on inter-caste love marriages?
A. Here we cannot do anything . . . It is not in our hands. The courts handle such cases all the time. We cannot stop someone from marrying someone else.

Q. One hears that biradari panchayats mete out punishments. Is this true?
A. We usually ask for a fine. For example, if a boy does not want to marry his childhood bride, we ask him to compensate the girl's family.

Q. Biradari panchayats impose a stringent punishment called *hukka pani band kardena* (social ostracism). Can you comment on this?
A. *(Laughs)* Look, do you know what this means? It means that your membership will be suspended or cancelled. Nobody will invite you to any functions or sit with you. That is all it means. *(He does not comment further).*

Q. What is the use of having biradari panchayats when there are police stations, courts, and several women's NGOs in Delhi?
A. The police are ineffective and people face a lot of harassment from them. The courts are expensive and time consuming. We take decisions and solve matters quickly. That is why people come to us.

Q. From where do you get your funding? Are you a registered organization?

A. We are not registered. We get our funding from donations and from the fines we impose. We take our share from that.

Q. Do you have any links with rural biradari panchayats?

A. Our biradari panchayats in Delhi have nothing to do with rural India.

BIBLIOGRAPHY

Agarwal, Bina. 1994. *A Field of One's Own: Gender and Land Rights in South Asia*. New Delhi: Cambridge University Press.

Ahearn, Laura M. 2001. *Invitations to Love: Literacy, Love Letters, and Social Change in Nepal*. Ann Arbor: University of Michigan Press.

Ali, Sabar. 1990. *Slums within Slums: A Study of Resettlement Colonies in Delhi*. Delhi: Har-Anand Publications.

Bairy, T. S. Ramesh. 2009. Brahmins in the Modern World: Association as Enunciation. *Contributions to Indian Sociology*. 43 (1): 89–120.

Basu, Srimati. 1994. Bengali in French Accent. *Manushi*. 83 (July–August): 38–9.

Becker, Gary. 1991. *A Treatise on the Family*. Cambridge MA: Harvard University Press.

Bennett, Lynn. 1983. *Dangerous Wives and Sacred Sisters: Social and Symbolic Roles of High-caste Women in Nepal*. New York: Columbia University Press.

Berreman, G. D. 1963. *Hindus of the Himalayas*. Berkeley: University of California Press.

Béteille, André. 1993. 'The Family and the Reproduction of Inequality'. In Patricia Uberoi (ed.) *Family, Kinship, and Marriage in India*, pp. 435–51. New Delhi: Oxford University Press.

Bhatla, Nandita, and Anuradha Rajan. 2003. 'Private Concerns in Public Discourse: Women-initiated Community Responses to Domestic Violence'. *Economic and Political Weekly*. 38 (17): 1658–64.

Busby, Cecilia. 2000. *The Performance of Gender: An Anthropology of Everyday Life in a South Indian Fishing Village.* London: Athlone Press.

Butalia, Urvashi. 2000. *The Other Side of Silence: Voices from the Partition of India.* London: C. Hurst & CO.

Carsten, Janet (ed.). 2000. *Cultures of Relatedness: New Approaches to the Study of Kinship.* Cambridge: Cambridge University Press.

Chanfrault-Duchet, Marie-Françoise. 1991. 'Narrative Structures, Social Models, and Symbolic Representation in the Life Story'. In Sherna Berger Gluck and Daphne Patai (eds.) *Women's Words: The Feminist Practice of Oral History,* pp. 77–92. London: Routledge.

Chant, Sylvia, (ed.). 1992. *Gender and Migration in Developing Countries.* London: Belhaven Press.

Chant, Sylvia. 2001. 'Men in Crisis? Reflections on Masculinities, Work and Family in North-West Costa Rica'. In Cecile Jackson (ed.) *Men at Work: Labour, Masculinities, and Development,* pp. 200–20. London: Frank Cass & Co.

Chowdhry, Prem. 1998. 'Enforcing Cultural Codes: Gender and Violence in Northern India'. In Mary E. John and Janaki Nair (eds.) *A Question of Silence? The Sexual Economies of Modern India,* pp. 332–67. New Delhi: Kali for Women.

———. 2004. 'Private Lives, State Intervention: Cases of Runaway Marriage in Rural North India'. *Modern Asian Studies.* 38 (1): 55–84.

———. 2007. *Contentious Marriages, Eloping Couples: Gender, Caste and Patriarchy in Northern India.* Delhi: Oxford University Press.

Cohn, Bernard S. 1987. *An Anthropologist Among the Historians and Other Essays.* Delhi: Oxford University Press.

Das, Veena. 1993 [1976]. 'Masks and Faces: An Essay on Punjabi Kinship'. In Patricia Uberoi (ed.) *Family, Kinship and Marriage in India,* pp. 198–222. Delhi: Oxford University Press.

De Haan, Arjan. 1994. *Unsettled Settlers: Migrant Workers and Industrial Capitalism in Calcutta.* Hilversum: Verloren.

Deliège, Robert. 1997. *The World of the "Untouchables": Paraiyars of Tamil Nadu.* Delhi: Oxford University Press.

De Neve, Geert. 2004. 'The Workplace and the Neighbourhood: Locating Masculinities in the South Indian Textile Industry'. In Filippo Osella, Caroline Osella and Radhika Chopra (eds.) *South*

Asian Masculinities: Context of Change, Sites of Continuities, pp. 45–67. Delhi: Kali for Women (Women Unlimited).

—————. 2005. *The Everyday Politics of Labour: Working Lives in India's Informal Economy.* Delhi: Social Science Press.

Donner, Henrike F. 2002. ' "One's Own Marriage": Love Marriages in a Calcutta Neighbourhood'. *South Asia Research.* 22(1): 79–94.

—————. 2008. *Domestic Goddesses: Maternity, Globalization and Middleclass Identity in Contemporary India.* Aldershot: Ashgate.

Dube, Leela. 1996. 'Caste and Women'. In M. N. Srinivas (ed.) *Caste: Its Twentieth Century Avatar,* pp. 1–27. New Delhi: Vistaar Publications.

Dumont, Louis. 1964. 'Marriage in India: The Present State of the Question'. Postscript to Part 1, 11. Marriage and Status, Nayar and Newar. *Contributions to Indian Sociology* (o.s.) 9: 90–114.

—————. 1970. *Homo Hierarchicus: The Caste System and Its Implications.* London: Weidenfeld & Nicolson.

Dupont, Veìronique. 2000. 'Spatial and Demographic Growth of India Since 1947 and the Main Migration Flows'. In Veìronique Dupont, Emma Tarlo, and Denis Vidal, (eds.) *Delhi: Urban Space and Human Destinies,* pp. 200–35. New Delhi: Manohar IRD.

Dwyer, Rachel. 2000. *All You Want is Money, All You Need is Love: Sex and Romance in Modern India.* London: Cassell.

Dyson, Tim, and Mick Moore. 1983. 'Kinship Structure, Female Autonomy and Demographic Behaviour in India'. *Population and Development Review.* 9 (1): 35–60.

Fuller, Chris J., and Haripriya Narasimhan. 2008. 'Companionate Marriage in India: The Changing Marriage System in a Middle-Class Brahman Subcaste'. *Journal of the Royal Anthropological Institute.* 14 (4): 736–54.

Gardner, Katy. 2002. Age, Narrative and Migration: *The Life Course and Life Histories of Bengali Elders in London.* Oxford, New York: Berg Publishers.

Geetha. V. 1998. 'On Bodily Love and Hurt'. In Mary E. John and Janaki Nair (eds.) *A Question of Silence: The Sexual Economies of Modern India,* pp. 304–31. New Delhi: Kali for Women.

Giddens, Anthony. 1992. *The Transformation of Intimacy: Sexuality, Love and Eroticism in Modern Societies*. Cambridge: Polity Press.

―――――. 1999. *Runaway World: How Globalization is Reshaping Our Lives*. London: Profile Books.

Gough, Kathleen E. 1993 [1956]. 'The Nayars and the Definition of Marriage'. In Patricia Uberoi (ed.) *Family, Kinship and Marriage in India*, pp. 146–76. Delhi: Oxford University Press.

Grover, Shalini. 1997. 'An Exploration into Contemporary Indian Feminism'. Masters dissertation, London School of Economics and Political Science.

―――――. 2006. 'Poor Women's Experiences of Marriage and Love in the City of New Delhi: Everyday Stories of *Sukh aur Dukh*'. PhD dissertation, University of Sussex.

―――――. 2007. Prem Chowdhry. 'Contentious Marriages, Eloping Couples: Gender, Caste and Patriarchy in Northern India (review)', 2007, pp. 1–347. Delhi: Oxford University Press, *Economic and Political Weekly*. XL11 (24): 2269–71.

―――――. 2009. 'Lived Experiences: Marriage, Notions of Love and Kinship Support Amongst Poor Women in Delhi'. *Contributions to Indian Sociology*. 43 (1): 1–33.

―――――. 2011. '*Purani aur Nai Shaadi*: Separation, Divorce, and Remarriage in the Lives of the Urban Poor in New Delhi.' *Asian Journal of Women's Studies*. 17 (1): 67–99.

―――――. 2014. '*Purani aur nai shaadi*: Separation, Divorce and Remarriage Amongst Delhi's Urban Poor' (reprint). In, Ravinder Kaur and Rajni Palriwala (eds.) *Marrying in South Asia: Shifting Concepts, Changing Practices in a Globalizing World*. pp. 311–32. Delhi: Orient BlackSwan.

―――――. 2016. 'Jural Relations of Middle-Class Marriage and Women as Legal Subjects in the Imaginary of "New India."' *The Australian Journal of Anthropology*. (TAJA) Doi:10.1111/taja.12188.

―――――. (Forthcoming). 'Marriage, Divorce, and Modernization from 1970 to Present-Day India.' *Contributions to Indian Sociology*.

Haddad, Lawrence, John Hoddinott, and Harold Alderman (eds.). 1997. *Intrahousehold Resource Allocation in Developing Countries: Models, Methods, and Policy*. Baltimore: Johns Hopkins University Press.

Haider, Saraswati. 1998. 'Dialogue as Method and as Text'. In Meenakshi Thapan (ed.) *Anthropological Journeys: Reflections on Fieldwork*, pp. 217–67. New Delhi: Orient Longman.

Hameed, Hala. 2003. 'Understanding Gender and Intra-household Relations: A Case Study of Shaviyani Atoll, Maldives'. PhD dissertation. UK: University of East Anglia.

Hart, Kimberly. 2007. 'Love by Arrangement: The Ambiguity of "Spousal Choice" in a Turkish Village'. *Journal of the Royal Anthropological Institute*. 13 (2): 345–62.

Hensman, Rohini. 2005. 'Revolutionising the Family'. *Economic andPolitical Weekly*. 40(8): 709–12.

Holden, Livia. 2008. *Hindu Divorce: A Legal Anthropology*. Aldershot, UK: Ashgate.

Iversen, Vegard, and P. S. Raghavendra. 2006. 'What the Signboard Hides: Food, Caste and Employability in Small South Indian Eating Places'. *Contributions to Indian Sociology*. 40(3): 311–41.

Jackson, Cecile. 1999. 'Men's Work, Masculinities and Gender Divisions of Labour'. *Journal of Development Studies*. 36(1): 89–106.

————— (ed.). 2001. *Men at Work: Labour, Masculinities, and Development*. London: Frank Cass & Co.

Jamieson, Lynn. 1998. *Intimacy: Personal Relationships in Modern Societies*. Cambridge: Polity Press.

Jankowiak, William R. 1993. *Sex, Death, and Hierarchy in a Chinese City: An Anthropological Account*. New York: Columbia University Press.

Jasinski Jana l., Nancy L. Asdigian, and Glenda Kaufman Kantor. 1997. 'Ethnic Adaptations to Occupational Strain: Work-Related Stress, Drinking, and Wife Assault Among Anglo and Hispanic Husbands'. *Journal of Interpersonal Violence*. 12(6): 814–31.

Jeffery, Patricia. 2001. 'A Uniform Civil Code? Marital Breakdown and Women's Economic Entitlement in Rural Bijnor'. *Contributions to Indian Sociology*. 35(1): 1–32.

Jeffery, Patricia, and Roger Jeffery. 1993. 'A Women Belongs to Her Husband: Female Autonomy, Women's Work and Childbearing in Bijnor'. In Alice W. Clark (ed.) *Gender and Political Economy: Explorations of South Asian Systems*, pp. 66–114. Delhi: Oxford University Press.

—————. 1996. *Don't Marry Me to a Plowman! Women's Everyday Lives in Rural North India*. New Delhi: Vistaar.

Jeffery, Patricia, Roger Jeffery and A. Lyon. 1988. 'When Did You Last See Your Mother. Aspects of Female Autonomy in Rural North India'. In John Charles Caldwell, Allan G. Hill and Valerie J. Hull (eds.) *Micro-Approaches to Demographic Research*, pp. 321–33. London: Paul Kegan International.

John, Mary E. 1998. 'Globalisation, Sexuality and the Visual Field: Issues and Non-Issues for Cultural Critique'. In Mary E John and Janaki Nair (eds.) *A Question of Silence: The Sexual Economies of Modern India*, pp. 368–96. Delhi: Kali for Women.

———. 2005. 'The Dialogue Continues (Marriage, Family and Community: A Feminist Dialogue)'. *Economic and Political Weekly*. 40 (8): 712–14.

Kabeer, Naila. 1994. *Reversed Realities: Gender Hierarchies in Development Thought*. New Delhi: Kali for Women.

———. 2001. 'Conflicts over Credit: Re-evaluating the Empowerment Potential of Loans to Women in Rural Bangladesh'. *World Development*. 29 (1): 63–84.

Kakar, Sudhir. 1989. *Intimate Relations: Exploring Indian Sexuality.* New Delhi: Penguin Books.

Kalpagam, U. 2008. 'Marriage Norms, Choice and Aspirations of Rural Women'. *Economic and Political Weekly*. 43 (21): 53–63.

Kandiyoti, D. 1988. 'Bargaining with Patriarchy'. *Gender and Society*. 2 (3): 274–90.

Kapadia, Kanailal Motilal. 1966. *Marriage and Family in India*. Delhi: Oxford University Press.

Kapadia, Karin. 1996. *Siva and Her Sisters: Gender, Class, and Caste in Rural South India*. Delhi: Oxford University Press.

Kapila, Kriti. 2004. 'Conjugating Marriage: State Legislation and Gaddi Kinship'. *Contributions to Indian Sociology*. 38 (3): 379–409.

Kapur, Promilla. 1970. *Marriage and the Working Woman in India*. New Delhi: Vikas Publishing House.

Karve, I. 1993 [1953]. 'The Kinship Map of India'. In Patricia Uberoi (ed.) *Family, Kinship and Marriage in India*, pp. 50–73. Delhi: Oxford University Press.

Kishwar, Madhu. 1994. 'Love and Marriage'. *Manushi*. 80 (Jan–Feb): 11–19.

———. 1999. 'Love and Marriage'. In Madhu Kishwar (ed.) *Off the Beaten Track: Rethinking Gender Justice for Indian Women*, pp. 192–208. Delhi: Oxford University Press.

Krishna, Anirudh. 2010. *One Illness Away: Why People become Poor and How They Escape Poverty*. New York: Oxford University Press.

Liddle, Joanna, and Rama Joshi. 1986. *Daughters of Independence: Gender, Caste and Class in India*. London: Zed Books.

Lynch, Owen. 1969. *The Politics of Untouchability: Social Mobility and Social Change in a City of India*. New York: Columbia University Press.

———. 1992. Sudhir Kakar. 'Intimate Relations, Exploring Indian Sexuality (review)' 1989, pp. 1–161. Delhi: Penguin Books. *American Ethnologist*. 19 (3): 613–14.

Magar, Veronica. 2000. 'Reconceptualizing Domestic Violence in Delhi's Slums'. Multidimensional Factors and Empowerment Approaches. PhD dissertation, University of North Carolina, Chapel Hill.

Mahmood, Saba. 2001. 'Feminist Theory, Embodiment, and the Docile Agent: Some Reflections on the Egyptian Islamic Revival'. *Cultural Anthropology*. 16 (2): 202–36.

Markova, Dagmar. 1994. 'Different Traditions'. *Manushi*. 82 (May–June): 41.

Marsden, Magnus. 2008. 'Love and Elopement in Northern Pakistan'. *Journal of the Royal Anthropological Institute*. 13 (1): 91–108.

Martin, R. 1995. 'The Companionship Trap'. In Christopher Clulow (ed.) *Women, Men and Marriage: Talks from the Tavistock Marital Studies Institute*, pp. 44–62. London: Sheldon Press.

McElroy, Marjorie M. 1990. 'The Empirical Content of Nash-Bargained Household Behaviour'. *Journal of Human Resources*. 25 (4): 559–83.

Merry, Sally Engle. 2006. 'Transnational Human Rights and Local Activism: Mapping the Middle'. *American Anthropologist*. 108 (1): 38–51.

Miller, Daniel. 1998. *A Theory of Shopping*. Ithaca, NY: Cornell University Press.

Mody, Perveez. 2002. 'Love and the Law: Love-Marriage in Delhi'. *Modern Asian Studies*. 36 (1): 223–56.

——— 2007. 'Kidnapping, Elopement and Abduction: An Ethnography of Love-Marriage in Delhi'. In Francesca Orsini (ed.) *Love in South Asia: A Cultural History*, pp. 331–47. New Delhi: Cambridge University Press.

————. 2008. *The Intimate State: Love-Marriage and the Law in Delhi*. New Delhi: Routledge.

Moore, Henrietta. 1992. 'Households and Gender Relations: The Modelling of the Economy'. In Sutti Ortiz and Susan Lees (eds.) *Understanding Economic Process*, pp. 131–48. Monographs in Economic Anthropology. University Press of America and Society for Economic Anthropology (No 10). Maryland: Lanham.

————. 1994. 'The Problem of Explaining Violence in the Social Sciences'. In Penelope Harvey and Peter Gow (eds.) *Sex and Violence: Issues in Representation and Experience*, pp. 138–55. London: Routledge.

Narayan, Kirin. 2004. ' "Honor is Honor, After All": Silence and Speech in the Life Stories of Women in Kangra, North-West India'. In David Arnold and Stuart Blackburn (eds.) *Telling Lives in India: Biography, Autobiography, and Life History*, pp. 281–318. Delhi: Permanent Black.

Nigam, Aditya. 2002. 'Theatre of the Urban: The Strange Case of the Monkeyman'. *Sarai Reader, The Cities of Everyday Life*, pp. 22–30.

Oldenburg, Veena Talwar. 2002. *Dowry Murder: The Imperial Origins of a Cultural Crime*. Delhi: Oxford University Press.

Osella, Caroline, and Filippo Osella. 1998. 'Friendship and Flirting, Micro-politics in Kerala, South India'. *The Journal of the Royal Anthropological Institute*. 4 (2): 189–206.

Osella, Filippo, and Caroline Osella. 2000a. *Social Mobility in Kerala: Modernity and Identity in Conflict*. London: Pluto Press.

————. 2000b. 'Migration, Money and Masculinity in Kerala'. *The Journal of the Royal Anthropological Institute*. 6 (1): 117–31.

————. 2006. *Men and Masculinities in South India*. London: Anthem Press.

Östör, Ákos, Lina Fruzzetti and Steve Barnett. 1982. *Concepts of Person: Kinship, Caste, and Marriage in India*. Cambridge, Massachusetts: Harvard University Press.

Palriwala, Rajni. 1991. 'Transitory Residence and Invisible Work: A Case Study of a Rajasthani Village'. *Economic and Political Weekly*. 30, 26 (48): 2763–77.

Panda, Pradeep, and Bina Agarwal. 2005. 'Marital Violence, Human Development and Women's Property Status in India'. *World Development*. 33 (5): 823–50.

Parashar, Archana, and Amita Dhanda (eds). 2007. *Redefining Family Law in India: Essays in Hounour of B. Sivaramayya*. New Delhi: Routledge.

Parry, Jonathan P. 1979. *Caste and Kinship in Kangra*. London: Routledge & Kegan Paul.

————. 1999. 'Lords of Labour: Working and Shirking in Bhilai'. *Contributions to Indian Sociology*. 33 (1–2): 107–40.

————. 2001. 'Ankalu's Errant Wife: Sex, Marriage and Industry in Contemporary Chhattisgarh'. *Modern Asian Studies*. 35(4): 783–820.

————. 2004. 'The Marital History of "A Thumb-Impression Man"'. In David Arnold and Stuart Blackburn (eds.) *Telling Lives in India: Biography, Autobiography and Life History*, pp. 281–318. Delhi: Permanent Black.

Philips, Amali. 2005. 'The Kinship, Marriage and Gender Experiences of Tamil Women in Sri Lanka's Tea Plantations'. *Contributions to Indian Sociology*. 39 (1): 107–38.

Prinjha, Suman B. 1999. 'With a View to Marriage: Young Hindu Gujaratis in London'. PhD dissertation, London School of Economics.

Raheja, Gloria Goodwin, and Ann Grodzins Gold. 1994. *Listen to the Heron's Words: Reimagining Gender and Kinship in North India*. Berkeley: University of California Press.

Rahman, Lupin, and Vijayendra Rao. 2004. 'The Determinants of Gender Equity in India: Examining Dyson and Moore's Thesis with New Data'. *Population and Development Review*. 30 (2): 239–68.

Reissman. Catherine Kolher. 2003. 'Analysis of Personal Narratives'. In James A. Holstein and Jaber F. Gubrium (eds.) *Inside Interviewing: New Lenses, New Concerns*, pp. 331–47. Thousand Oaks, CA: Sage Publications.

Searle-Chatterjee, Mary. 1981. *Reversible Sex Roles: The Special Case of the Benares Sweepers*. Oxford: Pergamon Press.

Searle-Chatterjee, Mary. 1994. 'Caste, Religion and Other Identities'. In Mary Searle-Chatterjee and Ursula Sharma (eds.) *Contextualising Caste: Post-Dumontian Approaches*, pp. 147–69. Oxford: Blackwell.

Sen, Amartya K. 1990. 'Gender and Cooperative Conflicts'. In Irene

Tinker (ed.) *Persistent Inequalities: Women and World Development*, pp. 123–49. New York: Oxford University Press.

Shah, Chayanika. 2005. 'Marriage, Family and Community: A Feminist Dialogue'. *Economic and Political Weekly*. 40 (8): 709.

Sharma, Rama. 1995. *Bhangi, Scavenger in Indian Society: Marginality, identity and Politicization of the Community*. New Delhi: MD Publications.

Sharma, Ursula. 1986. *Women's Work, Class and the Urban Household: A Study of Shimla, North India*. London: Tavistock.

Shih, Hsio-Yen. 1994. Trap of East vs West. *Manushi*. 83 (July-August): 37–8.

Shyamlal. 1992. *The Bhangi a Sweeper Caste: Its Socio-economic Portraits with Reference to Jodhpur City*. Madras: Sangham Books.

Singh, K. S. 1999. *The Scheduled Castes: Anthropological Survey of India*. Delhi: Oxford University Press.

Singh, Renuka. 1992. Sudhir Kakar. 'Intimate Relations, Exploring Indian Sexuality' (review) 1989, pp. 1–161. New Delhi: Penguin Books. *Journal of History of Sexuality*. 2 (4): 676–9.

Smith, Daniel Jordon. 2001. 'Romance, Parenthood, and Gender in a Modern African Society'. *Ethnology*. 40 (2): 129–51.

Srinivas, M. N. 1976. *The Remembered Village*. Delhi: Oxford University Press.

Srivastava, Sanjay. 2007. *Passionate Modernity: Sexuality, Class, and Consumption in India*. New Delhi: Routledge.

Surtees, Rebecca. 2003. 'Negotiating Violence and Non-Violence in Cambodian Marriages'. *Gender and Development*. 11 (2): 30–41.

Tapper, Bruce E. 1979. 'Widows and Goddesses: Female Roles in Deity Symbolism in a South Indian Village'. *Contributions to Indian Sociology*. 13 (1): 1–31.

Tarlo, Emma. 2000a. 'Welcome to History: A Resettlement Colony in the Making'. In Veìronique Dupont, Emma Tarlo, and Denis Vidal, (eds.) *Delhi: Urban Space and Human Destinies*, pp. 200–235. New Delhi: Manohar IRD.

————. 2000b. 'Paper Truths: The Emergency and Slum Clearance through Forgotten Files'. In Chris J. Fuller and Véronique Benei (eds.) *The Everyday State and Society in Modern India*, pp. 68–90. Delhi: Social Science Press.

Trawick, Margaret. 1992. *Notes on Love in a Tamil Family*. Berkeley: University of California Press.

Tyagi, Amita, and Patricia Uberoi. 1990. 'Adjustment is the Key: Postmarital Romance in Indian Popular Fiction'. *Manushi*. 61: 15–21.

Uberoi, Patricia (ed.). 1993. *Family, Kinship, and Marriage in India*. Delhi: Oxford University Press.

————— (ed.). 1996. *Social Reform, Sexuality and the State*. New Delhi: Sage Publications.

—————. 1997. 'Dharma and Desire, Freedom and Destiny: Rescripting the Man–Women Relationship in Popular Hindi Cinema'. In Meenakshi Thapan (ed.) *Embodiment: Essays on Gender and Identity*, pp. 147–73. Delhi: Oxford University Press.

—————. 1998. 'The Diaspora Comes Home: Disciplining Desire in DDLJ'. *Contributions to Indian Sociology*. 32 (2): 305–36.

—————. 2000. 'The Family in India: Beyond the Nuclear Versus Joint Debate'. *Occasional Papers in Sociology*. Institute of Economic Growth, University of Delhi. July 2000 (2).

Uchiyamada, Yasushi. 1997. 'Two Beautiful Untouchable Women: Sexuality, Desire and Becoming at the Margins'. In Yasushi Uchiyamada (ed.) *Postmodernism, Body and Marginality*, pp. 291–306. Foundation for Advanced Studies on International Development and International Development Research Institute (FASID-IDRI).

Vatuk, Sylvia. 1972. *Kinship and Urbanization: White Collar Migrants in North India*. Berkeley: University of California Press.

Vera-Sanso, Penny. 1995. 'Community, Seclusion and Female Labour Force Participation in Madras, India'. *Third World Planning Review*. 17 (2): 155–67.

—————. 1999. 'Dominant Daughters-in-Law and Submissive Mothers-in-Law? Cooperation and Conflict in South India'. *Journal of the Royal Anthropological Institute*. 5 (4): 577–93.

Vishwanath, Kalpana. 1994. 'The Real Issue'. *Manushi*. 82 (May–June): 40–1.

—————. 1997. 'Shame and Control: Sexuality and Power in Feminist Discourse in India'. In Meenakshi Thapan (ed.) *Embodiment: Essays on Gender and Identity*, pp. 313–28. Delhi: Oxford University Press.

Wadley, Susan S. 1994. *Struggling with Destiny in Karimpur, 1925–1984*. Berkeley: University of California Press.

Warah, Rasna. 1994. 'Strong Disagreement'. *Manushi*. 83 (July–August): 36–7.

Whitehead, Ann. 1981. 'I'm Hungry, Mum: The Politics of Domestic Budgeting'. In Kate Young, Carol Wolkowitz and Roslyn McCullagh (eds.), *Of Marriage and the Market: Women's Subordination Internationally and Its Lessons*, pp. 93–117. London: Routledge & Kegan Paul.

INDEX